Saints, Sinners, Saviors ∾

Strong Black Women
in African American Literature

Trudier Harris

palgrave

In loving memory of
Unareed Harris
(26 April 1914—8 January 2001)
one of the truly strong black women

SAINTS, SINNERS, SAVIORS
© Trudier Harris, 2001

First published 2001 by PALGRAVE™
175 Fifth Avenue, New York, N.Y. 10010 and
Houndmills, Basingstoke, Hampshire RG21 6XS.
Companies and representatives throughout the world

PALGRAVE is the new global publishing imprint of St. Martin's Press LLC
Scholarly and Reference Division and Palgrave Publishers Ltd (formerly
Macmillan Press Ltd).

ISBN 0–312–29300–3 hardback
ISBN 0–312–29303–8 paperback

Library of Congress Cataloging-in-Publication Data
Harris, Trudier.
Saints, sinners, saviors : strong Black women in African American literature
/ by Trudier Harris.
    p.   cm.
  Includes bibliographical references and index.
  ISBN 0-312-29303-8 (alk. paper)—ISBN 0-312-29300-3
  1. American literature—African American authors—History and
criticism.   2. Women and literature—United States—History—20th
century.   3. American literature—20th century—History and criticism.
4. African American women in literature.   5. Women in literature.   I.
Title.

PS153.N5 H29   2001
810.9'352042—dc211
                                                          2001036009

A catalogue record for this book is available from the British Library.

Design by Letra Libre, Inc.

First edition: December 2001
10   9   8   7   6   5   4   3   2   1

Printed in the United States of America.

Contents

Preface

I began work on this project in Fall 1992, when Ann Folwell Stanford of DePaul University asked me to contribute an article to a special issue of *Literature and Medicine* that she was coediting. The issue had been conceived to focus on illness in women's literature, and she wanted me to focus on African American women writers. Well, I said, that would be difficult to do, because African American women characters are usually so healthy. But I promised to think about the possibility and let her know something later. Then, in February 1993, I traveled to Guadeloupe with Citizens for International Understanding. While aboard a boat from one island to another—during which the boat was stopped and searched for drugs and illegal aliens—I concluded that strength in itself could have its problematic or diseased components. I came up with the phrase "this disease called strength" and wrote it on the back of my passenger ticket.

Upon returning home, I continued to think about the idea and began to make lists of possible writers and strong black female characters who could be included in such an article—at that point, I was still thinking only in terms of an article. The list included works by Zora Neale Hurston, Langston Hughes, James Baldwin, Lorraine Hansberry, Ralph Ellison, Nikki Giovanni, Toni Morrison, Alice Walker, Toni Cade Bambara, Ernest J. Gaines, J. California Cooper, Gloria Naylor, Tina McElroy Ansa, Octavia E. Butler, and several other contemporary African American writers, especially women. My work at that point resulted in an article that appeared in the Spring 1995 issue of *Literature and Medicine*.

In Spring 1993, I was invited to lecture at Florida A&M University, where I presented materials I had thought through to that point on the topic. After a lively discussion, Emma Waters Dawson commented that I clearly had a book project in hand instead of an article. Other projects, however, prevented me from pursuing that option for quite some time, though I continued to lecture on the topic. An invitation to lecture in Spain in August 1993 continued my interest in the subject. Several Spanish women in the audience commented that I could just as easily have been discussing them and their historical position at various times in Spanish culture; their comments were troubling and inspiring. I am grateful to Maria Frias, then of the University of Alcala de Henares, Madrid, for having extended the invitation.

These lecturing ventures increased my excitement for the topic, and I continued to add writers and strong black female characters to my list for study. During 1996–97, while I was a resident fellow at the National Humanities Center to work on what had by that time become a book project, I had extensive opportunities to develop my ideas further, including an invited presentation at the Center. Invitations from various colleges, universities, and libraries enabled me to move the project along. I am grateful to the many people inside and outside the country who have thus helped me to bring this project to fruition. They have listened, read, commented upon, or discussed the work with me.

I begin my acknowledgments by thanking Ann Folwell Stanford for encouraging me to take the journey. I thank Emma Waters Dawson, her colleagues, and the students at Florida A&M University who were the first to hear me working through these ideas and who heartily questioned me about them. Barbara G. Ladd and Mark A. Sanders of Emory University read and offered suggestions about the development of the article I published. Many individuals and organizations have provided lecturing opportunities for me to discuss this work. They include: Karla F. C. Holloway, Duke University; E. Patrick Johnson, formerly at Amherst College; Barbara Harris, University of North Carolina Women's Studies Program; Keith S. Clark, George Mason University; the Ford Foundation; John Rickard, Bucknell University; Susan Kask, Western Carolina University; Nancy Chick and R. Baxter Miller, University of Georgia; Ann W. Webb, University of Alabama, Tuscaloosa; Jean McIver, University of South Alabama, Mobile; Tracy M. Casorso and Friends of the Library of North Carolina State University; Speed Hallman and the Arts & Sciences Foundation of the University of North Carolina at Chapel Hill; Susan Cumings and the Southern Humanities Council; Susan Richardson, Denison University; and Mary Louise Smith and the Friends of the Pittsboro (North Carolina) Library.

I thank SallyAnn Ferguson of the University of North Carolina at Greensboro for reading the chapter on Lorraine Hansberry in January 1997 and challenging me to fine-tune several points. I thank Lovalerie King of the University of Massachusetts, Boston, for her careful reading of an earlier version of chapter 1; she pointed me to a couple of crucial sources and inspired me to offer a couple of explanatory footnotes. The Wintergreen women, of course, are always supportive, including Joanne V. Gabbin, Sandra Y. Govan, Karla F. C. Holloway, Joyce Pettis, Daryl C. Dance, Opal Moore, and Ethel Morgan Smith. I am particularly grateful to Daryl C. Dance for taking time from her busy schedule to read the entire final draft of the manuscript. Thanks, y'all!

Thanks especially to Kent R. Mullikin, W. Robert Conner, and the wonderful staff at the National Humanities Center who made my year there a memorable and productive one. I am particularly appreciative of the library staff: Eliza Robertson, Jean Houston, and Alan Tuttle. They made the difference in enabling me to bring this project to conclusion.

Thanks as well to the University of North Carolina at Chapel Hill and to William L. Andrews, former Chair of the English Department. Special thanks also to Jane Campbell of the University of Illinois, Calumet, and to Glenda E. Gill of Michigan Technological University.

I am grateful as well to students in two graduate seminars who discussed the project with me in Spring 2000. These include the students at Michigan State University who were enrolled in a seminar with Kenneth Harrow and those who were enrolled in a seminar with Beth Ferri and Vivian A. May at Texas Woman's College. I very much appreciate the invitations to lecture as well as the engaging seminar discussions.

As always, I thank my mother, Unareed Harris, for being my inspiration, and I thank all my relatives for their unwavering support.

Chapter 1 ∼

Introduction

The Black Female Body:
Seeing, Believing, and Perpetuating
Popular and Literary Images

> It is over thirty-five years since Autherine Lucy walked a gauntlet of white students screaming 'Kill her!' to enter a classroom at the University of Alabama; over thirty-five years since Rosa Parks sparked the Montgomery bus boycott by refusing to give her seat to a white man; thirty years since Fannie Lou Hamer was shot at by Mississippi nightriders for registering to vote. We in the United States have had at least three decades of powerful, passionate images of black women (and men) to complicate and challenge three hundred years of stereotypes, and yet the best-known black woman's face in the land looks out from a box of pancake mix.
>
> —Diane Roberts, *The Myth of Aunt Jemima*

Aunt Jemima is certainly one of the most prominent images of African American women in American culture, but it is not the only one. How this image of the large, strong, happy, asexual cook joined the mammy figure, the suprahuman endurer, and the Christian hard worker to dominate black female representation in a variety of genres is a fascinating strand in American history. The black female body—with passing connection to reality—was manufactured for white public consumption, whether in print or visual media, or on the stage. Even more fascinating is how such images, especially that of the strong black woman, were embraced within

African American culture and eventually found their way into and dominated female portrayal in African American literature. This embracing suggests that black acceptance of these images served financial, psychological, and cultural functions. The appearance of these images in African American literature and their evolution over more than a century suggests that African American writers were just as complicitous as the white-created mythology surrounding black women in ensuring that strong, asexual representations of black female characters dominated the literature in the twentieth century and threaten to continue that domination in the twenty-first century.

Images of asexual, culture-supporting black women in the American popular imagination and media are largely the construction of white Americans. From the vantage point of slavery and the history of black women's caregiving and other roles in relation to white Americans, it is understandable that such images would have been constructed to soothe the constructors. Designed to affirm the continued institutionalization of white power, comforting images of black women were favored over others and are therefore prominent in the American popular imagination. Those comforting images range from the large black women who keep black men in line for white Americans, to the very large black women who are eternally happy to be in the kitchen making pancakes for their white charges, to the mammy figures specifically conceived to provide broad bosoms of comfort for whites. If black women should fall into one of these categories, then they are in their "proper" roles, as defined by the scale of perception of black female bodies in American popular imagination. Another type of proper role, less altruistic—if such a conception could apply to the roles named—locked black women into the uncontained lustiness of sexuality and animalism in which they were stereotypically considered to lead upstanding, Christian white men astray during and after slavery. This hot momma figure, early on referred to as Jezebel, may still be seen in various media but without the obvious labeling.[1]

As Barbara Christian argued in *Black Women Novelists: The Development of a Tradition, 1892–1976* (1980), it was essential to the historical development of images of black women that the most acceptable images be stripped of sexuality, which was simultaneously an affirmation and a repression of reality. On the one hand, white women, the "proper" object of white men's sexual desires, were affirmed that black women were not sexually appealing to their white fathers, husbands, sons, and brothers. On the other hand, white males were prevented from having images projected before them that were positive enough to question their trespasses against black women's bodies. If popular representations of these bodies painted them as asexual, then white men could believe that they were innocent of wrongdoing, for how could they possibly be romantically drawn to women represented as physically unattractive? How the popular imagination and media portrayed black women thus enabled white men to separate daytime images from nighttime desires—the physically unattractive representation of objects whom they could maintain it was impossible to lust after from the reality of experiencing this lust. How could they possibly want to have sexual intercourse with women, so this logic went, who looked more like huge slabs of excessively dark ham masquerading as human than like desirable women? Who looked more like male wrestlers than women? Who could probably best them in a fist fight sooner than they could rock them into sexual ecstasy?

Slave labor, literary descriptions, photographs and sketches in popular magazines and other print media, stage, movies, and television have all been used to carve into and perpetuate in the public imagination these prevailing images of black women, and the entire country is still heir to this legacy early in the twenty-first century. Most of these images focus on strength and asexuality. The first commonly viewed images of black women, those in which they were pictured as working in the fields or caring for the babies of white women—though they might seem poles apart in range of tasks—nonetheless support the same conception of black female bodies and what is contained in those body spaces. Black women working on the plantations during slavery as "field hands" had their labor, and thus their strength, emphasized over anything else. Historical documentation makes clear that such women could be assigned tasks comparable to those of black men who were enslaved, such as picking 300 pounds of cotton in a single day. Black women were certainly subject to whippings comparable to those black men received, for their bodies were deemed equally capable of enduring as much pain.[2] The subhuman connotations attached to such actions are abundantly clear.

What may seem less appropriate at a glance would be how a similar connotation of subhumanity could be attached to black women assigned the tasks of caring for the offspring of white women. This seemingly preferable task ultimately placed the black woman's body in yet another position where her strength and perceived subhumanity were the primary traits. Black women caring for white children were expected not to give in to human conditions, such as fatigue or the need to sleep. They could get up in the middle of the night to soothe the cries of white children as the biological mothers slept without interruption. More than human—or less than human—however we read the implications, black women were expected to perform physically at a level that was seldom—if ever—required of the planter class of white women specifically or of white women generally. The constructed belief that black women were more nurturing, indeed natural nurturers, also highlighted the extrahuman quality attached to them and placed them in the realm of those animals who cared unconditionally for their offspring.

Therefore, whether in the fields or in the big house, black women were perceived as working beyond endurance, always giving, and capable of protecting others, but never themselves needing protection. Indeed, as Saidiya Hartman argues,[3] it was almost impossible for black women during slavery to convince anyone, certainly not lawyers and judges, that their bodies had been violated during sexual transgressions. The rock of the black woman's body, nonetheless pliable enough to be raped, could never claim, however, the public sympathy that could possibly accrue from such a violation. This combination of hardness and physical ability to work, combined with the pliability that allowed for picking cotton or changing baby diapers, yielded a black female body that could be transformed, managed, contained, or discarded at the whims of the controllers of black women's lives and images.

Early literary portrayal and visual images of black women make these points clear. Stereotypical black female characters appear throughout the nineteenth century in such works as John Pendleton Kennedy's *Swallow Barn* (1832), Harriet Beecher Stowe's *Uncle Tom's Cabin* (1852), and Thomas Nelson Page's *In Ole Virginia, or, Marse Chan and Other Stories* (1895).[4] Primarily, these characters serve white writers in preserving their mythological conceptions of the South and of black women's place in plantation culture (even Stowe, who ostensibly wanted change, could not achieve that objective without initially adhering to the type). In size, speech, labor, and actions, black female characters who appear in these works are placed outside the parameters used to define non-black females.

But photographs and sketches are more persuasive than words. Images of black women that dot the print landscape of the nineteenth and early twentieth centuries make impressively clear the physical perceptions, expectations, and requirements for black women. As a quick survey of popular magazines such as *Ladies' Home Journal, The Saturday Evening Post,* and *Good Housekeeping* in the first three decades of the twentieth century will illustrate, size, subservience, and a stylized role as servant were the foremost characteristics for black female representation.[5] There is simultaneously a hardness and a comfort implied in such images, both of which are designed to be in service to whites. Those excessively large bosoms of black women were never photographed to imply sexuality; they were instead tied to nurturing. To highlight strength over sexuality, large size was contained in clothing designed to efface the very body that size suggested was there. High collars, wrist-length sleeves, ankle-length skirts, and high-top shoes all ensured safe surface images of black women. "They can take care of your children," so the subtext might have gone, "but they can never take your husband. They can work hard in your service, but they cannot inspire rhapsodies of love from anyone."

When their images were first produced on the stage and in film, black women could not even represent themselves. White men dressed up as black women in minstrel shows, and in the film *Birth of a Nation,* white actresses added bosoms and derriere as the ironically stylized signals of the transformation into black female bulk.[6] At least in these instances, black "women" occasionally acquired voices, though that achievement came with the sad consequence that the voices were often ones of buffoonery. These managed images thus erased the black woman's authentic voice from the stage and film as assuredly as early images erased her sexuality and her authentic body. Stage and film thereby played their parts in the process of institutionalizing iconographic images of black women that separated them from their bodies as well as from their inner selves. With the strength usually assigned to them, however, black women were perceived as not suffering overly much from these separations and distortions.

A careful study of *Ethnic Notions,* a documentary focusing on popular images of black people in the American imagination from the 1820s to the 1970s, will reveal the impact of visual representation upon black female bodies.[7] In cartoons, movies, and television, the majority of black women have been presented as huge bodies in the process of working for and/or attending to whites, complaining about lazy black men, using their strength to correct black men, waiting for a long-anticipated heavenly retreat from earthly toil, and never once giving any attention to their love or sex lives. The images range from Louise Beavers in several films in the 1930s, including the well-known *Imitation of Life* (1934), to Ethel Waters in *Cabin in the Sky* (1942), to Hattie McDaniel in *Gone With the Wind* (1949).[8] These women seem to have been born into middle age, weighing an average of 250 pounds, and knowing instinctively how to wash, iron, cook, and care for white folks. When they have laments, they are centered in the realm of longing for heaven; they never complain about the work shunted off onto them, and they certainly never need rest and relaxation. Their major joys in life are taking care of whoever it is who most needs them at the moment.

Legacies given to us through minstrel shows and musical comedies sustained themselves sufficiently to find their way into television from the 1970s forward. A roll call of television shows popular during this period will reveal a plethora of fat black women, ones whose charges have usually changed from white children to black children and men who act like children. These include *The Jeffersons, What's Happening?, That's My Mama, Good Times, Amen,* and *Gimme A Break,* among others. There is nothing intrinsic to their roles that required any of these women to be overly large, yet they all were. Consider Nell Carter in *Gimme A Break.* Not only was she large, but she was an updated version of the screen mammy, taking care of the white children of the policeman for whom she worked and becoming so attached to one small boy that several episodes were built around that relationship. A product image will help to make my point. The cleaned-up, lipsticked, stylishly-scarved new version of Aunt Jemima on the pancake syrup container is the counterpart to what I mean about the modern mammy in Nell Carter.[9] But she was so funny, sang so well, and painted her nails so alluringly that few folks probably stopped to contemplate that, if she were stripped down to her essence, she would be one-half mammy and one-half clown.

Theresa Merritt certainly did not have to be large on *That's My Mama*, but the prevailing image of black women on comedy shows made fatness a cultural imperative for producers of such shows. The same point could be made about Esther Rolle in *Good Times;* there was no apparent reason for her to be cast as stout, but she was. Somehow, when those fat black women crack the jokes, they literally seem to carry more weight. And just think of those two fat church sisters on *Amen;* their size is essential to their conception, and a large portion of the laughter literally depends upon their body movements. Television producers therefore assuaged their stereotyped images with laughter, and the institutionalization of black women as very large, strong, Christian, and basically happy moved into a new era and a new medium of distortion. Many of these shows are twentieth century counterparts to the plantation tradition that we castigate Joel Chandler Harris, Thomas Dixon, Thomas Nelson Page, and Paul Laurence Dunbar for perpetuating.

In this society, which emphasizes health spas and health food—in a word, thinness[10]—it is amazing that black people in the media are encouraged to overeat for the sake of getting roles. In the 1980s, *Ebony* magazine featured an article in which the author discussed the stress upon black female bodies to comply with popular conceptions of how they should look in order to get roles in movies and on television. One woman maintained that she had been required to gain 30 pounds in order to get a particular role.[11] When I think of producer Michael Landon praising a young white woman for losing 11 pounds in one week (which I think is unconscionable, not to mention unhealthy) in order to get a role in a show he was directing, the gross incongruity in such practices is immediately obvious. The television and movie industry probably killed a lot of black women by forcing them to be overweight in order to coincide with the stereotype of the comforting, frequently funny black woman.

In the cultural imperatives that govern black female representation in the white media, stage, and popular imagination, black women are conceived so that somebody is always trying to get into their bosoms, that is, figuratively to the site of nurturance and comfort. For all those television images, if the women have 44-D's, the better. The larger they look, the more comforting they seem. They are literally perceived as being able to open their arms and comfort the world. Again, no white person would have anything to fear from these women. When necessary, however, they can command with the force of their voices and size, and many of them are commanding—though their directives are usually given to their children and husbands. Think of Claudia McNeil, who played the original Mama Lena Younger in Lorraine Hansberry's *A Raisin in the Sun* (1959).[12] Think of Esther Rolle again, who played Mama Lena Younger in the 31 January 1989 television production of *A Raisin in the Sun* as well as in the Alliance Theater's 1995 production in Atlanta. Think again of Ethel Waters, who in the 1920s was a gorgeous specimen of a sexy young blues singer; by 1942 and her appearance in *Cabin in the Sky,* she was a staunchly-moral, spiritual-singing, 250 pound bundle of comfort, happily scrubbing her troubles away in a scene during which she washed clothes in a galvanized tub on a scrubboard.[13]

What is equally if not more striking than the images themselves is the point at which black popular imagination intersected with white historical creations of black women to give sanction to these distortions. We do not have to look far to explain why white Americans may have needed such images, but why did black people accept them? Any survey of the numbers of uprisings that occurred during slavery easily debunks the notion that black people were content with their enslavement.[14] Yet whites needed that lie, needed to tell themselves that they were benign in their enslavement of blacks and that black people were content with the condition of slavery. It would have been difficult, indeed, for plantations to operate if whites could not sleep for fear that black people would break into the big houses and cut, rape, rob, kill, or maim the planters and their families. So they relied on the myths that black people were content, that black women who cared for their children really *loved* those children, and, mistresses especially wanted to believe that black women who came into constant contact with white men could not, except through animalistic, debased interactions, tempt those men away from white women, their perceived "rightful" partners. Perhaps all this rationalization can be capsuled in the need for the mammy myth. White people, male and female, saw this figure as the solace from their formative years as well as a measure of their status as well-bred planters. Scholars writing about such relationships in the South have noted that being raised by a mammy, especially among certain groups of Louisiana whites, was one of the truest signs of being to the manor born. The image of the mammy, therefore, wrapped in its large comforting size and asexuality, yet guided by Christian caretaking, became *the* preferred popular image of black women.

In the creation/production of their own bodies as well as in the roles they agreed to play in movies and on television, black women were complicit in their perpetuation of the dominant images of their conceptualization. And certainly they were helped along in that agreement, for economic factors were important considerations. In addition to being large, loud, and asexual, the women were expected to be buffoons in their own romantic interest, that is, if any courtship surfaced. Yet even those women who could *not* aspire to such public roles (the everyday, ordinary women, so to speak) nonetheless frequently manifested the same body types. Observers who focus on class, economics, and diet as factors in these appearances are certainly not incorrect in their observations, but they have consistently downplayed *choice,* an element that is also a factor. Many black women are themselves soothed by the images of large size and physical strength. I think especially of those gospel singers who maintain that they cannot perform well unless they are large, and I think of women who simply pride themselves in their love of food. They have all bought into the image of themselves as strong, nurturing, and physically enduring in spite of everything.

Their self-perceptions have also been enhanced by black males expressing their desire for women with "meat on their bones." Think of this image as it was iconized among blues singers of the 1920s and later:

> Big fat momma, meat shaking on her bones
> Big fat momma, meat shaking on her bones
> Every time she shakes that thing, some skinny girl lose her home.

These singers rewrote sexuality into size, but they nonetheless approved of the size. Consider, too, the emphasis upon hips in African American culture.[15] In order to get the hips that black men presumably find attractive and love, black women had to cultivate the accompanying generally larger physical size, which meant eating beyond basic dietary requirements. Thus southern culture and cuisine played their parts in encouraging black people, especially women, to accept stereotyped images of themselves. Before the 1980s, there was barely a black household in the South into which one could go and not find several of the following items on the after-church Sunday dinner menu: fried chicken; baked ham; barbecued spareribs; chitlins; collard greens, string beans, or other vegetables cooked with fatback or smoked ham hocks; fried corn; cornbread; potato salad; macaroni and cheese; candied yams or sweet potato pie; peach cobbler; and pound cake.[16] In more recent years, many national restaurant and cafeteria chains cater to soul food preferences, and black people can find these high cholesterol foods as plentiful outside their homes as inside, for a new social tradition, concomitant with increased economic resources, has instituted a growing trend of "eating out" after church on Sundays. And the danger of eating out may be greater because black people are eating the same quantities of food without even burning a few calories through the exercise involved in preparing it.

Southern hospitality is about food, and since the largest populations of blacks in this country were in the South well into the mid-twentieth century, the food culture contributed to the size and acceptance of large black women; tradition took over after that time as populations dispersing north and west carried the pattern with them and as memories of the Sunday dinner event were reinvigorated in the South. Such acceptance, however, did not necessarily mean that black people *intended* the concomitant acceptance of stereotypes, but that was inadvertently and at times willfully the case, for there is an obvious pride that black women take in their culinary skills and there is rarely any resistance to joining the prevailing cultural norms for size. Exchanges of recipes are commonplace, and almost every social occasion—birthday, funeral, wedding, card party, impromptu gathering, holiday—is an occasion for eating. Since Alex Haley's *Roots* (1976) sent millions of Americans on a quest for their roots, or at least inspired them to celebrate with relatives, family reunions have become the latest craze in overeating opportunities. Several hotels in the Atlanta area, for example, average one African American family reunion a weekend between May and September; hotel personnel have developed special black family reunion menus.[17] There are countless opportunities, therefore, for large size to prevail among black women and with little censorship connected to it.

Large size in black communities frequently brought with it an authority of sorts, and that may well have been an additional factor in forging oneself into the prevailing image. Few skinny women in African American communities are perceived as capable of directing the lives of others. Indeed, smaller women can be made fun of, if not outright rejected, as in the song, "Who'll Take the Woman with the Skinny Legs?"[18] Larger women who had the physical prowess to back up their directives with physical force usually held sway. The affectionate name assigned to grandmothers in this tradition makes clear the force of their size and their power; they are generally called "Big Mama."[19] Of course there are problems in this correlation between size and health, size and authority (some physically large women may be incapable of commanding anyone, and some small women may be absolute authorities in their household), but the overall pattern nonetheless holds sway.

The close ties between African American history and literature are undeniable, and that is no less the case for portraits of black women. Historically, African American women have been viewed as balm bearers, the ones who held a people together against assaults from outside as well as from within the community. They were towers of strength against the degradation of slavery. They were towers of strength against the abuse of husbands and the demands of children. They were towers of strength in taking care of their families, usually through domestic work. And they formed the pillars that supported the black churches that in turn demanded a tremendous strength from them. Indeed, historical African American communities could be viewed as having been in various states of ill health, having numerous diseases inflicted upon them by the ugly manifestations of racism. Black women were the spiritual as well as the physical healers, putting hearth, home, and family back together after the tragedy of lynching, nursing daughters brutalized by rape, and soothing children who were attacked when they tried to integrate Southern schools. Black women provided the bandages for the wounds, the solace for the stricken. We have applauded this strength—and certainly not without justification.

Seldom have we stopped to think, however, that this thing called strength, this thing we applaud so much in black women, could also have detrimental effects or consequences. Indeed the very virtue so praised historically can, in African American literature, become its own form of ill health, indeed a disease, as easily as it can be a safe, applaudable trait. Strength frequently perpetuates dysfunctionality in literary families, where the strong dispositions and actions of black female characters have negative impacts upon the lives of their relatives. Many readers and scholars—and even the other literary characters themselves—choose to ignore the problems inherent in the strength of these female characters in favor of highlighting the larger, sometimes positive, attributes of that strength. Strength continues to be praised as positive, and the subterranean consequences of the virtue that appears above the surface of the sea of literary relations is never fully examined. Strength becomes its own reason for being for these women and frequently for the characters around them as well.

Unfortunately, this development has been an almost innocent consequence of the convergence of historical and literary forces. It has manifested itself in a variety of incarnations. There is certainly an awesome quality about the black woman who kills her child rather than allow that child to be remanded to slavery. It is equally admirable when a woman takes the brunt of abuse that might be directed at her children and refocuses it upon herself. Or when she believes fervently in a supreme being who will one day right all the wrongs of the world. In representing these women who have never had the luxury of being put on a pedestal or incorporated into anyone's concept of what true womanhood meant, black writers presented these characters as perhaps freer to redefine themselves, or to "invent" themselves, as Toni Morrison asserts of *Song of Solomon*'s Pilate Dead.[20] Their re-creation, however, has bumped its head against the low ceiling of the possible virtues inherent in strength. Conceptualization of black female character, therefore, has fallen into the creative trap or paradox of finding a way out of traditional stereotypes by reinvigorating an old one whose myriad shades do not ultimately overcome the basic problem of limitation. The superficial attractions of strength have dominated portraits of black female characters to the detriment of other possibilities and have potentially stymied future directions for the representation of black women. This tradition of portrayal, therefore, has created as well as become its own form of stagnation.

The landscape of African American literature is peopled with black female characters who are almost too strong for their own good, whether that strength is moral or physical, or both. Historically, African American writers have assumed that strength was the one unassailable characteristic they could apply in representing black women. If black women could be attacked for being promiscuous, they certainly could not be attacked for being strong. If they could be criticized for acquiescing in their own debasement during slavery, they could certainly not be criticized for taking their burdens to the Lord and leaving them there. Unquestionably, strength was frequently the only virtue available to black women. Without extensive financial resources, militia, public opinion, or even mobs to protect them when threatened, they had only their minds and bodies (and these could obviously and easily be violated).

So, against the backdrop of unwritten taboos and efforts to avoid stereotypes, African American writers inadvertently created another stereotype—that of the black female character who was more suprahuman than human, more introspective—indeed, at times, isolated—than involved, more silently working out what she perceived to be best for her children than actively and warmly communicating those desires to them. At a glance these traits might seem more like virtues than problems until we consider the price the characters paid spiritually and emotionally, and until we realize that, in addition to detrimental effects strength had upon them, it was equally if not more harmful to others—the children, husbands, and other relatives of these females.

Along with the symptoms of suprahumanity, introspection, and keeping one's own counsel, there are other noteworthy features of strength that emphasize the problems inherent in it. Christian virtue (especially in the earlier literary portraits) and self-denial are prominent among them. So is silence. A pervasive taciturnity is a trait of several of these characters: they never feel the need to explain their motives or their actions to their offspring. They are not emotionally demonstrative and may, even by their offspring, be assumed to be emotionally unaffectionate. Yet there is an implied ideology of domination—emotional domination, though sometimes physical as well—in most of their interactions with their offspring. These representations of tyranny between mother and child, pictured as almost biologically determined, gain ongoing credibility from religious forbearance and personal sacrifices these women make for their kin. In such cases, these mothers may inadvertently replicate the power dynamics of masters over enslaved persons, for they seldom allow anyone to challenge their authority. In other cases, biology gives way to the stereotypically maternal as elderly black female characters in various literary communities assume a directive posture in the lives of younger blacks. Such characters ignore their own pains and troubles in favor of helping others.[21]

Physical and moral strength are standard for these characters. However, many portraits reach beyond those characteristics to add a new dimension to strong black female representation. In literary depictions in the 1980s and after, such women become otherworldly and mythical. These black female characters defy spatial and bodily limitations, commune with the dead, or die and continue to be sentient. Toni Cade Bambara's Minnie Ransom in *The Salt Eaters* (1980) converses with a ghost, sees a pantheon of *orisha* (gods and goddesses of African origin, specifically those derived from Yoruba cultures), and has out-of-body experiences, while Gloria Naylor's title character in *Mama Day* (1988) can cause unsuspecting men to fall in love, perform a ritual to ensure pregnancy for a barren woman, create a lightning storm to kill her grand-niece's enemy, and talk with the dead.[22] Tina McElroy Ansa's Mudear in *Ugly Ways* (1993) is dead but not dead, as she lies in a casket in a funeral home and transcends time and space by observing what her daughters and husband are doing in the days before her funeral.[23] While she was alive, she forced her three daughters to act out various pathologies, including licentious sexual behavior, because of the strength of personality that refused to nurture them but insisted that they nurture her. Alice Walker's Lissie in *The Temple of My Familiar* (1989) is reincarnated several times, across races, gender, and species, so that she has lives as a white man, a Pygmy, and a lion.[24] Finally, J. California Cooper's Clora in *Family* (1991) tries to take her children out of slavery by poisoning them and herself only to end up being the only one to "die" from the fateful meal, but she exists in a limbo space where she can observe her children for generations; her consolation is that her offspring flows like rivers and she is "mother" to all human beings.[25] Most worldly and several otherworldly phenomena are possible to these characters, and what they miss in emotional relationships, they more than make up for in power and the satisfaction of transcending human limitations. They are nearly complete unto themselves. Although they might pause, like Mama Day, to contemplate the consequences of interfering with natural phenomena, they seldom experience the rare moments of guilt or crises of conscience that we note in James Baldwin's Elizabeth Grimes, Langston Hughes's Hagar Williams, or Lorraine Hansberry's Mama Lena Younger.

These suprahuman female characters have been denied the "luxuries" of failure, nervous breakdowns, leisured existences, or anything else that would suggest that they are complex, multidimensional characters. They must swallow their pain, gird their loins against trouble (the masculine image coincides with the denial of traditional femininity to them), and persist in spite of adversity (they "keep on keeping on"). Black female characters have so frequently been called upon to be strong that strength has repeatedly over-shadowed their tenderness, overshadowed their softness, overshadowed the complexity of their femininity and humanity. We have really praised these literary figures for being suprahuman, certainly more than female, which means that often we have praised them for exhibiting traits that Western culture has traditionally designated as more masculine than feminine. Indeed, one of the criticisms leveled against the ones who still operate in the human realm is that their strength has crippled black men.[26] What they do—or not do—to men pales, however, in comparison to what they do to themselves. With strength as their primary trait, they exist in isolated, unchallenged realms of authority where their morality and physical prowess are all they have to comfort themselves.

And where does the literature get such portraits? A history of American literary and visual representation of black women certainly had a tremendous impact.[27] In addition to the documented history and the prevailing cultural myths, the portraits come from the biographies of the writers[28] as well as from reclaimed and often romantic conceptions of African American ties to Africa. Images of African women who trudge for miles with heavy loads of wood across their shoulders, or of regal women who carry huge pails of water on their heads, or of warrior queens who lead armies against intruders, or of women who till and cultivate their own fields, or of women who fight alongside their men during intertribal wars serve as ancestral inspiration for depictions of contemporary matriarchs and other strong black female characters.[29] Certainly, these characteristics convey difference from other racial and ethnic groups of women. But they simultaneously convey the trap into which black women (by their selective approval of certain stereotypes) and African American writers (by their desire to reject European American models) have been caught.

One striking instance of this representation of the physical strength of a black female character appears in Alice Walker's "Everyday Use."[30] Mrs. Johnson, Walker's narrator, describes herself in terms and through activities that we usually associate with males. I am certainly not suggesting that masculinity is to be equated with negativity. What I am suggesting is that the *process* of ascribing attributes to one's self that are usually identified with another gender in and of itself reflects a problematic conception of the self. Mrs. Johnson prides herself on her physical strength and her lack of the traditional squeamishness usually associated with women. In describing herself, she comments:

> . . . I am a large, big-boned woman with rough, *man-working hands.* In the winter I wear flannel nightgowns to bed and overalls during the day. I can kill and clean a hog *as mercilessly as a man.* My fat keeps me hot in zero weather.

I can work outside all day, breaking ice to get water for washing; I can eat pork liver cooked over the open fire minutes after it comes steaming from the hog. One winter I knocked a bull calf straight in the brain between the eyes with a sledge hammer and had the meat hung up to chill before nightfall. (48, emphasis mine)

There is no indication in the text that Mrs. Johnson *wants* to be a man. Yet the features that she emphasizes about herself and perhaps finds most attractive and affirming—size, physical endurance, and lack of emotion—are ones that, reflective of the values of her society, she associates with men. She is almost proud of the fact that she is not emotionally demonstrative; there is only one instance of affection shown in the story, and that is when she hugs the burn-scarred Maggie in identification with her values over those of her college-educated daughter who thinks that quilts are made only for hanging on walls as art work. That hint of softness quickly dissolves, and the mother returns to her emotionally aloof posture. It is indeed hard to imagine how she softened sufficiently to engage in the sexual activity that produced her two daughters.

When femininity or sexuality does enter the popular or literary equation, it leans toward excess, which, ironically, borders on evoking nineteenth-century stereotypes of sexually promiscuous black women. In a more contemporary version of this suprafemale quality, Whitney Houston asserts from the very popular 1992 soundtrack to the film, *The Bodyguard,* that she is "every woman." The title of the song, "I'm Every Woman," evokes images of a single human being who is physically, sexually, intellectually, and spiritually everything that the man in her life needs. "I'm every woman / It's all in me. / Anything you want done, baby, / I do it naturally."[31] The literary counterpart to this braggadocio is Maya Angelou's "Phenomenal Woman" or the persona of her poem, "And Still I Rise."[32] Though qualified by the word "like," the claims of Angelou's phenomenal persona are only slightly less fantastic than Houston's: "I laugh like I've got gold mines/Digging in my own back yard" and "I dance like I've got diamonds at the meeting of my thighs." Angelou revises in a romantic context a similar braggadocio that characterized the persona in Nikki Giovanni's poem "Ego Tripping" earlier in the 1970s.[33] Giovanni's persona blows her nose and brings oil to the Arab world; she drinks "nectar with allah"; Nefertiti is her daughter; the filings from her fingernails are semi-precious jewels; and she "can fly / like a bird in the sky."[34] It could be argued that these portraits are designed to reclaim black female strength and sexuality, that the writers intend them as positive, even light-hearted portraits. While these poetic versions of the myth might bring smiles of skepticism, the presumed strength of black women in the moral/physical realm has historically not been a laughing matter, either for the women or those around them.

When romance or marriage is relevant to literary conversations about strong black women, the emphasis upon strength that approximates manliness takes a different turn. Larger and stronger black female characters are painted as too much competition in wife-beating scenarios; therefore, black men have to use undue force and just knock them out or the men run the risk of being knocked out by the women. Think of Zora Neale Hurston's characters' responses to Tea Cake beating Janie in *Their Eyes Were Watching God;* Janie is unlike the common run of black women, they assert, because she shows her bruises, whereas "rusty" black women are too strong and tough for such marks:

'Tea Cake, you sho is a lucky man,' Sop-de-Bottom told him. 'Uh person can see every place you hit her. Ah bet she never raised her hand tuh hit yuh back, neither. Take some uh dese ol' rusty black women and dey would fight yuh all night long and next day nobody couldn't tell you ever hit 'em. Dat's de reason Ah done quit beatin' mah woman. You can't make no mark on 'em at all. Lawd! wouldn't Ah love tuh whip uh tender woman lak Janie! Ah bet she don't even holler. She jus' cries, eh Tea Cake?'

'Dat's right.'

'See dat! Mah woman would spread her lungs all over Palm Beach County, let alone knock out mah jaw teeth. You don't know dat woman uh mine. She got ninety-nine rows uh jaw teeth and git her good and mad, she'll wade through solid rock up to her hip pockets.'[35]

Sop-de-Bottom and his friends have thoroughly internalized the notion that most black women, with few noticeable exceptions, are just too strong for their own good. Think, as well, of Cholly and Pauline Breedlove in Toni Morrison's *The Bluest Eye* (1970) and of Sofia and Harpo in Alice Walker's *The Color Purple* (1982). Each husband/wife couple fights each other like two men (as Sop-de-Bottom implies is the case with him and his "woman"), not like husband and wife. "Rusty" Pauline is not dainty enough to be "properly" beaten; in fact, she finally knocks Cholly out with a frying pan. Sofia has learned fighting from her father and brothers and cannot imagine standing by passively when someone hits her. Celie specifically observes of Sofia and Harpo: "They fighting like two mens."[36]

Harpo, Cholly, and the men who admire Janie's bruises fall into the black folk rationale for African American men pursuing white women—black women are just too strong and non-feminine. Similar accusations of too much strength were reasons black women were asked to step into the background during the Civil Rights movement in order for black men to realize their wills to manhood.[37] A more recent literary example is Ruby Sanders' poem, "Hush, Honey," in which a presumed male voice is trying to get a loud black woman to be quiet:

HUSH!   YO' MOUTH
IT IS TIME TO BE QUIET
AND SOFT SPOKEN
WELL MANNERED
REFINED
SPEAKING SELDOM
AND ONLY WHEN NECESSARY . . .

YOU MAKE THE MAN FEEL SO SMALL
HE HAS TO KICK YOU KICK YOU
BEAT YOU   BEAT YOU
LEAVE YOU   LEAVE YOU
LEAVE YOU TO KEEP FROM KILLING
YOU[38]

Written from a Black Muslim perspective, the poem posits a constrained, respectful, pedestalized, and consequently weakened position for the black woman to counteract her loud, strong persona. Without such willful self-containment, black women would have provided too much competition for black men. This phenomenon supports the contention that black people, female and male, frequently accepted images of black women that had been planted outside black culture but that were wittingly nurtured within it.

The creation of strong black women as the prevailing popular and literary image is thus a thoroughly *American* collaboration on the parts of both African Americans and European Americans. While they assuredly had different purposes in creating and accepting such images, they have nonetheless shaken hands in a collaboration whose manifestation is, after visual representation in advertisements, movies, and television, most apparent in the African American literary tradition. The literature has become the primary site on which the myth acquired flesh and blood and began to believe in itself. Whether it is Ralph Ellison's Mary Rambo in *Invisible Man* (1952), Margaret Walker's Aunt Sally in *Jubilee* (1966), Big Laura in Ernest J. Gaines's *The Autobiography of Miss Jane Pittman* (1971), or Sophie Washington in Pearl Cleage's *Flyin' West* (1992)—the first a day worker, the second a plantation cook, the third a field hand, and the fourth a pioneer—black women are most often characterized in the literature as physically large, capable of almost superhuman strength, and without a sexual dimension. From nineteenth-century through mid-twentieth-century portraits, they are most likely also to be adherents of Christianity. These patterns have converged to form fascinating, problematic, and at times ambiguous representations in the literature. Indeed, the literature has provided the space in which the myth become substance has stubbed its toe. It is that problematic pause—when the virtue of strength metamorphoses into the virus of disease—that has informed the creation of black female character almost from its moment of inception in African American literature. The historically-informed myth become "reality" become questionable representation is the subject of this study.

The tradition of preferring black female strength in literature has become understandably self-perpetuating. Intertextuality is a powerful force in any literature, and African American literature is no exception. Recognizing foremothers and forefathers and what worked for them could lead to imitation as well as it could lead to revision or rejection. The strength of black women has most often inspired imitation with slight modifications. Zora Neale Hurston's claim, for example, that the black woman is "de mule uh de world" is one of the most often-cited quotations in the history of African American literature, and numerous writers have been inspired to show how that is or is not the case. Alice Walker is consistent in giving credit to Hurston as a source of inspiration, as Gloria Naylor is to Toni Morrison. In turn, Morrison's works have been discussed in the same breath with Ralph Ellison's and Toni Cade Bambara's. James Baldwin and Lorraine Hansberry shared conceptions of "witnessing" African American life and characters. And echoes of both Morrison and Naylor appear in the works of Tina McElroy Ansa. Revisions notwithstanding, intertextuality has ensured the perpetuation of the strength of black female literary representation.

Intertextuality as literary memory is as pervasive as the sacred auras with which we surround these strong black women. "They were women then," Alice Walker writes in her poem "Women," and we inadvertently conjure up "a time before" in the portraits and behaviors of black women and try to replicate that perceived strength and determination in whatever our literary present happens to be. We cling to a perception of inviolability about black women, even when we know it not to have been or not to be the case. We want them to have "battered down doors" and moved mountains in the past because that belief enables us to believe in the future. We need to celebrate their leading of "armies" "across mined fields" because we can then glimpse the paths available to us.[39] We mythologize black women as having been strong in the past because that myth can lead and guide us from where we happen to be to some unimagined but probable other space and place.

Strength can certainly be a virtue. In its current manifestations in black female characters in African American literature, however, it has metamorphosed into an unwavering line of development that, by its prominence, seems to cast aspersion upon other possible models. Current patterns seem to suggest that female characters like Octavia Butler's Anyanwu in *Wild Seed* (1980) are the beginning of a long line of protagonists who can claim goddess status at will, mate with other gods, set aside human morality, and manage to live almost forever.[40]

Within the textual worlds in which they exist, most of these characters find little familial or communal resistance to their strength. With the more traditional portraits, such as Hughes's Aunt Hagar Williams and Hansberry's Mama Lena Younger, there seems to be a *circle of acceptability* that encloses the women and makes it impossible for their offspring to truly challenge them. That circle of acceptability, I argue, also mirrors historical African American communities. Mothers are sacred, and grandmothers perhaps even more so. Even, as Hortense Spillers argues, when paternity is in question, *maternity* is always certain.[41] In history and legend, black mothers are painted as being nearly untouchable. We need but think of the tradition of playing the dozens to make the point. No young black man could or would insult his own mother, and he was duty bound to fight for her honor in cases where others dared to malign her.[42] It is no wonder that African American male athletes invariably greet their mothers instead of their fathers on national television.

Individuals and individual characters find it difficult to combat the implied familial, communal, and cultural respect that is inherent in the African American conceptualization of "Mama" or "Big Mama." It is therefore not surprising that Ernest J. Gaines's James in "The Sky is Gray" does his mother's bidding and kills the redbirds in spite of his objections to what he must do; the respect he has been taught to give to her is in the very cultural air from which his conceptualization is drawn. And the characters are certainly aware of their positions. They can consequently use the respect attendant upon their very positions as mothers to carve out impressive emotional, physical, and psychological spaces within their literary households. Thus the paradox of being annoyed with one's mother but not daring to show it or to tell her so parallels the paradox of black women's strength being both positive and negative. The cultural/historical circumstances out of which literary characterization of strong black women characters grows, therefore, imply a nonaccountability and nonreciprocal permissiveness from which even the most creative of twentieth century African American writers have not been able to escape. The cultural immunity granted to the traditional strong black woman has at its core an ingrained appreciation and respect for the motives of these women, the results they are able to achieve, and the actions they inspire. I recognize that immunity. I argue, however, that there is a *problematic continuum* between intent and outcome, that the ends cannot always justify the means. That problematic continuum, where violence, coercion, disrespect, and violation can occur, is the space from which I read the characters and texts covered in this volume.

This study, then, is an examination of selected African American literary texts in which strong and/or large African American female characters appear. I argue that strength can be a positive attribute as well as a problem for the characters who exhibit it as well as for the characters around them who must bear witness to and experience their strength. That paradox has informed the creation of almost every African American text in which such characters appear. I argue that African American female characters as constructed by African American writers of the twentieth century have been shaped in reaction to the larger society's conceptions of what black women were or should be. In trying to avoid playing into the hands of those who would malign black women, African American writers moved toward safe images, safe patterns of representations. The most dominant pattern led to the creation of strong black female characters. African American writers assumed strength to be a safe characteristic, safe in the sense that it could not be used to attack the morality of black women, their sexuality (or lack thereof), or their commitment to their families and to the American democratic ideal. Over the decades of the twentieth century, more and more female characters appeared in African American literature whose strength is their dominant trait. This pattern of development became so pronounced that it resulted in a self-perpetuating expectation. Above all else, black women characters were to be strong. I am not suggesting that other patterns did not develop as well. What I argue is that the portrait of the strong black woman character became the preferred representational pattern that has influenced African American writers for the past 150 years.

The basic organization of this study is a progression from moral and physical strength, to otherworldly strength, to futuristic strength, with a couple of regressions along the way. Within that conceptualization, female characters adhere to the designations of saints, sinners, or saviors. Characters in the first category, strictly adhering to type, bask in the saintly roles they play in and for their families. They range from Lorraine Hansberry's Mama Lena Younger in *A Raisin in the Sun* (1959), to Clora in J. California Cooper's *Family* (1991), to Tante Lou and Miss Emma in Ernest J. Gaines's *A Lesson Before Dying* (1993). Despite their claims to working exclusively for the interests of their families, objective—or at least other—standards might tend toward evaluating them as sanctimonious and perhaps even self-righteous.

I define strong black women characters as sinning against their families and their communities when their motives are more self-absorbed and selfishly *individualistic*, in spite of claims to the contrary. The moral base of the strength that defines the women in the saints category is submerged or warped with women in the sinners category. I place Ishmael Reed's Mammy Barracuda in *Flight to Canada* (1976) and Dorothy West's Cleo Judson in *The Living Is Easy* (1948) in this category. Mammy Barracuda's will to power and Cleo Judson's unscrupulous behavior separate them out from even a remotely altruistic portrait of strong black female characters, but they nevertheless show several of the traits of physical and mental strength that define other characters included in this study.

Cleo's actions against morality clearly condemn her. That is not the case with the women characters in Pearl Cleage's *Flyin' West* (1992), who collectively poison a man, or Sethe Suggs in Toni Morrison's *Beloved* (1987); these female characters fit somewhere in between the categories of sinners and saviors. By any moral standard of measurement, Sethe sins, but Morrison is able to surround the basic fact of Sethe killing Beloved with historical and biological imperatives that mitigate the absoluteness of any judgment that could be brought to bear upon her.

Other characters clearly attempt to use their strength for saving purposes. These include Minnie Ransom in Toni Cade Bambara's *The Salt Eaters* (1980), Baby Suggs in *Beloved,* and Lauren Olamina in Octavia E. Butler's *Parable of the Sower* (1993). Though their actions might be problematic, there is little ambiguity about the causes to which they put their strength to use. Lauren presents herself as savior to her band of displaced southern Californians. She will lead them north to safety in the futuristic *Parable of the Sower,* and she will not—though politely in comparison to Mama Lena and Cleo Judson—tolerate challenges to her self-actualized authority.

This is not a study exclusively about mammy figures or about what some scholars erroneously perceive as matriarchal black women. Strong black female characters as depicted in African American literature may have traits of the mammy or the matriarch, but that is not their whole story or the only context in which I find them of interest. I do not want to couch them primarily in the Daniel Patrick Moynihan or the Michele Wallace mode.[43] What is of greater significance is how African American writers have selected a pattern of portraiture that has its appeals and its detractions. These portraits of strong African American female characters, ranging across several decades of the twentieth century, make clear the attraction they hold for African American writers. Their attraction, however, must constantly be measured against the impact their strength has upon their families, their communities, our imaginations, African American artistic creativity, and the development of African American literature. In reexamining some texts that have achieved tremendous popularity and introducing others—and discussing them in the tradition of strong black women—I hope to expand the conversations about how fictional representation of black female character is achieved, how representation deliberately and inadvertently replicates itself, and how the politics of African American literary creativity sometimes handicaps the very tradition that it seeks to perpetuate.

Chapter 2 ~

A Raisin in the Sun

The Strong Black Woman as Acceptable Tyrant[1]

I begin my detailed commentary on literary portraits of strong black female characters with Lorraine Hansberry's Mama Lena Younger in *A Raisin in the Sun* (1959) because of the pivotal position that play holds in the development of African American drama. Hansberry scholar Steven R. Carter, for example, lists it "among the finest dramas of this century" and names it "the cornerstone of the black theater movement."[2] Critics and cultural historians tout the play as the moment in the development of the literature when the black female character received its most realistic portrait. Perhaps that could be modified to read when the black *working-class* female character received its most realistic portrait. Audiences identified with Mama Lena and her family because they recognized themselves in her or in members of her household. Her family's struggles to improve its lot in a racist society coincided with similar struggles of segments of the audiences viewing the play. Domestic workers were familiar to those black viewing audiences, as were chauffeurs. And Beneatha's first-generation college positioning in the play placed her in the company of many young black people in the 1950s whose family hopes rested on their potential educational successes. Perhaps James Baldwin put it most vividly when, after viewing the play with Hansberry in a pre-Broadway run in Philadelphia, he commented on it as well as on what happened afterward:

> What is relevant here is that I had never in my life seen so many black people in the theater. And the reason was that never before, in the entire history of the American theater, had so much of the truth of black people's lives been

seen on the stage. Black people ignored the theater because the theater had always ignored them.

But, in *Raisin,* black people recognized that house and all the people in it—the mother, the son, the daughter and the daughter-in-law, and supplied the play with an interpretative element which could not be present in the minds of white people: a kind of claustrophobic terror, created not only by their knowledge of the house but by their knowledge of the streets. And when the curtain came down, Lorraine and I found ourselves in the backstage alley, where she was immediately mobbed. I produced a pen and Lorraine handed me her handbag and began signing autographs. "It only happens once," she said. I stood there and watched. I watched the people, who loved Lorraine for what she had brought to them; and watched Lorraine, who loved the people for what they brought to *her.* It was not, for her, a matter of being admired. She was being corroborated and confirmed. She was wise enough and honest enough to recognize that black American artists are a very special case. One is not merely an artist and one is not judged merely as an artist: the black people crowding around Lorraine, whether or not they considered her an artist, assuredly considered her a witness.[3]

The play opened on Broadway 11 March 1959 at the Ethel Barrymore Theatre. Astonishingly, and true to Baldwin's assessment, the audiences were at times an unprecedented 50 percent black. Because of the high mimetic quality of the play, therefore, it has come to represent the moment of separation from *degradingly* stereotypical images (though stereotypes are certainly there) of black people that preceded it on the stage and in literature as well as from the more militantly drawn images of black character that followed it. The Youngers were not only recognizable characters; they were comforting. They contained racial struggle in the realm of the familial and the personal, and they made the monster of segregation appear to be not only something that could be tackled, but something that could be overcome. Their human struggles deriving from poverty placed them in the great American tradition of the underdog with whom even the most racist viewer could perhaps empathize. A significant factor in this acceptance scenario is Mama Lena's Christianity. Mama Lena is not a woman who would take revenge (perhaps by sabotaging their homes or mistreating their children while carrying out her duties as a domestic) if whites did not allow her family to integrate their neighborhood. She would simply take her own disappointment to the Lord in prayer, then pray for the souls of those whites, tell her family not to despair, and keep on keeping on. Religion and moral strength make her safe, and, as the head of her household, she will continue to instill those values in her family.

In the excitement and comfort of the play, in its obvious "firsts," and in the wake of its tremendous success and many awards, it would have seemed almost sacrilegious for anyone to dwell overly long on any faults with Hansberry's achievement.[4] Reviewers focused on the excitement attendant upon young Hansberry's dramatic success at 28, the "universal versus Negro" debate that raged about the play as well as in American society of the 1950s, whether or not the play should have received the New York Drama Critics Circle award for best play, the importance of its "firsts," and the high quality of acting by all cast members. Mama Lena's character seldom took up more than a sentence of reservation or complaint before reviewers heaped praises upon Claudia McNeil as well as upon other cast members. Typical is Gerald Weales, who called Mama Lena "a more conventional figure—the force, compounded of old virtues and the strength of suffering, that holds the family together."[5] Kenneth Tynan confronted the issue directly, then dismissed his own criticism as a "quibble": "Miss Hansberry's piece is not without sentimentality, particularly in its reverent treatment of Walter Lee's mother; brilliantly though Claudia McNeil plays the part, monumentally trudging, upbraiding, disapproving, and consoling, I wish the dramatist had refrained from idealizing such a stolid old conservative. . . . But elsewhere I have no quibbles."[6] Tom F. Driver perhaps commented on Mama Lena's typing more than other reviewers, but he ended his comments with a crescendo of praise: "The mother is a matriarch—tyrannical, though good-natured. . . . But the acting triumph of the occasion belongs to Claudia McNeil as the Mother. Large in body and heart, she makes the character's ignorance, dignity, and pathos entirely memorable." Her most powerful speeches, he concluded, "register with the full impact of theatrical fervor."[7]

A mold of critical commentary was thus set that exempts—more often than not—Mama Lena from the flaws identified with other stereotypically strong black female characters; indeed, it initially and paradoxically exempted her from the stereotype that reviewers recognized but mostly passed over. The logic apparently ran something like this: If we know so many women like her, if she evokes so clearly the ties between stage and life, and if she works only for the good of her family, how can we possibly not like her or approve of what she ultimately achieves? After all, she is not mean-spirited. She suffers and struggles along with the characters from whom she expects only morally-informed actions. This is one of the conspicuous instances in which the motives of the strong black female character are perceived to outweigh any potential criticism about *how* she achieves her objectives. Mama Lena is such a force in the play that she has perhaps overwhelmed and ultimately seduced the critics into behaving properly as much as she overwhelms her family members. One exception to this seduction is Ossie Davis, who, in arguing that Hansberry intended Walter Lee as the focus of the play, asserts:

Raisin was a great American play, and Lorraine was a great American play-wright because everybody who walked into the theatre saw in Lena Younger—especially as she was portrayed by Claudia McNeil, his own great American Mama. And that was decisive. . . . It was good for the great American audi-ence that all of the little guilt feelings and nagging reservations that are raised inevitably by the mere prospect of having to sit through a *Negro* play, could have been set so soon to rest by the simple expedient of seeing Lena Younger, and knowing she was in charge—that they could surrender themselves to her so completely, could find somebody they could trust absolutely up there on that stage—somebody so familiar to them—so comfortable.[8]

With Davis' comment as a point of departure and, in a less excited time, with clearer critical sight, it can be argued that Mama Lena Younger is as much a problem in the lives of her family as whites are, and her influence is more immediate and perhaps operates at a more insidious level. The source of that problem is her strength, which begins with her name and her physi-cal size and is very quickly bolstered by her Christianity. Hansberry herself gave Mama Lena the designation of matriarch, asserting that Mama Lena is "The Black matriarch incarnate: The bulwark of the Negro family since slav-ery; the embodiment of the Negro will to transcendence. It is she who, in the mind of the Black poet, scrubs the floors of a nation in order to create Black diplomats and university professors. It is she who, while seeming to cling to traditional restraints, drives the young on into the fire hoses and one day simply refuses to move to the back of the bus in Montgomery."[9] Hans-berry is perhaps more altruistic in the description of the matriarch than, as I will illustrate, her own characterization of Mama Lena warrants, for Mama Lena's good intentions are frequently overshadowed by the strong-armed methods she uses to achieve her objectives. Notably, however, Hansberry did admit the tendency to tyranny inherent in such figures, and she finds this possibility acceptable when measured against the ultimate good intentions of such women historically: "Not that there aren't negative things about it [the strong mother], and not that tyranny sometimes doesn't emerge as part of it. But basically it's a *great* thing. These women have become the back-bone of our people in a very necessary way."[10] Doris Abramson supports Hansberry's assessment by naming Mama Lena, as did original reviewer Tom F. Driver, "a tyrannical but good-natured matriarch."[11] J. Charles Washing-ton, writing in the 1980s, refers to Mama Lena's "overpowering personal-ity . . . particularly her moral rectitude and selfless nature."[12] Hansberry biographer Margaret B. Wilkerson recognizes Mama Lena's mold in the stereotypical, but suggests that Mama Lena breaks out of the mold.

Mama, who initially fits the popular stereotype of the Black Mammy, *seems* to be the domineering head of household. She rules everyone's life. . . . Mammy gives way to the caring, understanding mother, historic cornerstone of the black family. . . . While Mama may *seem* to be merely conservative, clinging to an older generation, it is she who, in fact, is the mother of revolutionaries; it is she who makes possible the change and movement of the new generation [emphasis mine].[13]

In these assessments, tyranny is altruistic. It begins, I argue, with a name. In the historical tradition from which her character is drawn, a woman like Mrs. Lena Younger would seldom be referred to as "Mrs. Younger." Instead, nonrelatives would usually call her "Miss Lena," and family members would adopt appropriate respectful titles. The honorary and respectful "Mama" designates a role and family position as well as a size (even the way those "m"s spread out in "M-a-m-a" seems to support this size argument). "Big Mamas," "Ma-maws," and "Nanas" populate the African American literary and historical landscapes and generally refer to black women who are usually third— but sometimes fourth and fifth—generation heads of households. These women, mostly widowed but sometimes married to mousy men who seldom earn the comparable appellation of "Big Papa," mind the business of *all* their family members.[14] From the perspective of their grandchildren, the title "Mama" makes clear that the authority of these women applies to but also bypasses their own offspring and has a direct impact upon this third generation. No one who is in the second generation of such a triad can expect to assert about a grandchild, "This is my child. I will tell him what to do," and believe that "Mama" is going to take it seriously. "Mama" highlights the biological connection across generations, thus demonstrating that authority follows biology and will not be interrupted by skipping a generation. The designation enables grandmothers like Mama Lena to engage directly with the third generation and dominate them usually as much and sometimes more than the second generation. It is important to note that the Youngers are sharecropper migrants from Mississippi. They would thus have been heir to southern factors that give rise to the creation of black family generations.[15]

It is no coincidence that the physically large Claudia McNeil was selected to play the role of Mama Lena Younger on the stage as well as in the 1961 Columbia Pictures film version of the play, for the mimetic quality extended from subject matter and characterization to cast selection.[16] Hansberry's description of Mama Lena probably influenced the selection of McNeil as well:

MAMA *enters. She is a woman in her early sixties, full-bodied and* strong. *She is one of those women of a certain grace and beauty who wear it so unobtrusively that it takes a while to notice. Her dark-brown face is surrounded by the total whiteness of her hair, and, being a woman who has adjusted to many things in life and overcome many more, her face is full of* strength.[17]

Throughout the play, Mama Lena's size and physical strength are focal points for action. On stage, Mama Lena towered over the women cast as Ruth and Beneatha; photographs from those productions make the contrasts strikingly obvious. In reading the play, her sheer force of will is apparent in contrast to everyone around her as it looms larger and carries more force. Body size and strength of character simultaneously operate to locate Mama Lena in the stereotype of the domineering strong black woman character as well as to lift her slightly out of it because she is literally the prototype for what later would be judged to be stereotypical.

This size factor is especially important in the scene that sets Mama Lena's biological tyranny in bas relief, that is, in the scene in which she slaps Beneatha for denying the existence of God. When Beneatha ends a tirade with "There simply is no blasted God—there is only man and it is he who makes miracles!," "(MAMA *absorbs this speech, studies her daughter and rises slowly and crosses to* BENEATHA *and slaps her powerfully across the face. After, there is only silence and the daughter drops her eyes from her mother's face, and* MAMA *is very tall before her)*" (39). Mama Lena combines physical size with moral strength when she forces Beneatha to repeat after her: "Now—you say after me, in my mother's house there is still God" (39). The reluctant Beneatha repeats the phrase in spite of her unwillingness to do so. And although Mama is "*too disturbed for triumphant posture*" as she leaves the scene, she has nonetheless made her point about where power resides in the family and who shapes reality. But she is not too disturbed to say as she departs: "There are some ideas we ain't going to have in this house. Not long as I am at the head of this family," and Beneatha meekly replies, "Yes, ma'am" (39). Mama Lena's way of looking at the universe is reinstated, verbally and physically if not substantively, and, in this setting, the physical forcing of verbal acquiescence seems to carry the day. As J. Charles Washington points out, Mama Lena's "actions rarely receive censure even though they are far less than ideal."[18] As African American scholar SallyAnn Ferguson asserts, the violence Mama Lena exhibits is an acceptable dimension of the woman in this tradition who is in charge of her household.[19] Ruth adds her brick to the wall of the status quo by asserting to Mama Lena after Beneatha's departure: "You just got strong-willed children and it takes a strong woman like you to keep 'em in hand" (40), a comment that encompasses the physical and the moral.

Mama's logic in reaction to Beneatha's blasphemy is centered upon the belief that no child borne of her body could have strayed so far from the moral values of its mother, a concept tied to the biblical notion that like trees bear like fruit ("By their fruits ye shall know them"). Beneatha therefore cannot remain unrecognizable because she has come from a recognizable source, thus Mama Lena presumably slaps her back into that familiar recognition.

It is the "Mama" position that has given Mama Lena the "right" to slap Beneatha, thereby making name, size, biology, and morality equal parts of the authority she wields.[20] Beneatha might assert after Mama Lena leaves the scene, "I see also that everybody thinks it's all right for Mama to be a tyrant. But all the tyranny in the world will never put a God in the heavens!" (40), but *in Mama Lena's presence,* Beneatha does as she is told.[21] Neither she nor Walter has the will to stand toe-to-toe, so to speak, with Mama, state a case, and win an argument. Mama's physical and moral power *as mother* are not to be challenged. She usually gets little resistance when she insists upon imposing her view of reality upon her family.

Mama Lena is like a hurricane that carves its path through any obstacles it encounters. That force, guided by the same attributes that determine her behavior with Beneatha, enables her to direct the lives of Travis, Ruth, and Walter Lee. Consider the scene in which Mama Lena questions Ruth about how she has prepared Travis' breakfast:

> MAMA . . . What you fix for his breakfast this morning?
> RUTH (*Angrily*) I feed my son, Lena!
> MAMA I ain't meddling—(*Underbreath; busy-bodyish*) I just noticed all last week he had cold cereal, and when it starts getting this chilly in the fall a child ought to have some hot grits or something when he goes out in the cold—
> RUTH (*Furious*) I gave him hot oats—is that all right!
> MAMA I ain't meddling. (*Pause*) Put a lot of nice butter on it? (RUTH *shoots her an angry look and does not reply*) He likes lots of butter.
> RUTH (*Exasperated*) Lena—(28–29)

At this point, Mama Lena simply turns the discussion to focus on Beneatha and the conversation she has been having with Walter Lee. That Ruth makes the transition with her is further indication that Ruth does not have the desire or the force of will to try to stand against Mama Lena overly long; besides, Mama Lena has made her point and, by reincorporating Ruth into a congenial conversation, she exhibits her power to disrupt as well as to soothe. In discussing Travis, Mama Lena not only ignores Ruth's anger and exasperation, but she makes it clear through her tone and persistence that no obstacle will prevent her from reaching her ultimate objective: confirmation that Travis has been fed in a way that Mama Lena would approve. It is not a conversation that Ruth will forget, and whether or not Ruth appreciates it, the conversation will influence the future meals she prepares for her son. By attempting to usurp Ruth's authority as Travis' mother, Mama Lena indicates that that relationship is merely nominal; the true "Mama" is Mama Lena.[22] She recognizes no boundary of presumed motherly authority in connection to Ruth that would prevent her from questioning Ruth, and she refuses to desist because Ruth is angry, offended, embarrassed, or otherwise made uncomfortable because Mama Lena is questioning her parenting abilities. She at least shapes her inquiries in the form of questions; more often than not, she speaks in the imperative voice.[23] Nonetheless, "the Mama"'s agenda supersedes everyone else's. The impact upon Ruth is apparent in her halting behavior throughout the play as well as in her relationship to Walter Lee; she is basically mousy, acquiescent. She can never claim a space as the primary woman in this household and is thereby pushed into a peripheral, ghostlike position. Ruth may also be referred to as "Mama," but her positional relationship in the family diminishes the use of that word in comparison to Mama Lena's power and position. Mama Lena's strength as mother and "wife" to Walter Lee and as "mother" to Travis nearly makes Ruth superfluous.

It is important as well to highlight again the physical space in which these exchanges occur and to note its possible impact upon these interactions. This is Mama Lena's space, *her house*. Ruth is therefore as much a guest as she is a daughter- or sister-in-law. This near outsider status and the knowledge that her husband, after the wedding ceremony, has simply taken her home to his mother's space may contribute its share to Ruth's character. Ruth has undoubtedly witnessed many scenes in which status by reason of space figures into the argument. Mama Lena uses ownership of this space on several occasions as the basis for demanding certain actions or acquiescence to her beliefs.

Mama Lena's biological tyranny and moral self-righteousness are keenly apparent in scenes in which Mama Lena directs the relationship between Walter Lee and Ruth. The first occurs when Mama Lena demands that Walter Lee talk with Ruth about her planned abortion, which is unfortunately just at the moment the long-awaited insurance check arrives:

MAMA Son—I think you ought to talk to your wife . . . I'll go on out and leave you alone if you want—

WALTER I can talk to her later—Mama, look—

MAMA Son—

WALTER WILL SOMEBODY PLEASE LISTEN TO ME TODAY!

MAMA (*Quietly*) I don't 'low no yellin' in this house, Walter Lee, and you know it—(WALTER *stares at them in frustration and starts to speak several times*) And there ain't going to be no investing in no liquor stores. I don't aim to have to speak on that again. . . .

WALTER I'm going out! . . .

MAMA (*Still quietly*) Walter Lee—(*She waits and he finally turns and looks at her*) Sit down.

WALTER I'm a grown man, Mama.

MAMA Ain't nobody said you wasn't grown. But you still in my house and my presence. And as long as you are—you'll talk to your wife civil. Now sit down. . . . [Walter Lee later jumps up] I said sit there now, I'm talking to you! (57–59)[24]

As many critics have pointed out, Mama Lena essentially treats Walter Lee like a little boy. He is being called into accountability as an adolescent might be who has just thrown a baseball through a window. What makes the scene so compelling in the strength scenario is the incongruity between the substance of the calling into accountability and the form it takes. Abortion is not a subject one would expect small children to be summoned to discuss, yet the summoning here is precisely in that seemingly innocent form. Mama Lena's control of her children's lives enables the summoning, and her moral superiority enables her to broach a subject that in this environment is usually not broachable.

This scene perhaps highlights Mama Lena's commanding presence more than any other in the play. However, as this sequence plays itself out, she gets less than she desires. She fully expects that Walter Lee, like Big Walter and like Mama Lena herself, will "do the right thing":

MAMA Son—do you know your wife is expecting another baby? . . . I think Ruth is thinking 'bout getting rid of that child.
WALTER (*Slowly understanding*) No—no—Ruth wouldn't do that. . . .
RUTH (*Beaten*) Yes I would too, Walter. (*Pause*) I gave her a five-dollar down payment.
(*There is total silence as the man stares at his wife and the mother stares at her son*)
MAMA (*Presently*) Well—(*Tightly*) Well—son, I'm waiting to hear you say something . . . I'm waiting to hear how you be your father's son. Be the man he was . . . (*Pause*) Your wife say she going to destroy your child. And I'm waiting to hear you talk like him and say we a people who give children life, not who destroys them—(*She rises*) I'm waiting to see you stand up and look like your daddy and say we done give up one baby to poverty and that we ain't going to give up nary another one . . . I'm waiting.
WALTER Ruth—
MAMA If you a son of mine, tell her! (WALTER *turns, looks at her and can say nothing. She continues, bitterly*) You . . . you are a disgrace to your father's memory. Somebody get me my hat. (61, 62)

The hurricane carves out its path; it does not pause to consider the house it topples or the tree it uproots. Family history and biology will not allow Mama Lena—at least not yet—to entertain the possibility that her actions might be detrimental to her son and her daughter-in-law. The position of "mama" enables her to violate privacy; indeed, the psychological violation of privacy is but the counterpart to the physical violation that ensues simply by virtue of the family's living quarters. Mama Lena's larger moral imperative does not grant to Ruth the power of alternative choices, for there can be no choice in Mama Lena's scheme except for her daughter-in-law to give birth to an unaffordable child, then love it—or pretend to—and raise it accordingly (and it is clear that Ruth would prefer not to go through with the abortion if she can help it). There is thus a simplicity inherent in Mama Lena's moral strength, a simple either/or formula that always figures right and wrong as clear-cut choices; there can be no gray areas. That simplicity adds another dimension to the strength formula; it makes control a clear-cut proposition just as it similarly makes reaction to control a simple and easy thing to do.

Anguish that Ruth may feel for having her burdening secret bluntly announced to her husband never figures in her or Mama Lena's actions, for Mama Lena's limited moral imperative denies the possibility of rejection of her righteous course of action. Embarrassment is not an allowable emotion in the strong black woman character's frame of reference. Hansberry seemingly gives Mama Lena the upper hand by not portraying overly much Ruth's reaction to the very drama that is intensely shaping her life. Certainly Ruth staggers and faints, but readers and viewers do not pause with concern about those occurrences for very long, for the larger issue is shaped by Mama Lena. Mama Lena can hold Ruth and soothe her in the staggering episode, but she has not created an environment in which Ruth could confide in her woman-to-woman and, indeed, their not being age peers might prevent that as well; she must therefore deduce that Ruth is pregnant. Once that knowledge is confirmed, Mama Lena can make it public, but she does not allow comparable public exposure of information about her. For example, when Walter Lee confronts her directly on the day she makes the down payment on the house, her response to his "Where did you go this afternoon?" and "What kind of business?" is "You know better than to question me like a child, Brother" (75, 76). Yet to Mama Lena, all the adults in her household are children. Ruth's pain, therefore, is Mama Lena's to manipulate as she wishes.[25]

Although Mama Lena seemingly "loses" in the scene in that Walter Lee does not avow his love for Ruth and his support for their unborn child, the traits that define her as the strong black woman character are nonetheless sharply apparent. Throughout, she directs—or attempts to direct—the action between husband and wife. She becomes marriage counselor, judge, and jury in addition to parent. Like Beneatha not being *allowed* to deny God, Walter Lee cannot possibly be *allowed* to deny the parental heritage bequeathed to him by Mama Lena and Big Walter. By pushing him toward identification with that, Mama Lena seeks again to reinstate the values most familiar to her. Again, the majority of the audience viewing the play in 1959 would have held similar attitudes toward abortion; therefore, this scene is especially compelling in the argument that would allow Mama Lena's point of view to prevail despite her domineering postures.

Yet there is a conflict here that Mama Lena obviously does not consider. She has raised her son Walter Lee, and although she now demands that he be a man, it is not apparent that she has previously allowed him to be so. Certainly he has observed the ostensible markers of manhood: marrying and fathering a child. But he has not assumed the responsibility of partnering that wife or raising that child, for Mama Lena has shouldered most of those responsibilities. Now a real crisis has arisen. It calls for action in keeping with Mama Lena's teachings but one that would assert an independence from her in Walter's desire to be a father in spite of the economic and family conditions. Walter is unable to respond. His lack of response, however, does not mean that the strong black woman character has been toppled from her position of family dominance. She has simply been temporarily thwarted from having her way in the lives of her children. After all, she ends the scene with a command: "Somebody get me my hat" (62), thereby still in control of many of the actions of those around her.

Thus the most noteworthy indications of Mama Lena's control as well as the effects of the impact of strength upon her offspring occur in her interactions with her son Walter Lee. Whereas Octavia in Gaines's "The Sky is Gray" wants to force her eight-year-old son to be a man, Mama Lena stretches out the childhood of her 35-year-old son. Racism and economic conditions have undoubtedly played important roles in Walter Lee living with his mother and sister instead of finding an apartment for his wife and child, but these have been compounded by Mama Lena continuing to treat him as if he were a wayward teenager or an irresponsible adolescent. Two scenes that occur late in the play illustrate these points as well as Mama Lena's attempt to rectify the situation. The first is the scene in which Mama Lena entrusts Walter Lee with the remainder of the money from her down payment on the house. She admits her negative role in Walter Lee's development and encourages him toward a different path. The scene occurs after the family learns that Walter Lee has been missing work and going to a bar instead because he sees all of his dreams smashed.

MAMA I've helped to do it to you, haven't I, son? Walter, I been wrong.
WALTER Naw—you ain't never been wrong about nothing, Mama.
MAMA Listen to me, now. I say I been wrong, son. That I been doing to you what the rest of the world been doing to you. (*She stops and he looks up slowly at her and she meets his eyes pleadingly*) Walter—what you ain't never understood is that I ain't got nothing, don't own nothing, ain't never really wanted nothing that wasn't for you. There ain't nothing as precious to me . . . There ain't nothing worth holding on to, money, dreams, nothing

else—if it means—if it means it's going to destroy my *boy*. . . . [She gives him the sixty-five hundred dollars to put in a bank.] It ain't much, but it's all I got in the world and I'm putting it in your hands. I'm *telling you* to be the head of this family from now on like you supposed to be. (86, 87; emphasis mine)

While we can certainly argue that African American cultural references would allow for Mama Lena to refer to Walter Lee as a "boy," her reference here and those earlier highlight again the power gap between them. She is definitely being altruistic in trusting the money to Walter Lee, and she seems genuinely remorseful, but she is simultaneously demanding, as she did in the scene earlier with Ruth, that he stand up to her expectations for him. She is *telling* Walter Lee once again to be a man, a man who is being shaped by the directive power of her voice. The mixture of behaviors that can define men/boys once again entangles control and love, but nonetheless continues to give Mama Lena the vocal and the moral upper hand.

When Mama Lena learns a week later that Walter Lee has naively given the money away, her physical strength is emphasized as she "*stops and looks at her son without recognition and then, quite without thinking about it, starts to beat him senselessly in the face. BENEATHA goes to them and stops it*" (109). Original viewers again probably focused less on the violence than on Walter Lee's wrongdoing and thus Mama Lena's "justified" righteous indignation. For all the emotional intensity of the scene, however, in resorting to violence Mama Lena shows kinship to Octavia in "The Sky is Gray" as well as to Eva Peace in *Sula;* what they cannot achieve by voice, they will achieve by hand.[26] We are similarly reminded of Mama Lena slapping Beneatha. The violence becomes "excusable" because of audience identification with Mama Lena and their general anti-atheist approach to the world. Beneatha's comments define tragedy for Mama Lena in belief, while Walter Lee's more immediately destructive action defines tragedy for her in family history. Walter Lee unseats, perhaps even borders upon erasing, her very basis for belief. Thus in the face of this tragedy, Mama Lena quickly resorts to prayer: "Oh, God . . . (*She looks up to Him*) Look down here—and show me the strength" (109), and she repeats the prayer for strength twice more before the scene ends. She wavers briefly in her certainty about planning her family's future, but her prayer serves as vocal affirmation of the role she must continue to play as head of her household.

However, she has one more low point to undergo with Walter Lee—the scene in which he plans to accept the money from Karl Lindner, the white man sent to buy out their interest in the house in all-white Clybourne Park. Mama Lena insists that Travis be on hand if Walter Lee is going to go through the minstrel act he has previewed for the family: "No. Travis, you

stay right here [instead of going downstairs]. And you make him understand what you doing, Walter Lee. You teach him good. Like Willy Harris
taught you. You show where our five generations done come to. Go ahead,
son—" (126). With those admonitions (strongly and powerfully directive
in spite of a presumably undermined Mama Lena), and with Travis' merry
expectations, it is impossible for Walter Lee to play the role of the minstrel
or to allow Lindner to buy his family's dignity. In the early stages of this
scene, Hansberry emphasizes twice that Walter Lee is *"like a small boy"*
(126, 127). It could be argued, then, that this small boy has lost his
mother's approval and, in a scene that parallels the first scene of the play between Ruth and Travis, must work to be restored to her good graces. The
"small boy" will finally—or seemingly so—be transformed into a man.
When Walter Lee tells Lindner that the Youngers will move into his neighborhood, "(MAMA *has her eyes closed and is rocking back and forth as though
she were in church, with her head nodding the amen yes*)" (128). The small
boy has indeed won his mother's approval.

In Walter Lee's presumed progression from boy to man, it is noteworthy
throughout the play how members of his family refer to him. Beneatha calls
him "Brother," while Ruth calls him "Walter" as much if not more than she
calls him "Walter Lee." Mama Lena refers to him as "Walter," "Brother,"
"Walter Lee," "boy," "baby," and "son," with at least the last three of these
designations reflecting her stunting of his growth; the use of "Walter Lee"
also raises some interesting possibilities. It could be argued that referring to
a 35-year-old man as "Walter Lee" is a carryover from southern traditions in
which parents routinely use first and middle names in referring to their children, but it could also be argued that retaining the middle name is a way of
retaining childhood, retaining control, and thereby stunting growth. It also
retains the southern heritage of black male acquiescence to voices of authority. On the occasions when both Ruth and Mama Lena use "Walter Lee,"
they are usually interacting with him in a directive mode, for example, when
Ruth is demanding that he get out of bed (13) or when Mama Lena is demanding that he not raise his voice in her house (57) or telling him to sit
down (58).[27] Ruth also uses it when Walter Lee humiliates her in front of
George Murchison (69, 71), thus he is acting less than manly. When she
drops the middle name, Ruth indicates her preference for the man instead
of the boy suggested by the two names. Ruth has thus on some level recognized—or hoped for—her husband's manhood from the point she married
him, while it is left to Mama Lena to name his growth into that state—and
thereby publicly decree it into a flexible reality (she can change it whenever
she wants)—after the scene with Lindner.[28]

When her family's actions are to her advantage and approval, Mama Lena
slides into the role supportive of those actions. Lindner tries to appeal to her,

only to be met with this comment from Mama: "I am afraid you don't understand. My son said we was going to move and there ain't nothing left for me to say. (*Shaking her head with double meaning*) You know how these young folks is nowadays, mister. Can't do a thing with 'em. Good-bye" (128). Since very little Walter Lee has said during the course of the play has been taken seriously (consider the breakfast scene with Ruth or his expressions of his dreams to Beneatha and Mama Lena), Mama Lena only supports his final position because it is in line with her own. And, no matter the nobility of Walter Lee's decision, perhaps Walter Lee has come to realize that making peace with Mama Lena is infinitely preferable to losing the respect of his entire family. Though Mama Lena claims to have lost her power of influence, it is clear immediately upon Lindner's departure that she is just as directive at the end of Act III as she was at the beginning of Act I: "Ruth, put Travis' good jacket on him . . . Walter Lee, fix your tie and tuck your shirt in, you look just like somebody's hoodlum" (128). The voice of power remains the voice of power, and the queen has not moved an inch from her throne.

This final scene reiterates a fact that has been true throughout the play: Mama Lena's assertion that she has done to Walter what the rest of the world has done to him. It is clear with Lindner that Walter will draw a line at willful humiliation in his interaction with whites. Lindner might perceive the family moving into Clybourne Park as a militant act, but Walter Lee is hardly capable of militancy.[29] He has lived a life of containment, and Mama Lena has been the primary shaper of that containment. Richard Wright suggests in *Native Son* (1940) that black women join with the white power structure in controlling black men, keeping them in subservient places in society.[30] Mama Lena has taught Walter the value of working hard (even at low-paying jobs),[31] the Christian-based value of loving one's neighbor, and general family values. All these good teachings mean that this black man will not be a problem for the larger white society. He will more than likely stay in the place assigned to him (being Mr. Arnold's chauffeur instead of Mr. Arnold) and though, like Bigger, he may have dreams of transcending, he will probably not disrupt the status quo to make his dreams reality. Mama Lena's good teachings, therefore, have ultimately become the white folks' gun at Walter Lee's head; they remind him of his limitations, of the bird cage in which he must reside, instead of pushing him to break the bars of that cage (his feeble attempt to redefine himself by losing the $6,500 in insurance money merely highlights his limitations). Mama Lena's role, like that of countless black women historically, is to save her son by instilling in him the values that will keep him safe—away from the white man's wrath, his violence, his jails. These applaudable intentions do not fail, however, to make clear where the power lines are drawn in the family. Mama Lena's and historical black women's originally protective instincts finally become stifling.

They muddle the fine line between protection and stunting a personality, and they therefore make power relationships that could be viewed altruistically seem, in the end, more self-serving and detrimental.

These chartings of the impact of strength upon the offspring of strong black women characters indicate that power and authority are so intertwined with self-sacrifice and love that is it is impossible at times to tease them out. The offspring of such women suffer mentally and physically, but the women themselves suffer as well. Consider Mama Lena's position in the play. The primary orbit of Mama Lena's existence is her small apartment and the homes of the whites for whom she works. If she has friends, they are not mentioned. There is a brief scene in the first movie in which Mama Lena interacts with her neighbor Mrs. Johnson, but no such scene is incorporated into the play. If Mama Lena is currently attending a church, that, too, is not mentioned; perhaps her moral fervor is a carryover from her religious days in Mississippi and the time before Big Walter died and need only be sustained now by memory instead of actual practice. Among her age and religious groups, then, Mama Lena is a loner. Her family thus fills a communal and friendship void, a fact that makes the intense involvement with them even more problematic because it does not have an objective or semi-objective outlet against which it can be placed in perspective. The absence of such outlets underscores again the self-sacrificing nature of the strong black woman character, the one who puts God and family above all else.

Mama Lena is in her 60s, and Hansberry writes that she is still a beautiful woman. In the current action of the play, however, she has no gentleman caller(s) and seems thoroughly devoted to the memory of Big Walter.[32] It is worthwhile to examine the legend of that relationship, for Mama Lena uses it in several instances to coerce her family to certain attitudes and actions. Though no mention of church going occurs in the current action of the play, Mama Lena comments, when she is confronted with Beneatha's blasphemy, that she and Big Walter took the children to Sunday School every Sunday; that memory is intended as a weapon to inspire Beneatha to tow the proper religious line. Mama Lena also uses Big Walter's example to inspire Walter Lee to accept his responsibility to Ruth and their unborn child, and memory of Big Walter's hard work provides the emotional depth of the betrayal when Walter Lee gives the money away. Yet what of the intimate relationship between Mama Lena and Big Walter? Has he been only a provider and concerned father? What of the privacy of their relationship? Certainly they had sex, but was there any romance there? Part of her heightened reaction to Ruth's contemplation of abortion is memory of the death of little Claude and how Big Walter responded to that tragedy. But that is precisely the area of concern in relation to her strength, for Mama Lena charts Big Walter's reaction to the death more so than her own, as if her strength has enabled her to endure the loss better than her husband—in spite of the child having issued from her very body.

More important, by making Big Walter larger than life, she diminishes his faults, and it is in those faults that we gauge what she has given up—or been forced to endure—in their relationship. She says: "Crazy 'bout his children! God knows there was plenty wrong with Walter Younger—hardheaded, mean, kind of wild with women—plenty wrong with him. But he sure loved his children. Always wanted them to have something—be something" (33). Mama Lena's intimate relationship with her husband is buried in the set aside phrase where she names his faults. What did his "hardheadedness" mean for her as his wife? How did his "meanness" affect her and indeed their children? And is "kind of wild with women" another one of those toning down expressions to which Mama Lena resorts to alter reality? Consider a couple of examples. When Walter Lee is suffering through the constant deferral of his dreams, he implores her, "I want so many things that they are driving me kind of crazy . . . Mama—look at me," with the clear intent of her seeing his pain. Rather than comply, she turns his anguish and his potential serious meaning in a superficial direction: "I'm looking at you. You a good-looking boy. You got a job, a nice wife, a fine boy and—" (60). Later, when the money is gone, she exaggerates the family's ability to make do in the space in which they currently live: "Been thinking 'bout some of the things we could do to fix this place up some. I seen a second-hand bureau over on Maxwell Street just the other day that could fit right there. . . . Would need some new handles on it and then a little varnish and then it look like something brand-new" (120). As Audre Lorde says her mother taught her, when you cannot change reality, change your attitude toward reality. Mama Lena can change reality on occasions, but she definitely changes her attitude toward it. These exaggerations and potential for changing reality thus raise questions about her relationship with Big Walter. How many women was he wild about? How frequently? And what kind of impact did infidelity have upon this strong black woman, in spite of her ability to contain it under her husband's ostensible love for his children? Whatever happened in the relationship with Big Walter, its relegation to memory now makes it pristine, and it makes Mama Lena's fidelity loom even larger.

In other words, by not showing any interest in men, Mama Lena is a *respectable* woman, so respectable that she does not even think of what it would mean to have a male companion/lover. And the setting of the play complicates that consideration. Where on earth would she and a man be intimate? While Hansberry allows for the modicum of privacy that Walter Lee and Ruth are able to have by allowing them a room to themselves, Mama Lena must share her room and bed with Beneatha, thus Hansberry has written out of the text any possibility for Mama Lena to have the privacy necessary to romantic relationships. By contrast, think again of Eva Peace in Morrison's *Sula*. Eva might be less than respectable by church ladies' estimations, but she refuses to deny her sensuality or her need for male companionship; even with one leg, she has several gentleman callers. For Mama Lena, the lack of consideration of the potential intimate/romantic part of her humanity merely places her more solidly into the self-sacrificial role of strong black women characters. Give up men. Give up sex. Give up privacy. Give up any thoughts of the flesh not immediately related to eating in preparation for work or feeling tired in response to work. Devote oneself exclusively to family. In exchange, earn the right to manage them with little course-changing objection.

Within as well as beyond her family, however, Mama Lena is a loner. That, too, is a serious consequence for the strong black woman character. As mostly undisputed head of her household, Mama Lena obviously has no peer. The hierarchy of power established within the family illustrates clearly that she has no one on earth to whom she can turn—even if she wanted to— for consultation about the decisions she makes. She might *look* "pleadingly" at her children and daughter-in-law on a couple of occasions to get them to *accept* her decisions, but she does not consult them in the decision-making process. Her position and power leave her without a shoulder to cry on, without a designated sympathetic soul mate. On the first brief occasion when she seems to falter (when she admits that she has been wrong and helped to hurt Walter Lee as much as the larger society has hurt him), she even argues with him in taking blame. "I been wrong," she says, to which Walter Lee, probably sarcastically, responds: "Naw, you ain't never been wrong about nothing, Mama." Still going it alone, she retorts: "Listen to me, now. I say I been wrong, son" (86). On the second brief occasion when she appears to falter—after Walter Lee has lost the money—she still has no worldly soul confessor to whom she can take her burden. Instead, she adopts another directive posture and orders the family to begin unpacking the things they have packed in preparation for the move. Even when she is apparently "*lost, vague, trying to catch hold, to make some sense of her former command of the world*" (118), she does not share that lostness with anyone; she continues to make decisions in spite of her seemingly diminished state. True to one of the primary tenets of the strong black woman character, she keeps on keeping on, more alone than not.

Another consequence of Mama Lena's strength that has a direct impact upon her physical well being is her size itself. Her large body is an indication of diet, which suggests that it is not one most conducive to good health. While Mama Lena is still strong and still able to work as a domestic, there are blatant signals in the text that her working days are limited. It could be argued that size is as much a factor as age in this anticipated conclusion to her working years. The acquisition of that size fits again into diet and the health issues surrounding the insistence in black communities that size is a reflection of strength and health. Mama Lena is as much concerned about food and the size of those around her as are the women in those historical communities. Remember her wanting Travis' oats loaded down with "lots of butter" (29) as well as her comment that Beneatha might catch a cold because she is "so thin" (28), and she is eager to prepare "some homecooked meals" (52) for Asagai.

Finally, the psychological pain that Mama Lena inflicts upon others is also hers to bear. That is apparent in her reaction to Beneatha's disbelief, in Walter Lee's refusal to be the man Mama Lena envisioned concerning the proposed abortion, and in her disappointment when Walter Lee gives away the insurance money. Those scenes pale, however, in comparison to those in which she is strong and dominating. By sheer volume of representation, the emphasis is on the side of seeming psychological health, so that the minor rips in that tightly worn garment are quickly repaired. The tight reins that Mama Lena holds on her family only *almost* unravel in her hands. I emphasize almost here because the strong black woman character seems always to recover, and that is no less the case with Mama Lena.

She is *the* classic example of the problematic nature of the black female character's strength. Mama Lena was so well-received in 1959 precisely because blacks were more concerned about *inter*racial issues than *intra*racial issues. If a strong black woman character like Mama Lena could make the case for acceptability of all black people, then why quibble, as one of the reviewers asserted, over her excesses of characterization? The facts that she was on stage, recognizable, and representative were sufficient unto themselves.

Since Walter, Ruth, Beneatha, and Travis all seem to respect Mama Lena, another question arises. If her way of raising them is so troubling to close readers, and if she has such an insidious impact upon them, why is their response to her not more negative? I would argue that, in the mold of expectation and community imperative that governs Mama Lena's behavior, the same governs her children. They cannot ultimately reject the impact of her parenting because they are also drawn to reflect a particular time and place: the circle of acceptability that informs their historical counterparts also informs Hansberry's creation of them. The culture has taught them to respect Mama Lena, in spite of her tyranny, just as it has taught her to throw her weight around. But in terms of her impact upon them, imagine the other characters beyond the time frame of the play. Walter is probably still going to be dependent upon the women. Beneatha will probably become a doctor, perhaps more in spite of than because of Mama Lena. And Ruth is still going to be mousy. Travis is a question mark, but he has seen enough of how his family operates to know that women are dominant, men have little power, and his father has had to acquiesce to Mama Lena's wishes in order to win her approval.

The play-going audiences' acceptance of Mama Lena's excesses depended in large part on what I call a communal moral imperative. As I mentioned earlier, the general consensus was that the majority of "Negroes" at the time were religious, did not believe in abortion, were aware of if not acquiescent in various forms of domestic violence (especially in terms of parents disciplining children), and accepted all the foregoing as the norm. Indeed, this was a period in African American history that one could conceivably refer to "the black community," for—primarily due to racial positioning—views were more consistent than divergent. Consequently, black people joined with whites in finding the physically and religiously comforting image of Mama Lena acceptable in spite of her violence and invasions of privacy. As Ossie Davis pointed out, the mere fact that this recognizable black woman character made it to the stage satisfied just about everybody. Therefore, the average black person viewing the play, or for whom the play was written, probably did not pause very long—if at all—to meditate on the fact that Hansberry had joined with many white writers in portraying African American women, with slight modifications, in a particular stereotypical way. Her collaboration was just as effective as those earlier ones in which black actresses played the stereotyped roles assigned to them. Through Hansberry's tremendously effective portrayal, then, blacks and whites fell in love with Mama Lena, who, despite her tyranny, served as a source of comfort to both groups.

Chapter 3 ~

Strength and the Battle Ground of Slavery I.

Even Parody: Ishmael Reed and Mammy Barracuda

From the middle 1970s to the 1990s, the antebellum South became one of the literary sites for portrayal of black female character, the strong as well as the not-so-strong. Ishmael Reed, Sherley Anne Williams, J. California Cooper, Charles Johnson, and Toni Morrison, among others, selected the arena of slavery as the territory on which to present their depictions of black female character.[1] While Williams, Johnson, and Morrison created works primarily in the realistic mode, and Cooper in the fantastic, Reed chose the satiric form that is his trademark. Even in his satire, however, black females are physically strong above all else. This is especially true of Mammy Barracuda, the character who, with Uncle Robin, literally runs the Swille plantation in Reed's *Flight to Canada* (1976).

An anachronistic meshing of historical times and personalities, modes of transportation, and nineteenth- and twentieth-century race politics, *Flight to Canada* is an amalgamation in which our expectations are consistently short-circuited and in which power roles are undermined and/or reversed. The tale of Massa Swille, Uncle Robin, Raven Quickskill, Mammy Barracuda, and others, the narrative centers upon a poem Quickskill has written as well as, in the tradition of many runaways who were enslaved, his flight to Canada. It also depicts Swille's encounter with Abraham Lincoln when Lincoln comes requesting funds for the Union cause, Mammy Barracuda's reinstatement of Ms. Swille as a southern belle, and Uncle Robin's general takeover of the plantation. In a narrative in which no one escapes the critical commentary on a plantation system gone awry and the race politics therein, the position of the black female character is particularly noteworthy and, in many ways, particularly offensive.

In this parodic treatment of the strong black female character, an aura of suspicion surrounds all her actions. Lacking the moral base that defined Mama Lena and earlier such characters, Mammy Barracuda is a sinful force set loose on the plantation household, its owners and servants, a force that will not be contained, not even by the ostensible master of the plantation who has unleashed it. As names are important with earlier portraits, so are they important here. "Mammy" touches on the traditional role of black women in plantation household societies and locates Mammy Barracuda in a familiar position in relation to the master, his wife, and children, as well as to other household workers, while "Barracuda" parodies any potential soft-ness in that image; barracudas are notorious for their violence, their ability to subdue fish and animals, including man, that are hundreds of times their size.[2] By assigning the character the two names, Reed gives substance to size. Mammy Barracuda is thus an image, a myth, brought to fictional life and al-lowed to act out all the characteristics that popular perception would have us believe actually occurred historically.[3] Reed endows her with power ru-mored to be associated with historical mammies, but that power was always a slippery, questionable condition in historical cases. In historical plantation households, the large black women identified as "mammies" seldom had power to go along with their large shapes. The comforting stereotypes that followed emancipation continued to cast such women in the role of nurtur-ers and self-sacrificing doers of white people's wills.

In physical presentation, Mammy Barracuda's character shakes hands only briefly with other representations of black female character cast in the stereo-typical role of mammy. Reed describes her at one point as wearing a scarf—with the incongruous indication that it is made of silk, and on another occasion she wears an apron. Her size, like so much of what Reed writes, is inferred rather than stated directly. Mamma Barracuda is tall enough to stand eye-to-eye with most of the men she encounters, including the lanky Abra-ham Lincoln. She is strong enough to be observed at one point executing a "half nelson"[4] on Ms. Swille, and on another occasion, when Ms. Swille slips and falls on her way to taking the bath Mammy Barracuda is forcing upon her, "Barracuda picks her up as though she were a child and throws her into the tub" (113). In every scene in which she appears, Mammy Barracuda ex-udes a strength that pervades the very air of the text, whether physical ges-tures are involved or not. The stereotypical aura of strength that surrounds her holds sway even when the specific traits identified with that aura are not made explicit. The success of her physical characterization rests upon the knowledge that Reed was sure his readers would bring to the text from their saturation in American popular mythology, including their perceived notions of slavery and their popularly derived notions of the size connected with strong black women. To bolster that popular mythology, Reed uses a series of descriptive verbs that also highlight Mammy Barracuda's strength and power. Mammy Barracuda never does anything in a soft or quiet way; instead, she "smacks" (38), "throws" (111), "knocks," "grabs," "presses" (112), "knees," "shoves" (113), and "gives orders" (117).

Mamma Barracuda's apparently legendary position in the Swille plantation household, however, is tied to real power as much as it is tied to real physical strength. It is a legendary status that Mammy Barracuda perpetuates for herself and one that has apparently been so successful over the years that Massa Swille has given her the leeway to do pretty much as she wants. Consider her interaction with other black women in the Swille household. Bangalang, the young girl who works with Mammy Barracuda, is clearly afraid of her, and Mammy Barracuda has no difficulty getting other servants to recite a catechism with which they are probably quite familiar.

'Who da boss?'
'You are, Mammy Barracuda.'
'Who?'
'You.'
'Let me hear it from all of you,' she said, her hand cupping her ear.
The girls say, 'You are, Barracuda. You the boss. Our leader . . .' (117)[5]

Massa Swille allows Mammy to do as she pleases because she represents his interests completely. There is absolutely no separation of her identity from plantation politics. What the slaveholders want is what Mammy Barracuda wants. No mask-wearing exists here, no identification with black people who have been wrongfully enslaved.[6] Reed writes Mammy Barracuda as white power in blackface, white institutions in the servant role, and white values in the kitchen. By depicting her so thoroughly as behaving to the detriment of her biological if not psychological or spiritual kin, Reed puts another brick in the wall of "evidence" against black women who use their positions among whites to keep other blacks in place.

With Mammy Barracuda, Reed therefore takes to its logical absurdity the mythology surrounding black women who did nothing more than give, give, give. Mammy Barracuda gives to the whites constantly, even when it is ostensibly harmful to her or to those like her. But since she is a shell of representation, absent a reflective life, there is no sense of what the cost to her actually is or could be. Reed then redefines the image of the giving black woman by creating a power hungry, hulking, predatory, and rapacious personality in Mammy Barracuda. Size, strength, and power become the primary definers of this re-creation. It is clear from first mention of her in the text that Mammy Barracuda generally works against the interests of black people. *Who* she is is made clear from the references other characters make to her. Just as reader impressions of a character like Gabriel Grimes in James Baldwin's *Go Tell It on the Mountain* are formed before he enters the text, so too are impressions of Mammy Barracuda. Once she appears, all she has to do is illustrate what has already been asserted about her. The fact that she has occupied the head spaces of other characters sufficiently for them to comment on her is yet another testament to the role she plays in the plantation household.

Initially, as Raven Quickskill prepares to write "Flight to Canada," which is chronologically at the beginning of the book but after the events it relates, he queries Bangalang on the whereabouts of Mammy Barracuda, to which she replies: "Last I heard, she sang before the last reunion of Confederate Soldiers. . . . She sang a chorus from 'Dixie.' Well, I have to tell you when she got to those lines that go 'Will run away—Missus took a decline, oh / Her face was de color ob bacon-rine-oh!', the old soldiers took Mammy on their shoulders and marched her out from the convention hall" (14). Upholding the slavocracy even as she is upheld, Mammy Barracuda is an anachronism in the post-slavery South, but it is precisely the belief in that kind of anachronism that led in part to twentieth century representations of strong black female character. Revered for the strength of her conviction that she should side with the planter class,[7] Mammy Barracuda reaps the rewards of that wise decision, or that sellout—depending on the vantage point from which her actions are evaluated. Except for Cato the Graffado, Mammy Barracuda's mulatto sidekick from their plantation reign, the reunion of Confederate soldiers is a gathering of white men and *a* black woman. As the novel develops, the significance of this alignment becomes increasingly apparent.

In singing "Dixie," Mammy Barracuda situates herself in a culturally erasing role instead of a culturally defining role toward the other African American characters, but a culturally supporting or affirming role toward whites. Compare her, for example, to Aunt Sally in Margaret Walker's *Jubilee* (1966) or to Big Laura in Ernest J. Gaines's *The Autobiography of Miss Jane Pittman* (1971). Aunt Sally's singing on the plantation, her appropriation of food to take to other blacks in the quarters, and her caring for young Vyry all paint her in the role of affirming African American life and cultural traditions while she works as the subversive trickster within the Dutton household. There is a clear separation between who she is as a black woman and the people who attempt to define her as property. The same is true of Big Laura. In fighting white paterollers in an effort to save herself and black children when they dare to leave the plantation after the Emancipation announcement, Laura aligns herself with blacks and freedom. She gives her life rather than be enslaved. Neither she nor anyone else takes a romantic or white cultural attitude toward their enslavement. By contrast, in singing "Dixie," Mammy Barracuda not only separates herself from black culture and historical causes, but from the very black women who were in the same or similar positions in plantation households. Yet the substance of her erasure is contained within a very traditional black female form.

When Mammy Barracuda makes her initial appearance, her political identification with Massa Swille is evident from the familiarity he has granted to her. Believing that they are alone, she refers to him as "Arthur" before she sees Uncle Robin and makes an attendant adjustment. And realizing that Massa Swille, not his wife, is the ultimate source of power on the plantation and indeed in the United States, Mammy Barracuda elects to tattle to him about the actions of Ms. Swille. Instead of mailing a suffragette letter Ms. Swille has written and with which she has been entrusted, Mammy Barracuda gives it to Massa Swille. Noting that Uncle Robin is staring during this exchange, Mammy Barracuda asks threateningly, "What you lookin' at?" (21). The image is not far removed from the directive black women actresses pictured in *Ethnic Notions,* and the insistent, demanding tone is not appreciably unlike what we might hear from Mama Lena. Uncle Robin's profession of admiration for Mammy Barracuda's new apron in response to her question is unsatisfactory, for Uncle Robin is privy to something she did not anticipate. She unhesitatingly agrees to destroy the letter, but is concerned enough about Robin to ask Massa Swille, "What about him?" To her mind, there are two powerful characters in the room, and Uncle Robin is not one of them. Indeed, she considers him expendable in this scenario, and she appears ready to do violence against him. Swille's reply that he trusts Uncle Robin "second only to you, Barracuda" earns only a "Humph" and other noises from her as she exits—in bas relief against the lingering rumor that once "she stared a man to death." Swille's designation of her as a "wonderful old soul," to which Uncle Robin can only agree, obviously works as much in Swille's best interest as it does in Mammy Barracuda's. She not only keeps the household in order for Swille, but she allows him to live out his mammy fantasies with her. "Lying curled up fetuslike in your lap," he says to her, "is worth a hundred shrinks on Park Avenue" (21).

Her identification with Swille enables Mammy Barracuda to be prepared to put Uncle Robin in his place, which means that her strength and power are again in the service of the white plantation system. The dynamic being worked out here between the strong black woman and the black man brings to the surface the suggestion that black women are willing to harm black men for white men.[8] Unlike the cage in which Walter Lee is confined, however, Reed allows Uncle Robin an escape. Except for superficial interactions, he does not recognize a need to deal with Mammy Barracuda. Instead, he too goes to the source of power in working to achieve freedom from Swille and slavery (as Swille's bookkeeper, he alters the will so that he inherits the plantation). The mask that Mammy Barracuda does not want or need enables Uncle Robin to acquire vast quantities of property upon Swille's demise. In this scene, however, Mammy Barracuda has the upper hand, and achieving her objective leads her to ensure that Uncle Robin can in no way interfere with it.

Interestingly, the white woman and the black man—at least at a glimpse—are presumably under the thumb of the white man and the black woman. Perhaps Reed is playing here with the popularly perceived notion that white men and black women are the freest of these racial pairings in American society. Forming a partnership would seem a logical extension of that perception. That partnership, based in public power (as opposed to Uncle Robin's surer, quieter use of power behind the scenes) and exploitation, depends as much on the black woman's strength as it does on the white's man financial and social power. This unholy matrimony and its ugly consequences make the representation of the strong black woman character particularly unsettling in Reed's hands.

The liberties that Mammy Barracuda takes with Arthur Swille are duplicated in her brief interaction with Abraham Lincoln. She is respectful, then allowably directive (Swille gives her that power, not Lincoln):

> 'Oh, Mr. Linclum! Mr. Linclum! I admires you so. Now you come on down to the kitchen and let me make you and your party a nice cup of coffee.'
> 'But I have very important business to do on *The River Queen,* the tide of battle . . .'
> 'Shush your mouth and come on down here get some of this coffee. Steaming hot. What's wrong with you, man, you gone pass up some of this good old Southern hospitality?'
> Lincoln shrugs his shoulders. 'Well,' he says, smiling, 'I guess one little cup won't hurt.' She waltzes around with Abe Lincoln, who follows awkwardly. She sings, 'Hello, Abbbbbe. Well, hello, Abbbbbe. It's so nice to have you here where you belong.' (38)

Here, in the role of entertainer, Mammy Barracuda parallels her role with the Confederate soldiers for whom she sings "Dixie." On the surface, her seeming appreciation for Lincoln might be viewed as typical of a black person who understood Lincoln's role in African American history. However, since Mammy Barracuda has little if any identification with that history, her ostensible appreciation for Lincoln is perhaps tied more to an identification with power. Since Swille and Lincoln are in cahoots, Lincoln can effectively be equated to Swille in this interaction. For Mammy Barracuda to welcome Lincoln so effusively, therefore, is in effect to welcome Swille's spiritual brother.

On the other hand, and in keeping with her later chastising blacks for listening to a speech by Lincoln, it is perhaps more logical to assume that Mammy Barracuda's interaction with Lincoln constitutes a stalling ruse designed to thwart, as least temporarily, his effectiveness as commander-in-chief of the Union forces. Under the guise of southern hospitality, therefore, Mammy Barracuda can appear innocent in her request for Lincoln to enjoy the pleasures of her kitchen. This alternate interpretation would nonetheless still be consistent with her position in relation to Massa Swille. It is a protective gesture toward him personally as well as toward the southern values that he upholds. This might be the one exception in the text in which Mammy Barracuda appears to adopt a mask, though it is a mask that binds or blinds rather than liberates, and it is light years away from the personal political stance that Uncle Robin takes.

What is perhaps most fascinating about Mammy Barracuda is how her strength is directed toward her white charge, in this case Ms. Swille herself. Her interactions with Ms. Swille are a perverse combination of gender revenge, vicarious self creation, and cruelty, traits not usually assigned to the altruistic mammy figure. I offer the phrase gender revenge because of the hints of possible sexual interaction between Mammy Barracuda and Massa Swille. Usually portrayed as asexual, the mammy can have children but, paradoxically, no sex life. The text hints that Mammy Barracuda is lusty in all her appetites and that the latitude Massa Swille allows her might derive from her sexual encounters with him. However, even if this were true, the racial protocol of the plantation is enough in effect that there can be no public display of affection—or sexuality—between Massa Swille and Mammy Barracuda.[9] Her gender revenge thus ties into the vicarious self creation, for she transforms Ms. Swille into what she, Mammy Barracuda, can never be—public, sexual partner to Massa Swille. Simultaneously, Mammy Barracuda can never be thin, either in life or mythology, so she creates a thin self in Ms. Swille.

Consider also how Mammy Barracuda's clothing fits into this gender revenge motif. In incongruously matched attire, she exhibits a propensity for a social and class station beyond her own, yet in the very mismatching of her outfits, she shows her inability to be at home in that class. Clothing and jewelry that she will force Ms. Swille to wear to perfection are not things that she herself can similarly effect to good taste. Two descriptions of her clothing illustrating her penchant for velvet and large jewelry[10] will serve to illustrate the point. "Barracuda has a silk scarf tied about her head. A black velvet dress. She wears a diamond crucifix on her bosom. It's so heavy she walks with a stoop" (20) and "Barracuda . . . wore a purple velvet dress with silver hoops, a pongee apron with Belgian lace, and emerald earrings" (109). Her attire might be identified with the wealthy class, but Mammy Barracuda is nonetheless in service to Arthur Swille. In fact, the crucifix she wears around her neck is a blatant symbol of her having sold out to white power. In exchange for the image being given life and substance, she has given her soul for the money and power that accrue to her. The crucifix is therefore as conspicuous a symbol as the mythical mammy being brought to life. Both serve simultaneously to put air into questionable legends and to deflate them, for Mammy Barracuda has certainly not been resurrected for any altruistic purpose.[11] In relation to Ms. Swille, Mammy Barracuda can smooth out the bulkiness in her own appearance by forcing Ms. Swille to look the part that she cannot. Indeed, there might be another manifestation of the "Etheric Double" concept at play in the narrative, this time between Mammy Barracuda and Ms. Swille.[12] Displacement, vicarious self creation, revenge, and cruelty all become the servants of power as Mammy Barracuda forces Ms. Swille into her corseted role.

Superficially, Mammy Barracuda's transformation or reclamation of Ms. Swille approximates the mythical notions of what mammies were allowed to do on historical plantations. They presumably had moral and social control over their young white charges. They supervised their dress, guided them in the development of morals and manners, and "approved" their beaux.[13] Mammy Barracuda was with Ms. Swille long before she met and married Arthur; though their relationship has progressed chronologically from Ms. Swille's childhood to her adulthood, Mammy Barracuda shows that she still views Ms. Swille as a child when she takes charge and makes her behave in the role that southern society, with Mammy Barracuda's approval, has carved out for her. That role is a combination of the frivolous and the superficial. In this text, southern belles arrange flowers, pass judgment on menus served to guests, arrange their bodies into the height of artful beauty, and make appearances before southern gentlemen in order to be praised in the tradition of the "to the Ladies" toast. When Ms. Swille decides that she is going to become a suffragette and "goes on strike" against her prescribed role, Mammy Barracuda tolerates it for awhile, then gets Swille's permission to reclaim Ms. Swille. In this reclamation process, Mammy Barracuda reinstates Ms. Swille in the role of obedient child/frivolous southern lady and thereby viciously reasserts her own position as the physically strong black mammy.

The reclamation process compares to a ritual of conversion as Ms. Swille must be restored to her former bellehood in body as well as in mind. Mammy Barracuda has the power of command—her voice as well as the help of the other servants—in getting the job done. In the cleansing process, Mammy Barracuda insults Ms. Swille by ascribing to her traits usually not identified with southern white women. She "enters the Mistress' room. Surveys the scene. Puts her hands on her hips" (111) in a classic strong black commanding female gesture, and asserts that Ms. Swille stinks by calling her a "lazy bourgeoise [*sic*] skunk."[14] Ms. Swille's attempts to assert sisterhood with Mammy Barracuda only lead to Mammy Barracuda placing her in the role of a child to be commanded. Mammy Barracuda ignores Ms. Swille's pleas for understanding, pulls the covers off her, and raises the window to air out the room. She "grabs her by the hair and yanks her to the floor" (112) and proceeds toward the unwanted bath while heaping a series of epithets upon Ms. Swille: "'Now move, you old motherfukin she-dog. You scarecrow. You douche-bag! You flea-sack drawers! . . . Look like shit. On strike. I got your strike, you underbelly of a fifteen-pound gopher rat run ober by a car. Sleep with a dog, he let you. You goat-smelling virago, you gnawing piranha, worrying that man like that" (113). Mammy Barracuda is inside the license of permissibility in attending to Ms. Swille and insisting that she change, but she is far outside the limits of such license in the language she uses to effect that transformation. This violation of verbal restraints again shows the position Mammy has been able to earn from Arthur Swille, for it illustrates that she has violated all linguistic and psychological limitations masters might expect from enslaved persons, an illustration that carries Reed's point of breathing life into the mammy myth so that it out-Herods itself. Mammy Barracuda can thus, in violent and ugly language, heap upon Ms. Swille accusations about the lack of concern for feminine and bodily hygiene that popular mythology usually associates with black women.

"That man" being worried is Arthur Swille, and his interests—and the interests of those like him—guide Mammy Barracuda consistently throughout the text. The planter class that Swille represents demands a certain image in the women of that class, and Mammy Barracuda uses her strength to create that icon. She, Bangalang, and the other women proceed to create the artful illusion in hair and clothing with the newly washed Ms. Swille, as well as the accompanying expectations in actions. Hair brushed to perfection, Ms. Swille is told to wear "a bonnet and a cloak and some jewelry" for the "garden poetry reading of Edgar Poe" (115) and similar appropriate dress when a famous military man comes to visit the next evening. In preparation for that visit, Mammy Barracuda supervises as "Ms. Swille sits in the chair facing the huge mirror. The slave girls and the pickaninnys are applying makeup, combing, brushing, manicuring; others are bringing out the wardrobe, *preparing to put Ms. Swille in it.* She sits at the dressing table, in her slip" (117; my emphasis—notice the forced passivity here). In terms of actions, the belle must pick violets, host a tea for the neighbors, attend a cookie sale for charity, personally supervise the making of the meal for the military man, and make the obligatory appearance for the men to recite the "Ode to the Southern Belle." Fulfillment of these expectations is the outward sign of the power Mammy Barracuda wields, and she is not willing to relinquish it because Ms. Swille is a reluctant participant.

Mammy Barracuda therefore wants to make sure that Ms. Swille's mind is where it should be. In order to achieve agreement from Ms. Swille with what she has been forced to do, Mammy Barracuda initially employs the sentimental approach by drawing upon the "mother/child" relationship she has always had with Ms. Swille.

> 'Barracuda hates to do what she had to do with her darlin, but her darlin was letting her darlin self go. Barracuda no like that. Barracuda no like. Come from a proud fambly. Good fambly. Remember when you used to help fix waffles for your Daddy and Mr. Jefferson? "Can I help, Mammy Barracuda?" you used to ax. Bless yo little soul.' . . . Mammy Barracuda is preening and plaiting the Mistress' hair, looking googly-eyed toward the ceiling. She pauses a minute. 'You try to raise them and look what they done done. Marry a rich man like that. Arthur Swille III. Anybody else would be proud. Proud. Like a fairy queen in one of them Princess books.' (114, 115)

When nostalgia does not encourage Ms. Swille to get into the appropriate role, Mammy Barracuda resorts to administering Valium. And to be absolutely sure that Ms. Swille knows who is in control, Mammy Barracuda ends her catechism with her helpers by turning to Ms. Swille for verbal recognition of her power:

> 'I didn't hear one person say it [that Barracuda is the boss].'
> The girls stop. They stare at Ms. Swille.
> 'Barracuda, please don't . . . don't humiliate me before the girls . . . '
> 'You've given up your respect. . . . Now I give you one more chanct. Who the boss?'
> 'You are, Barracuda.' (117–118)

Moving freely from Aunt Thomasina to dictator, Mammy Barracuda uses both sides of her personality to retain control over the household. The urge to dominate, to slap, throw, kick, and punch Ms. Swille (she also threatens Bangalang on one occasion) consistently keeps Mammy Barracuda walking a tightrope of her own construction and one that allows her to maintain an absolute balance of power.

Certainly—by objective standards—violence and cruelty are significant parts of Mammy Barracuda's transformation of Ms. Swille. What motivates the cruelty? Perhaps the answer is in a simple lust for wielding power, which is the same impulse that engaged southern planters throughout slavery. As Frederick Douglass observed, masters and mistresses were just as negatively affected by the system of slavery as were the black people themselves. The love of power, and the freedom to wield it *unchallenged,* motivates Mammy Barracuda as assuredly as it motivated overseers who lashed black people and then poured salt into their wounds. In yet another perverse transformation, therefore, Mammy Barracuda becomes "master" of Ms. Swille's life, treating her in effect as "property." Ms. Swille does what Mammy Barracuda demands of her because she has no recourse in the face of the strength and power that refuse to recognize any legitimate claims on her part. She is as helpless as any enslaved person who might be sold "down the river" for invoking the displeasure of his or her master.

In reshaping Ms. Swille into the southern belle, Mammy Barracuda is ostensibly upholding southern plantation mythology. That mythology, however, is so warped and absurd in the presentation in this text that what Mammy Barracuda is upholding is barely worth the effort—except from the point of personal satisfaction, and perhaps that is all that is necessary in a satiric text. Massa Swille's plantation is clearly a house of cards, with perversities—including his own incestuous desire for his sister—abounding. The Civil War is being fought in the background, which will bring an end to the slavocracy, and enslaved persons, including Raven Quickskill, 40s, and Stray Leechfield, are disappearing as fast as they can into the Union lines as well as into Canada. It is a short-lived mythology from which Mammy Barracuda derives her pleasure, and there is little suggestion in the text that she lives for anything beyond this temporary gratification, for she is ultimately drawn with more fluff than substance—beyond the fact of her strength.

The strength Arthur Swille allows Mammy Barracuda to exhibit in the narrative might also be read as an elaborate revenge tale in which Reed manipulates black female character and allows it retaliation for historical wrongs. As numerous cultural historians, sociologists, and other scholars have documented, black women went into the homes of white women to work during and after slavery. These black women were more often than not at the mercy of the white women—as well as the white men—for whom they worked as domestics. White women could make unreasonable labor demands upon them, and black women had little redress if they wanted to work. White men could take sexual advantage of the women and suffer no repercussions. On a daily basis, however, it was primarily the white women who made black women's lives difficult if not downright miserable. To reverse those circumstances, as Reed does in *Flight to Canada,* would seem to be a plus. Unfortunately, as in the historical scenarios, both black and white women are still ultimately controlled by the white man's economic, political, and social power. To reverse the situation might, on the surface, serve a tolerable and perhaps even understandable revenge motive. However, in achieving that objective, Reed strips the strong black female character of the attributes that might have made her tyrannical strength historically acceptable.

Mammy Barracuda finally does not work for black community or for perpetuation of black life and health. Her strength is used merely for her own satisfaction. She does not have the justification of a Bigger Thomas in Wright's *Native Son* (1940) or Guitar Bains's Seven Days in Morrison's *Song of Solomon* (1977); she just seems to be having fun. By taking the strong black woman character out of church, out of family ties, out of history, Reed succeeds more than anything else in highlighting the pathology that informs my larger discussion. The dissonance Reed creates in Mammy Barracuda's personality raises questions about her mental health. If indeed she likes to inflict pain and is cruel simply because she has the power to do so, then she becomes psychologically warped, neurotic even, and not appreciably unlike Walker Vessels in Amiri Baraka's *The Slave* (1964). Black people, the so-called revolutionary Vessels argues, are under no obligation to be better than whites if they should come into power; it would simply be their turn.

Mammy Barracuda's turn is destructive to other black characters as well as to the representation of black female character. At the reading of Massa Swille's will, the Judge reveals that Massa Swille has left Mammy Barracuda in charge of a school for black people. In the objects he leaves with the school, it is clear how Mammy Barracuda will operate it. Swille has written: "I have set aside a quantity of land in Washington, D.C., for the erection of a Christian training school for the newly liberated slaves, who, without some moral code, will revert to their African ways and customs known to be barbarous and offensive to the civilized sensibility. In this school, Mammy Barracuda will see to it that the students are austere and abstemious. So that this school might be truly structured, I leave my closetful of precious whips and all of my fettering devices to Mammy" (168), where upon "Mammy Barracuda lit up, raising her feet from the floor. She rubbed her hands and smiled at Cato" (168). In this barely coded message, Mammy Barracuda receives orders in keeping with her singing "Dixie" for the reunion of Confederate soldiers. No Christians will come out of her school because neither she nor Swille has been concerned about moral principles, although Swille does mention at one point that it was "helpful" of Mammy Barracuda and Cato "to end all them cults and superstitions and require that all the people follow only the Jesus cult" (53); the concern here is with control, not moral development. No independent thinking will emerge because Mammy Barracuda will beat all such signs out of her charges (and notice the oxymoronic "liberated slaves"). Definitely no offense will occur because Mammy Barracuda will create generations of "safe" colored people who will adhere to the status quo and remain mentally enslaved far beyond the fact of Emancipation. She rubs her hands in anticipation of the pain that she knows she will be able to inflict unchecked.

An anti-race woman, Mammy Barracuda will continue to create a race of slaves. Her philosophy is clear in her reaction to Aunt Judy and other enslaved persons in the Swille household. Aunt Judy comments:

'Barracuda came into the kitchen, and we turned off the radio because we were listening to Mr. Lincoln's address, but she caught us. She asked us did we know what Emancipation meant, and we sort of giggled and she did too. Then Barracuda showed us the Bible where it say "He that knoweth his master's will and doeth it not, shall be beaten with many stripes." . . . She said that we were property and that we should give no thoughts to running away. . . . As for Canada, she said they skin niggers up there and makes lampshades and soap dishes out of them, and it's more barbarous in Toronto than darkest Africa, a place where we come from and for that reason should pray hard every night for the Godliness of a man like Swille to deliver us from such a place.' (57)

The feature of Mammy Barracuda's personality that would encourage her to create a race of slaves, combined with other features presented throughout the text, makes her antithetical to the historical necessity for the strong black woman but perversely validates the very thing she subverts (that is, strong black women allegedly trained generations of acquiescent young blacks). Her running of the school, therefore, will be detrimental to every black person who encounters her. Here will be no mother herding her children into integrated environments. No inspirer of learning, as the mother does in Hughes's "Mother to Son." No nurturer of revolutionaries, as Hansberry claimed for Mama Lena. Here instead is an anomaly whose tendency to violence is expressed at the will reading when she "stood and shook her fist" (167) at Uncle Robin when the judge announces that Massa Swille has left his plantation and much more to Robin. Motivation for Mammy Barracuda remains in the realm of personal pleasure and sadomasochistic satisfaction (especially in knowing she is literally doing her master's will), and it is that realm that makes her a backward-looking representation of black female character.

Reed seems to take such pleasure in portraying Mammy Barracuda as a buffoon at points that it raises questions about his like or dislike for his own character—or at least his manipulation of that character. He seems to set her up in order to take potshots at characteristics popularly associated with black women, especially the assumption in recent history that they have a distinct dislike of certain black men. Since Reed does not depict any interaction between Raven Quickskill and Mammy Barracuda, Uncle Robin becomes the representative black male stand-in. Inexplicably—except that he is not white and seemingly not in control—Uncle Robin evokes a strong dislike in Mammy Barracuda. It can only be surmised that the role in which he finds himself must contribute to her assessment of his worth. He works in the plantation house, where he is visibly a eunuch, asexual and powerless, and he mouths the stereotypical sentiments supportive of slavery that Massa Swille requires (scenes with his wife, Aunt Judy, easily contradict these surface impressions). Since Mammy Barracuda ostensibly does the same, her displeasure seems to be centered in some kind of competition. She seems to have more power with Arthur Swille than Uncle Robin, especially in terms of the daily running of the household, but Uncle Robin is still someone to whom Arthur devotes attention when perhaps Mammy Barracuda thinks that Uncle Robin is not worthy—or *should* not be worthy—of such attention. She is distinctly unimpressed when Arthur Swille remarks that he trusts Uncle Robin almost as much as he does Mammy Barracuda.

What is striking is that for all his obsequiousness, Uncle Robin is redeemed, for Raven Quickskill's narrative makes it clear that Robin is merely playing a role to gain access to Swille's will and property. Readers thus respond to Robin's trickery with a measure of warmth and acceptance. His objectives for reinstating the "old cults" (171), giving complexity to African American culture that Christianity does not allow, earns consideration if not approval from readers. In not allowing Mammy Barracuda a similar complexity in characterization, Reed and Raven Quickskill paint her as fullblown evil, comparable to Alice Walker's initial portrait of Mister, which has earned similar criticism. While Walker allows Mister to be redeemed, however, Reed lets Mammy Barracuda remain as she was when she entered the novel—ever ready to serve the purpose of her demonic former enslavers, ever ready to inflict violence, ever ready to use her strength against other black characters. Uncle Robin even aligns Mammy Barracuda with some of his and Reed's perceived negative features of Christianity by avowing that she sings spirituals and by asserting that her favorite expression is "God helps those who helps themselves" (170), which he has executed in the property-acquiring literal mode. By damning Mammy Barracuda, Reed does not challenge or damn a history of black female representation; he merely damns certain black women. While it would be difficult to be sympathetic to Mammy Barracuda, it might not be difficult to understand her in the context of the circumstances that have created such an anomaly. Reed does not give readers the history that would justify that option, electing instead to retain his sick monster of strength as the backdrop against which the actions of the very likable black male characters are judged. It could reasonably be argued that even Stray Leechfield in his northern perversity (he makes porno films) is a more acceptable character than Mammy Barracuda.

The Christian morality that guided previous literary portraits of strong black women is irrelevant to Mammy Barracuda, and Reed does not allow any associations with it to redeem her.[15] In connection with morality, again the second part of Mammy Barracuda's name is conducive to this conclusion. She achieves the kind of amoral godhead associated with tricksters such as Brer Rabbit (though she herself is not a trickster) and that we might identify with Eva Peace in Morrison's *Sula*. Her elision of morality is apparent in her willingness to do something (*what* is left unspecified) to Uncle Robin when she thinks he has heard too much. It is also apparent in her willing-ness to administer drugs to Massa Swille (109) as well as to Ms. Swille (116). For all her physical strength and power in the text, there is no indication that Mammy Barracuda actively engages questions of right and wrong. She is a force, more acting than acted upon, just as willing to pursue her course as any morally-directed strong black female character. What Reed has taken away from her, therefore, has not significantly changed the character type in its ability to ignore or crush others as it blasts its way to achieving what it wants. Mammy Barracuda can never conceive of Canada—any Canada, ei-ther in mind or body—let alone make a flight in that direction.

Flight to Canada is ultimately a meditation on images gone awry, images carried to the absurd conclusions that popular mythology suggests about them. This is especially the case with the plantation master, the plantation mistress, and particularly the plantation mammy. The popular, cultural, and historical images and stereotypes bred in slavery and developed for 100 years after have enabled Reed to tap into that well of mythology and create his rec-ognizable monster. At a glance, Mammy Barracuda is everything white peo-ple, but especially white men, in the antebellum South were taught to believe about black women; she is hard, coarse, violent, "nurturing," visually asexual, visually a contrast to the white woman. She is portrayed as more masculine than feminine, and whatever sexual desire she may inspire in Swille is hidden in the nighttime lust he may share with his historical counterparts. In the image of the mammy made flesh, Mammy Barracuda fully executes the im-plicit desires of the status quo—that is, of white supremacy. While many photographs of historical mammies picture them with white babies and thus imply their lack of concern for their own offspring and thereby their support of white supremacy, here Mammy Barracuda acts out that support by deni-grating other African Americans. By making her character such a despicable puppet to the ideology of the slaveholding South and the beliefs it passed into American culture, Reed finally suggests that some black women were so well trained during slavery in their white culture-supporting, denial-of-black-progress roles that their descendants in the twentieth century cannot possibly have denuded their psyches of such desires. Pathologically strong black women especially, Reed posits, are anathema to racial advancement, not be-cause they are forced to be, but because they love whites and white society enough to willingly perform that function.

Chapter 4 〜

Strength and the Battle Ground of Slavery II.

Survival Beyond Survival: The Price of Strength in *Beloved*

In *Annie Allen* (1949), Gwendolyn Brooks describes her protagonist as "taming all that anger down"[1] in response to a series of mythical scenarios of romance and love from which dark-skinned girls like herself are usually excluded. This control mechanism enables Annie Allen to swallow her anger and disappointment when her "man of tan," home from World War II, deserts her and their children by disappearing into the arms of another, lighter-skinned woman. She must move her anger aside when the man of tan returns to her, broken and dying. She also tames all that anger down in trying to raise her children alone in a society that does not value them. She speaks of "fighting" before "fiddling," but she is finally merely "polite" and looks to ancestors for guidance. If Annie Allen, who is in many ways an acquiescing, unassuming, self-effacing, and sometimes deliberately weak female character, nonetheless gathers the emotional forces necessary to tame all that anger down, then even more so is that the case with black women characters whose strength and determination are their foremost characteristics. For fictional black women who survive slavery, such as Toni Morrison's Baby Suggs and Sethe Suggs, Sherley Anne Williams's Dessa Rose, and J. California Cooper's Always, taming the anger down is perhaps more important than the occasions on which they explode with rage, for they can explode.

Controlling rage is understandably a survival mechanism. I do not refer here simply to the expected anger that might ensue from beatings, rape, or other personal injury that an individual might receive during slavery. I also include the rage that is quietly attendant upon watching the beating or sale of a loved one, in knowing that the master is planning to sell one or one's child, or in knowing that slaveholders control one's life so effectively that the very air smells like slavery. That is the kind of rage that Baby Suggs and Sethe Suggs experience in Morrison's *Beloved* (1987). They are contrasting portraits in taming the anger down versus letting it explode. In both cases, their characterization as strong black women is the key to understanding them and the strategies they adopt for survival. An older woman, Baby Suggs has been in slavery much longer than Sethe, and she has understandably had more opportunities during which to develop strategies for surviving the assaults upon her humanity that were daily accompaniments to her enslavement. With Baby Suggs, questions that logically warrant asking are, how much can a human being take before she says "No."? Or, "I give up. I quit. I'll take my own life"? How much loss, suffering, and dehumanization can an individual endure before she breaks?—*if* she breaks? The answers to these questions are contained in the fact that Morrison imbues Baby Suggs with the same characteristics inherent in many of her literary ancestors. With strength as her primary virtue, Baby Suggs—for most of her life—is not allowed to give up. Even when she ostensibly quits, strength remains the defining feature of that decision.

Physically, Baby Suggs is not an extraordinarily large woman; certainly no size comparable to Mama Lena Younger or Mammy Barracuda is implied. She is presented more in reference to injury and loss than to physical size. Her strength, as with some of the literary women before her, might in fact be characterized by a deformity. Just as Miss Thompson in Paule Marshall's *Brown Girl, Brownstones* (1959) has a sore on her leg as the indication of her moral strength in saying no, and just as Sethe carries a "tree" of whip scars on her back to mark her resistance to the institution of slavery, Baby Suggs has a deformed leg that conveys a similar message. We learn that, at Sweet Home, she is "exempted from the field work that broke her hip and the exhaustion that drugged her mind"[2]; the hip injury has left her with a walk "like a three-legged dog" (141).

A woman without a romantic partner, Baby Suggs takes the defining part of her name from her "husband," who, according to the pact upon which they had agreed, took his chance to run away from slavery and never looked back. It was he who taught her to make shoes. He cannot find her, she surmises, if she resorts to using the name "Jenny Whitlow" that Mr. Garner points out is on the bill of sale. She defines herself, therefore, by a romantic absence, a lack, one that highlights her keeping on in spite of the apparent (and understandable) desertion by her husband. Some readers could view her retention of the name as a positive attribute, for by insisting upon "Baby," Baby Suggs defines herself in a way that the slaveholders cannot control. Even when they persist in calling her Jenny, she knows that she is Baby.

The pleasant sound of that word, however, is a contrast to its connotations of struggle and loss in this woman's life. Rather than conveying intimacy, it conveys yet another dimension of the strength of the enslaved black female character. It is tangible recognition of the mental strength against degradation, the ability to tame the anger down and keep on keeping on. Like Charles W. Chesnutt's 'Liza Jane in "The Wife of His Youth," Baby Suggs will remain faithful to the absent partner and retain a state of celibacy against the possibility of his return.[3]

Baby Suggs's ability to keep on keeping on is particularly manifest in the tale of her children being sold away from her. Since most of these strong black female characters thrive on the sacrifices they make for and the relationships they have with their children, Baby Suggs's position as mother is especially noteworthy. Over the course of many years, she has seen seven of her eight children sold away from her. There is no more striking passage in all of African American literature that conveys the strength of black women characters, what they had to endure and keep on going on, than the following description of Baby Suggs's losses during slavery:

> Anybody Baby Suggs knew, let alone loved, who hadn't run off or been hanged, got rented out, loaned out, bought up, brought back, stored up, mortgaged, won, stolen or seized. So Baby's eight children had six fathers. What she called the nastiness of life was the shock she received upon learning that nobody stopped playing checkers just because the pieces included her children. Halle she was able to keep the longest. Twenty years. A lifetime. Given to her, no doubt, to make up for *hearing* that her two girls, neither of whom had their adult teeth, were sold and gone and she had not been able to wave goodbye. To make up for coupling with a straw boss for four months in exchange for keeping her third child, a boy, with her—only to have him traded for lumber in the spring of the next year and to find herself pregnant by the man who promised not to and did. That child she could not love and the rest she would not. (23)

Mothering, one of the solid bases of the strength of the black woman character, has thus been severely compromised with Baby Suggs. In a set of circumstances where black women historically and literarily could define themselves as mothers *only* from the biological perspective, Baby Suggs's nurturing qualities have been short-circuited with her own children. And she grew to distance herself as much as she could from potential emotional involvement with children she knew would be sold away from her (something that Sethe is unable to do). That Halle was allowed to remain with her is one of the joyous mysteries of her life. When he does not show up in Ohio at the appointed time, she has already steeled herself against the possibility of his death; "she had been prepared for that better than she had for his life"

(139). Slavery has taught her—as Paul D tries to teach Sethe—that letting go of loved ones is frequently necessary to sanity, or simply necessary to survival. In spite of lost opportunities, however, Baby Suggs manages to "mother" in the tradition of Ralph Ellison's Mary Rambo and Gloria Naylor's Mattie Michael. She becomes the comforter to other ailing souls, whether they are children or adults.

Her opportunities come with Sethe and her children as well as with the newly freed blacks on Bluestone Road in Cincinnati, Ohio. Baby Suggs's response to Sethe's bloody back evokes intertextual comparison to Mattie Michael's washing of Ciel's tortured body in Gloria Naylor's *The Women of Brewster Place* (1982) as well as to the more benignly inspired cleansing/bathing of Avey Johnson in Paule Marshall's *Praisesong for the Widow* (1983). The nurturing women in the washing roles must repair the bodies as well as the minds of the women who come under their restorative laying on of hands. For Baby Suggs, cleaning Sethe's body is a washing away of the immediate impact of the ugliness of slavery along with the bloodiness of beatings. Baby Suggs chokes back her anger as she assumes the mothering role with Sethe, and she painstakingly, lovingly repairs the damage schoolteacher and his nephews have done to Sethe. She heats pans of water and washes Sethe's body in sections—face, hands, arms, legs. "She cleaned between Sethe's legs with two separate pans of hot water and then tied her stomach and vagina with sheets. Finally she attacked the unrecognizable feet. . . . Roses of blood blossomed in the blanket covering Sethe's shoulders. . . . wordlessly the older woman greased the flowering back and pinned a double thickness of cloth to the inside of the newly stitched dress" (93). So effective is Baby Suggs's healing ability that Sethe will note after Baby Suggs's death that "nine years without the fingers or the voice of Baby Suggs was too much" (86), for Baby Suggs has been perhaps the most soothing, comforting force in her life.

Baby Suggs's laying on of hands not only restores Baby Suggs to the role of strong and supportive mother that had been wrenched away from her during slavery, but it also affirms a space of survival, a spiritual place where black women can go to tune out the destructive forces of the world; its physical counterpart is comparable to the chicken house to which Cooper's characters retreat in *Family*. As Sethe recognizes, for 28 days the house at 124 Bluestone Road is a haven, unviolating and unviolated. There is a community of supportive women who make her briefly forget about what she has so recently endured in her escape from slavery. The atmosphere is almost otherworldly because the created space is so comforting, so spiritual. Baby Suggs is primarily responsible for that sense of well-being. I emphasize spiritual here because Baby Suggs's psychic space is not based in conventional—and perhaps expected—Christianity. Certainly she talks with and about God, and she even prays to Him, but she also creates godhead.

From naming herself Baby to founding a religion, Baby Suggs puts into reality what Eva Peace only hints at. In the process, she becomes mother/priest, a potential savior, to a generation of suffering and undirected newly freed black humanity.[4]

In further naming herself "holy," Baby Suggs shapes an alternative reality to the historically confining system of slavery. Having come to maturity in an institution that found nothing of value in blacks beyond their physical labor, Baby Suggs adds a metaphysical dimension, a self-defining condition to go along with her newly acquired freedom. She thereby adds a strength of imagination to her former determination to keep on keeping on. By inspiring the black characters around her to see themselves as new creatures in body and mind, she serves the mother/god role in shaping/nurturing new life. In a transformed usage of power, Baby Suggs assumes the role of encouraging in her black neighbors a strength similar to the kind she has had to rely upon throughout her life.

Her conceptualization of strength is tied to the physical condition and the physical bodies in which these formerly enslaved persons find themselves. Formerly unloved persons must learn to love themselves; that is the primary lesson Baby Suggs teaches. Love for the self—from bone marrow to skin—and love for others within the group become bulwarks against potential destructive forces that rage outside the community. In the Clearing where she holds her meetings, Baby Suggs instructs her people in a modified, improvised sermon:

'Here,' she said, 'in this here place, we flesh; flesh that weeps, laughs; flesh that dances on bare feet in grass. Love it. Love it hard. Yonder they do not love your flesh. They despise it. They don't love your eyes; they'd just as soon pick em out. No more do they love the skin on your back. Yonder they flay it. And O my people they do not love your hands. Those they only use, tie, bind, chop off and leave empty. Love your hands! Love them. Raise them up and kiss them. Touch others with them, pat them together, stroke them on your face 'cause they don't love that either. *You* got to love it, *you!* And no, they ain't in love with your mouth. Yonder, out there, they will see it broken and break it again. What you say out of it they will not heed. What you scream from it they do not hear. What you put into it to nourish your body they will snatch away and give you leavins instead. No, they don't love your mouth. *You* got to love it. This is flesh I'm talking about here. Flesh that needs to be loved. Feet that need to rest and to dance; backs that need support; shoulders that need arms, strong arms I'm telling you. And O my people, out yonder, hear me, they do not love your neck unnoosed and straight. So love your neck; put a hand on it, grace it, stroke it and hold it up. And all your inside parts that they'd just as soon slop for hogs, you got to love them. The dark, dark liver— love it, love it, and the beat and beating heart, love that too. More than eyes or feet. More than lungs that have yet to draw free air. More than your life-holding womb and your life-giving private parts, hear me now, love your heart. For this is the prize.' (88–89)

Baby Suggs locates the power to save one's self within the confines of one's body and the strength of one's mind, thereby denying to slaveholders the very structure, the very frame they have claimed as property. The mind can conceive, *imagine*, a state of grace that is finally the only thing that matters. The collective minds of her formerly enslaved comrades can confine slavery and its effects to the category of "yonder," far removed from them. In the wooded sanctuary of the Clearing, they have effectively "cleared" a space to reconstruct themselves and the values that can sustain them.

Yet a question arises as to whether or not Baby Suggs practices what she preaches. In this set-aside space of the Clearing, perhaps she does, but there is little other evidence to support her loving herself, her very flesh. She is burdened down by the abuses of white folks. She does not seem responsive to possible romantic gestures from Stamp Paid. Though she focuses on the beating of her heart and the sound of her breathing when she initially arrives in free territory at the Bodwin household in Ohio, she seems to forget the sermon she preaches when she steps outside of the body she professes to value to focus exclusively on color. In the Clearing scene, however, her sermon seems strong and confident.[5]

Approaching a traditional conception of blasphemy in her teachings—in that she directs black people away from God to the divinity within themselves—Baby Suggs essentially founds a religion or at least a different brand of spirituality. In her imperative voice and directive posture here, she shares kinship with Hansberry's Mama Lena Younger and anticipates Butler's Lauren Olamina in assuming that she knows what is best for her "children." Because she has not been able to save her biological children, she resorts to trying to save others. She assigns authority to herself in ways comparable to that of other strong black women characters. Importantly here, in assigning authority to herself, she thereby diminishes or denies the authority that slaveholders have wielded over her and her people throughout their period of exploitation. Whereas they would confine her to the "servants, obey in all things your masters" portion of the scriptures, she centers the former servants, makes their bodies the priority, makes their wishes prominent, and sanctifies them and herself in the process.

More specifically, Baby Suggs encourages Sethe to give up her hatred and move to a different psychological and spiritual space. "Lay em down, Sethe. Sword and shield. Down. Down. Both of em down. Down by the riverside. Sword and shield. Don't study war no more. Lay all that mess down. Sword and shield" (86). In contrast to what this advice may seem at a glance, strength is inherent in the directive. For Sethe to lay down the horrors that are burdening her is not a directive for her to give in, but a directive for her to transcend. If Sethe can transcend the horrors of slavery, transcend the pain of having her milk taken from her, of having lost her husband, of having killed her child, then and only then can she move toward envisioning a life, a future, beyond that defined by her enslavers. As Alice Walker's Grange Copeland tries to teach his son Brownfield, if Brownfield blames everything on white folks (including his beating his wife and children, poisoning streams, and being generally mean and evil—ostensibly because of the sharecropping life into which he has been forced), if he allows white people to occupy such a central space in his head, then he makes gods of them. " . . . [W]hat I'm saying is *you got to hold tight a place in you,*" Grange urges, "*where they can't come.*"[6] And if someone else is occupying the place of divinity within an individual, that pushes the essence of self into a degraded space. Baby Suggs's advice to Sethe, therefore, does not in any way mean giving in, but a moving toward and a saving of the best in herself. The strength that it will take to move beyond the pain is greater than the strength required to live with the pain. Paul D will offer Sethe a comparable healthy possibility for movement into the future at the end of the novel when he asserts that she is her own "best thing."

In order to keep on living after her children were snatched away from her, to keep on going on when any overseer or any other white man demanded that she "lay" with him or with designated black men, to retain a sense of humanity even in the face of rejecting progeny conceived through acts of inhumanity, Baby Suggs has had to find an unearthly strength. And her resolve has certainly been challenged at times. There are occasions when her faith in her abilities seems to falter and when she sinks into placing blame. These occasions must be measured against her nurturing of Sethe and her love for Halle and her grandchildren, as well as against her teaching of self-love to other black people. She recalls that "those white things have taken all I had or dreamed . . . and broke my heartstrings too. There is no bad luck in the world but whitefolks" (89). Despite multiple psychological and physical injuries, Baby Suggs is still strong enough to accept Halle's loss and possible death as well as to take care of Sethe, wise enough to recognize the injury she has caused her neighbors that in turn precipitates their desertion of her, and imaginative enough to encourage formerly enslaved black folks to recreate themselves.[7]

When she does decide to make her exit from painful circumstances, that departure is similarly based in a strength that comes from within. While others—readers and characters—might read Baby Suggs's taking to bed to contemplate color as a giving up, I would argue otherwise (for the time being, at least). Consider Sethe's assessment of what is happening to Baby Suggs. Sethe's guilt over killing Beloved leads Sethe to believe that Baby Suggs's extended demise is a response to her action, never mind the fact that many years passed between the "Misery" identified as the events surrounding Beloved's death and Baby Suggs's own death. Stamp Paid finally concludes of Baby Suggs that "the whitefolks had tired her out at last" (180) and that she dies as a result—though it takes her eight years to do so. From his point of view:

> Her marrow was tired and it was a testimony to the heart that fed it that it took eight years to meet finally the color she was hankering after. The onslaught of her fatigue, like his, was sudden, but lasted for years. After sixty years of losing children to the people who chewed up her life and spit it out like a fish bone; after five years of freedom given to her by her last child, who bought her future with his, exchanged it, so to speak, so she could have one whether he did or not—to lose him too; to acquire a daughter and grandchildren and see that daughter slay the children (or try to); to belong to a community of other free Negroes—to love and be loved by them, to counsel and be counseled, protect and be protected, feed and be fed—and then to have that community step back and hold itself at a distance—well, it could wear out even a Baby Suggs, holy. (177)

The fact that *she decides* when to make her exit is important in the consideration of how strong Baby Suggs is. For all those catastrophes Stamp Paid enumerates, none singly has broken Baby Suggs's spirit. She has always found the strength to go on. The fact that she decides when to die gives her an ultimate triumph over the forces that have tried to beat her down. She steps out of their responses to time and claims the right to a leisurely death, something that no enslaved person—or person whose mind is enslaved— could claim. This notion of an ultimate triumph stands even against the narrator locating blame for her death:

> Baby Suggs grew tired, went to bed and stayed there until her big old heart quit. Except for an occasional request for color she said practically nothing— until the afternoon of the last day of her life when she got out of bed, skipped slowly to the door of the keeping room and announced to Sethe and Denver the lesson she had learned from her sixty years a slave and ten years free: that there was no bad luck in the world but whitepeople. 'They don't know when to stop,' she said, and returned to her bed, pulled up the quilt and left them to hold that thought forever. (104)

Two things are important here. First, it takes Baby Suggs *eight* years to die. I would argue that that is as much choice as her leading the ceremonies in the Clearing. She has exempted herself from the time frame by which enslavers quickly killed rebellious black people or maimed them for life. She takes time to go quietly into that good night and thereby sets herself outside the frame of the world that designated her "slavewoman."

Second, while it is true that she asserts that white people are the only bad luck in the world, that they do not know when to stop, she has not acted in response to this assertion. It is important, therefore, to note that the *rhetoric* of quitting is substantially different from the *fact* of that condition. Baby Suggs has advised Sethe to give up the hatred, and her contemplation of color—perhaps searching for the most soothing, least harmful or disturbing shades—has been the instance of her following her own advice. Contemplation of color parallels a desire for peace in her world, a desire to move away from the horrors of slavery and what they have wrought. Her ability to achieve her purpose is her own quest for transcendence. If the religious substitute that has come from her has not given her the peace she needs, then an alternative quest is equally valid. That alternative quest is not merely reactive, it is also, in its own way, fulfilling. Her quest for color may well be an extended ritual in which she attempts to save the best in herself.

It is also an elaborate ritual in trying to find meaning when all the bases propping up her world seem to have fallen down. If Baby Suggs has spent many years preaching, during which she placed so much value on the power of speech, then why should she not try the alternative—the power of silence? She is alone with her own thoughts and those inspired by the harmless colors she contemplates. Stamp Paid asserts that Baby Suggs has been unable to "approve or condemn Sethe's rough choice" (180) of killing Beloved; that might be a source of her contemplation. Other places in the narrative assert that she is violated by the fact that, even though she is presumably free in Ohio, white men still come into her yard to take her daughter-in-law and grandchildren back to slavery. Perhaps that is something else she contemplates.

It is important to note that most of the interpretations of Baby Suggs's responses to the tragedies in her life are offered by other characters. They perhaps draw their conclusions from what they would have done or how they would have felt under similar circumstances. In many ways, therefore, Baby Suggs remains a source of mystery, which is another factor that leads us to think of her as a link between the known world and the unknown. The few lines we get from Baby Suggs in reaction to whites or to Sethe do not lead us to conclude that her strength is substantially diminished by the force of what she must endure. Nor do they suggest that she has been warped psychologically because of difficult, brutal circumstances. The partial silence she holds for eight years, therefore, is not appreciably unlike the silent spaces surrounding her motives and actions; in those spaces is the possibility for numerous interpretations. It is also comparatively like other strong black women characters, notably Mama Lena and Octavia, who have no confidants, seek the counsel of no one.

An accompanying point in the pathology analogy in connection to strength is that Baby Suggs actually takes to her bed, the space generally recognized as essential to the recovery of disease. This is an unusual move, because few of the strong black women characters actually end up in bed. The fact that Baby Suggs does does not presage a diminishing of her strength or renewed attack from the forces that have inspired her strength. More psychological than physical, her strength, like so many of her literary foremothers and descendants, is also her forte. As she rests from her trials and tribulations, she also contemplates them and gathers new strength during this pausing period. In this scenario, Baby Suggs is strong enough to transform the bed of affliction, the place of disease and death, into a long-considered gateway into another state of being.

This strong woman character does not experience the quick exit of a Pilate Dead, and there is meaning in that extension. Perhaps this is an extension of Baby Suggs laying down her own sword and shield, finally accepting the advice she has given Sethe and preparing for what lies in the next world. I would argue that Baby Suggs is not merely preparing to die; she is preparing to make a transition from this world into the one in which Beloved resides. Indeed, on a couple of occasions, Denver believes that Baby Suggs's demise has enabled Beloved's appearance. This is not a position I find acceptable, however, because it would be hard to imagine Baby Suggs assisting in Sethe's punishment for having killed Beloved. Also, the time lapse between Baby Suggs's death and Beloved's appearance at 124 is long enough for the events not to be immediately related. The transition, instead of having such a specific objective, enables Baby Suggs to move into eternity, to move into a realm from which, like Clora in Cooper's *Family,* she can watch over her generations of offspring.

Lest this seem farfetched, consider her intervention when Denver has difficulty moving from the porch of 124 to seek food and work from neighbors after Beloved has taken over Sethe's will. Denver is understandably afraid because it has been more than ten years since she left the immediate surroundings of her small world. As she hesitates, Baby Suggs makes a significant return:

> . . . Denver stood on the porch in the sun and couldn't leave it. Her throat itched; her heart kicked—and then Baby Suggs laughed, clear as anything. 'You mean I never told you nothing about Carolina? About your daddy? You don't remember nothing about how come I walk the way I do and about your mother's feet, not to speak of her back? I never told you all that? Is that why you can't walk down the steps? My Jesus my.'
> But you said there was no defense.
> 'There ain't.'

Then what do I do?
'Know it, and go on out the yard. Go on.' (244)

This is not the directive of a female character beaten down by the horrors of her life and the slaveholding world in which she has lived for 60 years. This is the directive of a character who knows the possibilities of her own strength and who recognizes that her granddaughter shares in her bloodline (note, too, that Baby Suggs speaks of herself in the present tense, another indication that her demise is merely a transition into something else). Baby Suggs takes on, once again, the nurturing role she has had throughout her life in spite of the fact that she has been able to nurture only one of her eight biological children. She has certainly told Denver all of the things she mentions, and she now uses them as examples to make it clear that whatever Denver must face could not possibly be equivalent to what her family has already endured, to what has brought them to this point. Like Baby Suggs, Denver will survive.

Alternatively, then, if all this works so well, a necessary question arises in the strength paradigm. How is the pathology of strength apparent in Baby Suggs's death? She provides the ultimate sacrifice for those in her household whom she has "mothered" by literally willing herself to death. I term it a sacrifice because she chooses to die rather than pass judgment on Sethe killing Beloved. To say Sethe has done wrong is to reject a woman who was in desperate circumstances as well as in desperate need of spiritual if not moral support. So Baby Suggs dies rather than say to Sethe, "You have violated the principles by which human beings need to live." Baby Suggs therefore considers herself stronger, better able to withstand the contradiction inherent in a love strong enough to kill. She in effect executes the same pattern. By killing herself, she essentially asserts that she loves the memory of her son Halle and what Sethe meant to him enough to die rather than confront the rejection of Sethe that must necessarily invade her moral universe if she passes judgment on Sethe killing Beloved. Imagine, too, the impact on Sethe and Denver of Baby Suggs taking eight years to will herself to death. She is immune to the reactions that her extended demise has on them, and she does not discuss her decision with them.

By committing suicide, Baby Suggs also shows the effect of strength of mind directly upon her body. She becomes as godlike as Sethe in deciding who lives and who dies. In this battle of mind and body, the body loses. Baby Suggs's seeming weakness on her bed of affliction is really the finest manifestation of her strength. Instead of praying to endure the troubles of this world, she simply exits. By so doing, she shares traits with her literary sisters such as Minnie Ransom in manipulating the very forces of the universe to her advantage. In controlling her entry into the plane between life and death, as well as beyond that plane, and by returning from the other side to instruct Denver, Baby Suggs turns the pathology of strength into an otherworldly celebration of it. She thereby anticipates more of her otherworldly literary sisters.

Baby Suggs's laughter from the other side, her very merriment about the events that have made her life "intolerable" (4), allows for the interpretation that her toleration has indeed been with the certainty of better things and thus favorable qualities of her strength are reinstated. Comparable to Native Americans and Alaskan Eskimos who *will* themselves to death, Baby Suggs is linked to cultures and peoples who have endured in spite of the efforts to obliterate them from the face of the earth. The legendary qualities of the strength of mind that we assign to such peoples similarly define Baby Suggs. The mind can "whip it all," or, as Ralph Ellison's narrator in *Invisible Man* (1952) discovers, it can whip the individual. Baby Suggs whips it all and ends up in a space that anticipates her literary sisters of the 1990s, those women who traverse freely the boundaries between life and death, the known world and the unknown. In her characterization of Baby Suggs, therefore, Morrison moves from the physical realm of the black woman's strength to primarily the psychological realm.

In positing strength as Baby Suggs's major characteristic, Morrison has constructed Baby Suggs as another iconographic testament to the endurance of strong black women characters. Unquestionably, black women's choices were limited during slavery. Among them were death, acquiescence in their own debasement, disobedience and its consequences, or the strength to endure. Even when it was frequently unclear *why* one should endure, most did. They had no certainty of freedom through escape, no certainty of freedom through legal means, no certainty that their children would remain with them, no certainty that they would not be sexually and physically violated, no certainty that death was anything but more slavery. Yet many of them elected to endure, to "take low," to tame all that anger down with nothing more for reward than their sense that slavery was an insult to human existence, an insult to human will, and that someone, somehow, with no more evidence than their battered bodies, should survive as evidence in a story that must be told.[8] So they endured beyond endurance, survived beyond survival and became examples not only in their families but also in their contributions to history and literature.[9]

Sethe Suggs, an actor rather than a silent sufferer like Annie Allen, explodes into rage early in *Beloved* but ends up taming as much anger down as does Baby Suggs. Sethe's strength begins with her mental toughness, with her ability to carve out little spaces of quiet defiance between the interstices of slavery. The only available black woman at Sweet Home in the company of five sex-starved black men, she nonetheless takes her time—more than a year—in choosing a partner from among them. Similarly, although she knows the tradition of marriage through broom-jumping and the lack of dress-up clothing for the weddings of persons who are enslaved, she nonetheless insists upon some distinction. She manages to "borrow" the materials and sew a dress for her wedding in spite of the expectation that she should be satisfied simply to be allowed to choose a man, since most enslaved women, Baby Suggs included, were not allowed to make such a choice.

These traits noticeable in this girl/woman character of uncertain origins mark an independence not usually witnessed among enslaved persons. They also foreshadow Sethe's actions throughout the novel. Against the grain of expectations, she will assert that she is a mother, that her children need her milk, that she has responsibility for them, and that she is the sole arbiter over their worldly condition. In other words, she ascribes to herself much of the authority that slaveholders believed was their exclusive right. This mental toughness is apparent in the first few pages of the novel, when, without knowing anything of Sethe's history, we see her willingness to confront the powers of the unknown by inviting the baby ghost to appear at her house (4). She treats the possibility of an otherworldly encounter as normal, the first sign that she is perhaps just a bit different from the usual formerly enslaved black woman.

Her mental strength is immediately joined to the physical, with her ability to perform whatever act is necessary in a given circumstance, as is apparent in her granting sex to the chiseler of Beloved's headstone. In order to pay for the word "Beloved," Sethe leans on tiptoe against one of the stones, "her knees wide open as any grave," "rutting among the headstones with the engraver, his young son looking on" (5). Here is a woman who, in the process of making the ultimate moral commitment to her children, is willing to sacrifice morality for them, willing to degrade herself, willing to separate her mental self from the physical abuse of her body. This image, long before we read of the physical act of Sethe killing Beloved, locks her in our memories as a character of unusual mental resolve, one who challenges slavery as effectively as Baby Suggs commits herself to endure beyond endurance. It also locks her into our memories as a woman character for whom it is not easy to distinguish between actions that could be judged to be sinful and those that are designed to save.

How other characters remember or perceive Sethe is also relevant in this evaluation of her strength. Paul D remembers her as "Halle's girl—the one with iron eyes and backbone to match . . . irises the same color as her skin, which, in that still face, used to make him think of a mask with mercifully punched-out eyes" (9).[10] After he hears of her killing Beloved, Paul D thinks of Sethe:

The prickly, mean-eyed Sweet Home girl he knew as Halle's girl was obedient (like Halle), shy (like Halle), and work-crazy (like Halle). He was wrong. This here Sethe was new. The ghost in her house didn't bother her for the very same reason a room-and-board witch with new shoes was welcome. This here Sethe talked about love like any other woman; talked about baby clothes like any other woman, but what she meant could cleave the bone. This here Sethe talked about safety with a handsaw. (164)

Known but unknowable, Sethe will engage the imaginations of many characters around her. Denver remembers her mother as "queenly" and as

> The one who never looked away, who when a man got stomped to death by a mare right in front of Sawyer's restaurant did not look away; and when a sow began eating her own litter did not look away then either. And when the baby's spirit picked up Here Boy and slammed him into the wall hard enough to break two of his legs and dislocate his eye, so hard he went into convulsions and chewed up his tongue, still her mother had not looked away. She had taken a hammer, knocked the dog unconscious, wiped away the blood and saliva, pushed his eye back in his head and set his leg bones. (12)

As Sethe's neighbors believe after the events of the "Misery," "she could do and survive things they believed she should neither do nor survive" (47). They are duly negatively impressed by her self-presentation after Beloved's death: "Sethe walked past them in their silence and hers. She climbed into the cart, her profile knife-clean against a cheery blue sky. A profile that shocked them with its clarity. Was her head a bit too high? Her back a little too straight? Probably" (152). In the years after her release from prison, her neighbors wait "for Sethe to come on difficult times. Her outrageous claims, her self-sufficiency seemed to demand it" (171). From the perspective of her neighbors, Sethe, whom they consider an egregious sinner, is too proud, and she is surviving too well. On the path that leads to Baby Suggs's haven in Cincinnati, that survival begins with Sethe's determination to escape from slavery.

Legendary accounts of black people finding their way from slavery to freedom populate slave narratives and the folklore surrounding historical escapes. Henry "Box" Brown mailed himself to freedom while Frederick Douglass used the borrowed papers from a seaman to effect the same result. William and Ellen Craft, disguised as a white man and his "slave," "ran a thousand miles for freedom." In literature, William Wells Brown's Clotel disguises herself as a man in order to escape to freedom. Morrison's Sethe has no time for the polish of disguise; she literally puts her feet in the road, in the tradition of so many of those who walked to freedom with Harriet Tubman, and takes her chances with her own very pregnant body. Her strength of mind and body are apparent in this feat, for shortly before her departure, the milk that she needs for her "crawling already?" baby is taken from her laden breasts, and she is beaten when she dares to tell Mrs. Garner what has happened.

Those brutal acts, both designed to alter her resolve to be a mother in fact as well as in biology, only strengthen her desire to leave the Garner plantation. Her intent upon leaving what many judge to be a rather benign form of slavery is a measure of her unwillingness to suffer any longer any form of servitude. The physical price she pays manifests itself in a beating historically reflective of those reserved for pregnant women during slavery. Sethe is forced to lie down upon the ground, over a hole that has been dug to accommodate the "property" in her stomach, and is whipped so unmercifully that the wounds scar into the shape of a tree on her back. This is punishment for her daring to presume that any one, even a white woman, has authority to alter the circumstances Sethe's so-called owners have designated for Sethe.

Her decision to escape takes it toll upon her body, but it does not weaken her resolve. She sets out with her bloodied back and a belief that escape or death is preferable to Sweet Home, schoolteacher, and his nephew with mossy teeth. The belief of her neighbors that Sethe can survive anything is applied in the negative context of the "Misery"; however, one literal interpretation of that evaluation occurs during her trek in the wilderness. Alone, pregnant, bleeding, having lost contact with her husband at their prearranged rendezvous point, Sethe nonetheless intends to survive. When her strength has given out momentarily, and she has fallen by the wayside, she still intends to fight when she believes she has been discovered by a "whiteboy." "She told Denver that a *something* came up out of the earth into her—like a freezing, but moving too, like jaws inside. 'Look like I was just cold jaws grinding,' she said. Suddenly she was eager for his eyes, to bite into them; to gnaw his cheek" (31).

This bloodied pregnant woman, recently beaten and lying flat on her back, nonetheless has the will to fight against reenslavement. The iron eyes that characterized her earlier are matched by an iron will. That iron will is also what gives her the physical strength to keep on when she has thought she cannot keep on. The person who discovers her is a white girl, Amy Denver, who leads Sethe to the shelter of a lean-to for the night:

> So she crawled and Amy walked alongside her, and when Sethe needed to rest, Amy stopped too and talked some more about Boston and velvet and good things to eat. . . . Nothing of Sethe's was intact by the time they reached [the lean-to] except the cloth that covered her hair. Below her bloody knees, there was no feeling at all; her chest was two cushions of pins. It was the voice full of velvet and Boston and good things to eat that urged her along and made her think that maybe she wasn't, after all, just a crawling graveyard for a six-month baby's last hours. (34)

In her physical endurance, Sethe personifies the perceived archetypal suprahuman strength of black women in slavery as well as after slavery.

Driven by mother love, she is willing to give her last ounce of strength to get milk to her baby girl in Ohio. What she endures physically might be the counterpart to Mama Day looking into the well at the other place in Gloria Naylor's *Mama Day* (1988) and experiencing, in an almost overwhelming rush, all the psychological loss and death of generations that have preceded her. It is difficult for those not placed in comparable positions to imagine the toll such physical and mental pain takes upon the persons who bear such burdens.

Sethe's burden-bearing continues in the actual delivery of Denver. Even as she is releasing the burden of the child from her body, that very release brings with it attendant burdens. Forced, like an animal, to flee for her life, she is similarly forced to give birth under circumstances that do not usually define the human species. The pain of releasing Denver forces Sethe to face the increased possibility for discovery; her previous psychological and physical pain are now intensified, for the gaping wound of birth marks her, the baby can only slow her down, and the urgency with which she desires escape because of the baby writes the danger even larger. And yet this woman does not even remotely entertain the possibility of not moving forward. Her extrahuman determination and strength in this instance equate her to basic animal instinct—survive even when chances for survival are significantly against you.

In spite of a fever from birth (for which she is thankful because it keeps her baby warm) and in spite of having little idea as to how to get across the river, Sethe keeps on keeping on until she meets Stamp Paid. She sits until he directs her about crossing the Ohio. "Too tired to move, she stayed there, the sun in her eyes making her dizzy. Sweat poured over her and bathed the baby completely. She must have slept sitting up. . . . The clanging was back in her head but she refused to believe that she had come all that way, endured all she had, to die on the wrong side of the river" (90). And she does not die. Stamp Paid delivers her to Baby Suggs's house, but Sethe has made the arduous journey from Sweet Home with only her iron will to propel her forward. Awareness of Sethe's ordeal highlights even more Baby Suggs's role in washing away the pain and part of the memory that set Sethe on a course for Cincinnati. Sethe is a fascinating study in the power of belief, in the possibility of imagination. Never mathematically certain that she would reach Ohio, yet always believing that she would, she has imagined a world comparable to the grace that Baby Suggs teaches her followers to imagine.

Sethe's mind and body get her to Ohio, but the losses she has suffered in Kentucky and will suffer in Ohio perhaps leave her with more strength of mind than strength of body. The novel centers upon the force of will that enables a mother who undoubtedly loves her children to injure two of them, kill one of them, and try to kill the fourth rather than see them remanded to slavery. Arguably, the act of killing is the ultimate expression of love. Equally as arguably, it is the ultimate expression of strength, of sheer mental determination. Also, it could be assumed to be the greatest sin or the greatest attempt at saving. What enables a mother to roughly saw open the tiny neck of a toddler? How could she have continued that act after the first spurt of blood? What force raised the hand to the saw and the saw to the neck? And what force led her to continue in the attempt to kill another of her children after the first one was dead? What must have been the psychological weight of killing the *one child* for whom she had suffered so much in her own personal wilderness and dark night of the soul? In the shed behind Baby Suggs's house, Sethe refuses to tame all that anger down. Unfortunately, she makes her children the object of its raging consequence.

Sethe paradoxically comes out of the ordeal even stronger than she was before. The assertions of her neighbors that she survives things she should not might be accurate from a certain point of view, for she transcends the consequences of her own actions into a near suprahuman ability to endure suffering. That ability takes her into a realm in which she is an exclusive occupant, constantly enduring the almost impossible psychological pain of her rememories from slavery, but enduring nonetheless. Although Sethe may sometimes want a displacement of mind from memory, what she gets is a strengthened mind that accommodates harsh memories. By the time Paul D arrives at 124 Bluestone Road with his tale of Halle having watched Sethe being milked by schoolteacher's nephew, she cannot retrain the mind that is already accustomed to enduring whatever it needs to endure. The news about Halle watching, however, challenges Sethe to wonder about the very strength that has sustained her.

> She shook her head from side to side, resigned to her rebellious brain. Why was there nothing it refused? No misery, no regret, no hateful picture too rotten to accept? Like a greedy child it snatched up everything. Just once, could it say, No thank you? I just ate and can't hold another bite? I am full God damn it of two boys with mossy teeth, one sucking on my breast the other holding me down, their book-reading teacher watching and writing it up. I am still full of that, God damn it, I can't go back and add more. Add my husband to it, watching, above me in the loft—hiding close by—the one place he thought no one would look for him, looking down on what I couldn't look at at all. And not stopping them—looking and letting it happen. By my greedy brain says, Oh thanks, I'd love more—so I add more. And no sooner than I do, there is no stopping. . . . Other people went crazy, why couldn't she? (70)

But insanity is seldom an option for Morrison's women characters. With the exception of Pecola Breedlove in *The Bluest Eye,* they deal with the horrors and pains of their lives and go on. Violet Trace in *Jazz,* for example, does not end up in a mental institution after attempting to deface the corpse of her husband's young lover; she reaches for reconciliation and moves forward.

Sethe may believe that the news about Halle makes her falter, but in reality it does not:

> . . . if she could just manage the news Paul D brought and the news he kept to himself. Just manage it. Not break, fall or cry each time a hateful picture drifted in front of her face. Not develop some permanent craziness like Baby Suggs' friend, a young woman in a bonnet whose food was full of tears. Like Aunt Phyllis, who slept with her eyes wide open. Like Jackson Till, who slept under the bed. All she wanted was to go on. As she had. Alone with her daughter in a haunted house she managed every damn thing. Why now, with Paul D instead of the ghost, was she breaking up? getting scared? needing Baby? The worst was over, wasn't it? She had already got through, hadn't she? With the ghost in 124 she could bear, do, solve anything. Now a hint of what had happened to Halle and she cut out like a rabbit looking for its mother. (97)

A temporary questioning is not ultimately a faltering, and Sethe continues rather calmly in her relationship with her daughters as well as with Paul D. And a temporary worry about sanity is not a reduction of sanity. With reduced expectations—or none at all—Morrison's women characters carve out spaces to be. Sethe's complaints about what her mind will accept or about her running for help (to Baby Suggs's Clearing) can only be measured against her ability to keep on track when she should, by all rights, have fallen by the wayside.

Diminished expectations perhaps become another feature of the problematic nature of strength in this instance, for Sethe is forced to stand so frequently on her own that she is skeptical of the possibility of someone making a commitment with or to her, especially in terms of romance. Paul D unsettles her expectations by leading her to hope that there can be life after slavery and the death of a child, but one encounter with him reveals that she is very much capable of returning to being solely on her own, totally self-sufficient. The incident occurs after Paul D's sexual liaison with Beloved; out of guilt, he meets Sethe at Sawyer's restaurant and intends to tell her everything. His announcement that Sethe "won't like" what he has to say allows for her lessened expectations to surface.

> She stopped then and turned her face toward him and the hateful wind. Another woman would have squinted or at least teared if the wind whipped her face as it did Sethe's. Another woman might have shot him a look of apprehension, pleading, anger even, because what he said sure sounded like part one of Goodbye, I'm gone.

Sethe looked at him steadily, calmly, already ready to accept, release or excuse an in-need-or-trouble man. Agreeing, saying okay, all right, in advance, because she didn't believe any of them—over the long haul—could measure up. And whatever the reason, it was all right. No fault. Nobody's fault. (128)

Paul D's awareness of Sethe's "diminished expectation" leads him to ask her to become pregnant instead of telling her about Beloved. Sethe exhibits here what is common with several of the strong black literary women, that is, the ability to convey—without words—the inadequacy, or certainly the lacks, in the men in their lives.

Diminished expectation becomes a reality for Sethe when Paul D actually leaves her. Informed by Stamp Paid that Sethe killed Beloved, and after listening to her *almost* tell what happened, Paul D offers the nearly unforgivable response that "You got two feet, Sethe, not four" (165). Paul D joins many of his historical and literary counterparts in passing judgment on Sethe. She is too strong for Paul D, more of a "man" than he could ever imagine being. For this special Sweet Home man to join with the slaveholders in labeling her animal and then pretend that he is not in fact leaving her only evokes the sarcastic in Sethe: "Sweet, she thought. He must think I can't bear to hear him say it. That after all I have told him and after telling me how many feet I have, 'goodbye' would break me to pieces. Ain't that sweet" (165). Sethe withdraws into the protective arenas of her mind and house, the mind that has protected her from the past even as it has flooded her with it, and the house that has protected her from her accusing, unforgiving neighbors. The encounter with Paul D makes clear to her that, once again, she must be sufficient unto herself. That resolve meets its biggest challenge, however, in the presence of Beloved.

More than anything else in the novel, Sethe's interaction with Beloved raises questions about her strength, yet, simultaneously, it also makes clear the final nature of that strength. Beloved is able to do what no one else in Sethe's history has been able to do: unsettle Sethe so completely that she is transformed mentally and physically. Sethe's one vulnerable spot throughout her life has been her children. It was for them that she risked life and limb in escaping from slavery. It was for them that she risked jail and eternal damnation. It was for them that she set aside morality in getting Beloved a proper headstone. It was for them that she has endured the ostracism of her neighbors and the knowledge that she has caused Baby Suggs almost unbearable pain.[11] It was because of them that she has had no love life before Paul D arrives and no expectation of a future. Her most desired objective in life has been to be a mother in spite of the slaveholders' determination that she not so designate herself.

Motherhood is therefore her sacrificial realm of weakness, for although she has been strong enough to do any number of things for her children, it is precisely the mothering role in which she is most vulnerable to attack, especially from one of her children. Although it is with Beloved that critics usually focus on Sethe's mothering, questions could also be raised in connection with her relationship to her sons, so she is vulnerable to attack from readers as well. With the departure of Howard and Buglar, Sethe loses an additional 50 percent of what it meant to her to be a mother. Losing them must have been painful, but we are left to surmise that emotional impact upon Sethe. In the true pattern of keeping on keeping on, she never utters a word about their departure or sends up a prayer for their good fortune. Indeed, it is only through the narrator and Denver that we know anything of the boys after slavery. Sethe operates so firmly in the mold of handling with grace everything that happens to her that, in relation to the boys, she almost negates the very role—mother—through which she initially defined herself against the horrors of slavery.

It is also noteworthy—if we can trust Denver—that Sethe's strength and fixation on the baby ghost have led the boys to leave. Sethe's mothering apparently goes more dramatically toward her female children than her male ones, for the males are depicted as being afraid of her (Denver initially experiences some fear as well). The fact that the boys and Denver play "Die Witch" as a balm against Sethe potentially harming them is worth remembering. She is so strong unto herself that she sometimes forgets the impact of her actions upon her offspring.

In the extended look at her mothering, Sethe is noticeably defenseless against the child who accuses her of exactly what she has done. Beloved is thus able to engage Sethe's guilt to the point that Sethe makes another sacrifice for her child, this time her own health and well being. Paradoxically, in Sethe harming herself, she is still trying to be the ultimate mother, still trying to explain to her child why her actions were necessary and why, in spite of those actions, she loved and still loves Beloved. Her greatest challenge is to convince Beloved.

> Beloved accused her of leaving her behind. Of not being nice to her, not smiling at her. She said they were the same, had the same face, how could she have left her? And Sethe cried, saying she never did, or meant to—that she had to get them out, away, that she had the milk all the time and had the money too for the stone but not enough. That her plan was always that they would all be together on the other side, forever. Beloved wasn't interested. She said when she cried there was no one. That dead men lay on top of her. That she had nothing to eat. Ghosts without skin stuck their fingers in her and said beloved in the dark and bitch in the light. Sethe pleaded for forgiveness, counting, list-

ing again and again her reasons: that Beloved was more important, meant more to her than her own life. That she would trade places any day. Give up her life, every minute and hour of it, to take back just one of Beloved's tears. (241–42)

Shrinking in size and becoming increasingly will-less, Sethe is during these events the weakest she has been in the book. Having overcome being milked like a cow, having escaped slavery alive when she could easily have died, and having found the strength to kill her baby daughter, she now has no obvious resource upon which to draw to make Beloved understand.

However, because Sethe *deliberately* makes herself weak in her efforts to get Beloved to understand her actions, it could be argued that, even here, there is strength in weakness, or deliberate weakness becomes a kind of strength. Sethe is resolved, no matter the damage to herself, to keep the well being of her child as her primary focus. Undoubtedly, her judgment is skewered, and undoubtedly she focuses totally on one child to the neglect of the other. At the base of her temporary lack of proportion, however, is the same impetus to sacrifice for her children that has guided all of her actions in the narrative. From this perspective, she could very easily, like Baby Suggs, will herself to death if that is the length to which she must go to convince Beloved of her love. Her interactions with Beloved emphasize even more clearly the sometimes pathological nature of strength. Such female characters risk harming themselves internally, psychologically, and occasionally physically by the choices they make for their children. On the smaller scale, Sethe gives food to Beloved instead of eating herself, and on the larger scale, she is prepared to give over her very sanity and life. What appears to be weakness on the surface, therefore, might be viewed alternatively in this strength paradigm.

The most powerful indication that we are still dealing with strength versus a complete diminishing of strength is Sethe's belief that Beloved is indeed her deceased daughter. This final nature of Sethe's power reflects a strength of mind comparable to Baby Suggs willing herself to death—or the strength of imagination again in conceptualizing only an idealized, individualized grace. In a world in which several characters have experienced encounters with the world beyond, it is not farfetched that Sethe would respond to its demands. After all, she has recognized the baby ghost for years and willfully invited it to share her household. She is thus open, as Gloria Naylor would conclude, to the possibilities inherent in dissolving the lines of demarcation between this world and the next. It is not a far leap from this openness for Sethe to welcome Beloved as her long-dead daughter and to believe fervently that that is indeed the case. The passages in which Sethe reflects upon the accuracy of her surmising that Beloved is her daughter are not illogical; they are reasoned responses to what the circumstances would suggest. Sethe has the willing mind, therefore, to make the necessary leap of imagination and arrive in the space where belief and substance are one, where she makes no distinction between a living daughter and one returned from the dead.

In the realm that ties her most directly to her literary counterparts, Sethe exhibits traits on a more mundane level that are comparable to Gaines's Octavia as well as to Mama Lena Younger and several other strong black women characters. She shows the biological tyranny that characterizes many of these women. She directs Denver more than simply speaking to her, as illustrated most vividly when Denver, out of her jealousy of the Sweet Home connection, is impolite to Paul D upon his arrival on Bluestone Road. "I don't want to hear another word out of you," Sethe yells when Denver questions how long Paul D is planning to stay, and "Hush! *You* make tracks. Go somewhere and sit down" (43) when Denver tries to persist with her questions. Although Sethe wants Denver to be independent (57), she is not willing to tolerate authorial challenges from her. Sethe directing Denver, who is 18, is not appreciably unlike Mama Lena telling Beneatha or Walter Lee what to do.[12] Such directions are a part of Sethe claiming Denver as daughter, again reflective of the mothering beyond the biological stage that slaveholders tried to deny to enslaved black women. Her ultimate biological tyranny is in taking Beloved's life.

To recover from all that she has endured—loss of a husband, death of a daughter, loss of two sons, death of a saintly mother-in-law, loss of a ghostly daughter, the ever-present memories of slavery—requires a strength from Sethe unlike anything that she has shown before. To keep on going on, to see a future when the past seems so dominant, to be trusting enough to allow a man who has provided the ultimate insult to reenter her life are the challenges for Sethe at the end of the narrative.[13] When Paul D asserts that *she,* not Beloved, is her "best thing," Sethe's "Me? Me?" can reflect a first stage (disbelief) as well as a second stage (acceptance). She finally accepts no choice but to go forward, and that choice is in keeping with the strength she has exhibited throughout the text. For all her losses, for all her pain, she, like Baby Suggs, tames all that anger down in the end and is the stripped down essence of the strong black female character ever capable of withstanding the human as well as the otherworldly challenges directed toward her.

Chapter 5 ~

Commanding the Universe

I. More Than Witch:
Bambara's Minnie Ransom

In critical discussions of Toni Cade Bambara's *The Salt Eaters* (1980), Velma Henry holds a respectful center as a strong black woman character. Before she slit her wrists and stuck her head in an oven—which must have taken its own peculiarly Sethe Suggs kind of strength—she has held a job that it takes *seven* people to fill once she is no longer there. She has endured infidelity, assaults upon her psyche, and the physical pain of attempted suicide. As the narrative begins, she sits on a stool in the Southwest Community Infirmary in Claybourne, Georgia, facing Minnie Ransom, a well-known healer, who sits on another stool; they are surrounded by a 12-membered group (representing the signs of the Zodiac) providing spiritual support for Minnie as well as by a collection of medical doctors and curious onlookers. While Velma has received and is certainly deserving of much critical attention, Minnie Ransom is equally important to the narrative, and I will center this discussion upon her as instituting a new breed of strong black women characters. She might qualify as a savior in the extranatural tradition.

Minnie, Velma's spiritual healer, who is less tangibly aligned to this world than Velma is initially, shares with Baby Suggs and other literary women in the 1980s and 1990s an ability to transcend temporality. Not only does she glimpse that other world, but her body is a direct conduit to it. Minnie is the first in a long line of African American female characters whose strength is cast in the more than human. Like Cooper's Clora and Naylor's Mama Day,[1] she does what no one else in her world can. Various forms of the extranatural provide the source for her powers and enable her to "ransom" or save Velma Henry's spiritual well being, but she is able to engage those powers only because of the special relationship she has to the people and the world around her.

The extranatural traits place her a notch above characters such as Mama Lena Younger and Mammy Barracuda, but Minnie Ransom is also set apart by the responses of other characters to her rumored healing abilities. In this sense, the *reputation* that she holds in her community elevates her in the tradition of many conjure women throughout African American history and literature.[2] In this scenario, what people and characters around them *believe* about conjure women—and I include healers in this group—is as important an indicator of their power as what the women are actually able to accomplish. As to accomplishments actually dramatized during the course of *The Salt Eaters,* Minnie Ransom does very little, it seems, until the very end. As to accomplishments rumored to have been effected, she holds the legendary role that many such historical women held. Descriptions of her lend credibility to this evaluation. She is initially referred to as the "fabled healer"[3] of Claybourne, Georgia, and is described as wearing "kenti cloth" and "a minor fortune of gold, brass and silver bangles" that immediately tie her to African and West Indian cultures. Those connections hint at the supernatural powers identified with African gods and goddesses referred to as *orisha* and their new world counterparts in the West Indies, specifically the *loa* that inhabit Haiti more than the United States. By using these descriptions, Bambara is quickly able to set Minnie apart, note her legendary healing abilities, and place her in a range of powers that exceeds Western rationalism, for it is in the context of a broader range of cultural bases that Velma's healing will take place.

Minnie is also described as a "legendary spinster" and an "ole swamphag" (4). The first description, from the narrator's perspective, captures the sense of mission that has been Minnie's life, for even in her stronger than strong capacities, her life has still been one of service to others; she has not been married, and she does not have children. Her extranatural abilities have given her the power to heal, and she has put them to service in helping her "family," which might reasonably be assumed to be any of the inhabitants in the town of Claybourne, Georgia. She specifically becomes "mother" to Velma during the healing process, for Velma's godmother, M'Dear Sophie, leaves the healing room, and her biological mother, Mama Mae, is on a church retreat when Velma tries to kill herself.[4] Velma's assertion that Minnie is an "ole swamphag" separates Minnie and emphasizes her special powers; it also indicates how blind Velma is at this point in her healing process (she will shortly see Minnie as "a farmer in a Halston, a snuff dipper in a Givenchy" [8], another indication that she is still focused on outward appearances and not yet ready to move toward the inner substance that will enable her to share in her own healing process). Swamphag, with its witchlike connotations, is partly accurate, for it ties Minnie to the forces of nature that are a significant part of her power. It also evokes comparison to Charles R.

Johnson's Swamp Hag in *Faith and the Good Thing* (1974), a tale of another fabled "seer beyond sight" who has powers not of this world.[5]

To Fred Holt, the bus driver who inadvertently wanders into the healing room, Minnie Ransom is a source of fascination and transformation. Fred is having his own crisis of the soul as a result of his best friend having been murdered, and he is as much in need of healing as Velma. In fact, Velma is a microcosmic representation of various ills in her community, those physical and emotional (as is the case with Fred), as well as those spiritual and political; if she can be saved, then she in turn can save her community. Minnie is the key to unleashing the energy in Velma that will reach all the others. Although Minnie does not touch Fred physically, she touches him spiritually. Indeed, his past impressions of her give way before what he witnesses when he enters the room. Initially, he thinks: "So this was the mojo lady he'd heard about. Kind of frisky-looking, he thought. Seemed like she should have some old-looking clothes on, beat-up slippers, and look like a frog" (270). Fred's stereotypical expectations of how a person with unusual powers should look are not appreciably different from Velma referring to Minnie as a swamphag, yet he is drawn to what he does not understand. He moves from the back of the room toward Minnie and Velma, and "the longer he looked at the two women, especially the classy old broad, the better he felt" (270). Neither Fred nor Nadeen, a young pregnant onlooker, can articulate precisely what it is about Minnie that inspires change in them, but they are both touched by the work she does. From expecting Minnie to look like a frog, to perceiving her as "classy," Fred moves further along his journey toward healing; it will culminate simultaneously with that of Velma and several other characters in the community.[6]

For Nadeen, who is receiving treatment at the Southwest Community Infirmary where the healing takes place and who is invited to witness it, Minnie Ransom is the key to her new sense of self. Devalued by her older lover and considered an immature child generally, Nadeen seems to have little sense of self; that self-perception alters as Minnie inspires Velma to change. When Nadeen, who has watched with "riveted" eyes, sees Velma's wrists healed from the suicidal slashes, she "felt a movement at the base of her stomach. Something leaped in her, like the baby Jesus leapt when Elizabeth, big with John, saluted Mary" (111). Without understanding what has happened, Nadeen nonetheless recognizes it as "the real thing" in healing, and she adds her own history of knowledge of Minnie Ransom to the general perceptions of Minnie as powerful and different: "Miss Ransom known to calm fretful babies with a smile or a pinch of the thigh, known to cool out nervous wives who bled all the time and couldn't stand still, known to dissolve hard lumps in the body that the doctors at the county hospital called cancers. This was the real thing. Miss Ransom in the flouncy dress and hip shoes with flowers peeking out of her turban and smelling like coconut Afro spray" (113). Nadeen's recital of Minnie's abilities evokes comparison to Naylor's Mama Day, who has similar as well as much more extensive powers. Her witnessing of "the real thing" ties Nadeen to all community members who are transformed by Minnie's interaction with Velma, and Nadeen resolves to be more forceful in her encounters with a "bossy" nurse.[7]

Nadeen's function here is not simply to serve as validating witness to the current action, but also to validate the traditions from which Minnie is drawing to heal Velma. Nadeen recounts many instances in which she has seen revival healing, which "was just not it. The rolling in sawdust, the talking in tongues, the horns blaring and people crying, folks tearing off their clothes, the little kids whimpering. . . . That was not the real thing" (112). Neither, she asserts, is the real thing connected to "them spooky sessions in the woods her younger cousin used to dare her to" (112). By inauthenticating presumed Christian and some secular traditions of healing, Nadeen invites readers to consider the alternative that is the basis of Bambara's book. By placing such observations in the eyes and minds of a character as "innocent" as Nadeen, Bambara achieves a validation for Minnie's work that she might not have achieved as effectively through another character. Minnie's reputation is thus enhanced from an unexpected source.

As a strong black woman character whose strength derives from the supernatural, Minnie shares with Mama Day the appearance that she has lived far beyond expected years. Cora Rider, one of the "old-timers" in the 12-membered Master's Mind that oversees the procedure as Minnie undertakes the task of healing Velma, describes Minnie as being "a hundred, if she's a day" (16), a description that belies Minnie's power just as George takes Mama Day's tiny stature as being synonymous with a lack of ability. On the other hand, the 100 years could also signal the knowledge that Minnie has stored up for use in just such cases as the current one with Velma. They also indicate that time in this text and in Minnie's and Velma's lives cannot be measured in the usual way; that fact again sets them outside Western traditions and enables the healing that occurs.[8] In spite—or because—of her figurative 100 years, therefore, Minnie holds in her fingertips the pathway to conducting healing energy from the universe. She has been selected as a conduit in a process that resembles the call to preach in many historical African American communities.

The process of being selected for special powers ties Minnie to African American folk practices as well as to African and West Indian ones. Like many African American preachers or others selected for special anointing, Minnie is troubled at an early age by forces she does not understand. Persons so singled out may be "worried" by or with something; they might be temporarily ostracized from their communities because they engage in actions their communities do not understand. Minnie's transformation, the unfolding of her gift of healing, had provided several occasions for her family and neighbors to be concerned.

> They called her batty, fixed, possessed, crossed, in deep trouble. Said they'd heard of people drawn to starch or chalk or bits of plaster. But the sight of full-grown, educated, well-groomed, well-raised Minnie Ransom down on her knees eating dirt, craving pebbles and gravel, all asprawl in the road with her clothes every which way—it was too much to bear. And so jumpy, like something devilish had got hold of her, leaping up from the porch, from the table, from morning prayers and racing off to the woods, the women calling at her back, her daddy dropping his harness and shading his eyes, which slid off her back like slippery saddle soap. The woods to the path to the sweet ground beyond, then the hill, the eating hill, the special dirt behind the wash house. (51–52)

Through these turbulent times, Minnie is guided by Karen Wilder, who, after her death, becomes Minnie's spiritual guide. Karen serves as the helper for Minnie to go through the transition of being chosen. Indeed, this process of a gift being made known to the recipient is not unlike what Octavia Butler portrays in several of her novels when characters with psionic powers must be "brought through" (the Christian-based phrase in African American communities) to a stable state of being able to use those powers. While the giver of such power in the Christian tradition is God, and the god-like Doro in Butler's works, with Minnie the powers come from a combination of forces, none of which is named as being directly responsible; the *loa* are mentioned on several occasions, and the old-timers draw upon numerous Christian forms, including prayer and long-metered singing. The very universe seems to be as much a giver of her gift as the other forces.

With her connection to the *loa*, Minnie is cast as a priestess and keeper of their temples and their memories. In a world where they are not as valued as they were at one time, they desire the attentions of someone like Minnie. As a keeper of ancestral flames, she does not forget them; indeed, she makes the requisite libations and offerings to them that keep them enthroned on inhospitable American soil. There is a venerable "Old Tree where Minnie Ransom daily placed the pots of food and jugs of water for the loa that resided there" (145). Minnie sights them (though most mortals cannot) making entrances at various points during Velma's healing; in fact, they assist Minnie in the healing process by "setting up to make music for Velma to dance by" (62). Music and dancing are key to Velma being in synch with the universe and with the rhythms of healing that are conveyed through Minnie's hands.

Velma proves a difficult case for Minnie, and one explanation for that springs from the loa. Old Wife asserts:

> 'Maybe you've met your match, Min.'
> 'What you say?'
> 'Say she sure is fidgetin like she got the betsy bugs.'
> 'She one of Oshun's witches, I suspect. What's Oshun's two cents worth on the matter? Maybe she'd like to handle this Henry gal herself.'
> 'I don't know about the two cents cause I strictly do not mess with haints, Min. I've always been a good Christian.'
> 'When you gonna stop calling the loa out of their names? They are the laws alive. Seems to me you need to slough off a lot more of the nonsense from this plane if you're going to be any help to me. Some spirit guide.'
> 'Leastways I know that Oshun ain't studyin this problem, Min, cause I hear Oshun and Oye prettyin up to hop a bus to New Orleans. Carnival in this town ain't fancy enough for them. Town gettin too small for some other proud spirits I could name too.'
> 'Bus? What are you talking about—the loa on some bus?'
> 'I'm talkin about them haints that're always up to some trickified business. They ride buses just the same's they ride brooms, peoples, carnival floats, whatever. All the same to them. What they care about scarin people with they ghostly selves?' (42–43)[9]

If the *loa* have an interest in Velma, then that is another argument for her being selected to follow in the extranatural healing footsteps of Minnie Ransom. Old Wife, Minnie, and Velma therefore form another transgenerational grouping, like Baby Suggs, Sethe, and Denver and Beloved, to mark the strength and power of black women characters. Although Bambara uses this small part of the healing as an occasion to position Western beliefs against non-Western beliefs, it is simultaneously an opportunity to make clear the multiple sources of Minnie's power, Minnie's relationship to her spirit guide, the multiple planes on which the healing must occur, and the limitations of Minnie's own—though awesome—saving powers.

Bambara's placing of the *loa* side by side with Christianity—and indeed giving the non-Christian a slight edge—echoes Uncle Robin's desire to bring back the "old cults" in Reed's *Flight to Canada*. Whereas Uncle Robin imagines that the reinstitution of such cults will curb the black woman character's power (as exemplified in Mammy Barracuda), Bambara posits them as providing an additional source for power. For Bambara, there is less a clash of cults than a synthesizing of them, a syncretism reminiscent of what Zora Neale Hurston observed about African religions and Catholicism in New Orleans in the 1920s (that syncretism is also apparent in Nadeen evoking Elizabeth, John, and Jesus in one context and denying the validity of so-

called Christian healing shortly thereafter). Bambara's black women characters therefore use all forms of belief known to them in order to influence
their worlds. Minnie is thus as physically syncretized with her natural and
supernatural worlds as Bambara's text is philosophically integrated across
cultures and belief systems. For Minnie, "over the years it had become routine: She simply placed her left hand on the patient's spine and her right on
the navel, then clearing the channels, putting herself aside, she became available to a healing force no one had yet, to her satisfaction, captured in a
name" (47).

But how do Minnie's powers actually operate in the text? They are a combination of her gift, Old Wife's advice, the attendance of the *loa* and the
music they provide, and what may be generally referred to as the rhythms of
the universe. Certainly she places her hands on Velma in the manner she describes, but she receives "messages" from unexplained sources, and Old Wife
provides information to which Minnie does not have direct access. For example, in the passage about the *loa*, Old Wife seems to be able to "see" more
into their ways and doings than Minnie can, but Old Wife, because of her
identification with Christian traditions, does not reveal every detail to Minnie. Also, Old Wife, in the tradition of many helpers, can herself be playful
at times—in the sense that, because her wisdom enables her to know more
expansively and over a greater part of eternity than Minnie, she is not as immediately ruffled when Velma does not seem to be making the progress that
Minnie expects. Further, because Old Wife perhaps already knows the outcome of Velma's situation, she leaves Minnie on her own at crucial moments;
in fact, her actions suggest that she trusts—or is at least more comfortable
with—Minnie's powers at times than Minnie herself does and is.

For Minnie, wellness and health are contained in the musical images and
references that saturate the text. Human existence is a dance, one that has
multiple dimensions. Illnesses interrupt the dance, put the body out of
synch with itself, make the song it sings unintelligible. Minnie's job is to
eliminate whatever interferes with the music and the dance. The following
passage captures the philosophy and typifies the significance of dancing and
music throughout the text and in the lives of all the characters.

> Calcium or lymph or blood uncharged, congealed and blocked the flow,
> stopped the dance, notes running into each other in a pileup, the body out of
> tune, the melody jumped the track, discordant and strident. And she would
> lean her ear to the chest or place her hand at the base of the spine till her foot
> tapped and their heads bobbed, till it was melodious once more. And often
> she did not touch flesh on flesh but touched mind on mind from across the
> room or from cross town or the map linked by telephone cables that could
> carry the clue spoken—a dream message, an item of diet, a hurt unforgiven

and festering, a guilt unreleased—and the charged response reaching ear then inner ear, then shooting to the blockade and freeing up the flow. Or by letter, the biometric reading of worried eyes and hands in writing, the body transported through the mails, body/mind/spirit out of nexus, out of tune, out of line, off beat, off color, in a spin off its axis, affairs aslant, wisdom at a tangent and she'd receive her instructions. And turbulence would end. (48–49)

This planetary model suggests that the bodies of the characters reflect the universe, a theory in keeping with Bambara's microcosmic location of Velma Henry. Once she is freed or saved from the blockage caused by her suicide attempt, the community will begin to be free of its many internal political and social splinterings. Minnie must inspire in Velma the desire to return from the way of death, then give her the healing energies that will completely eliminate the blockage to her healthier dance.

Velma's *desire* to be well is key to Minnie's ability to work, for she cannot force health upon Velma if she does not want it. The narrative is the documentation of Velma's reasons for wanting to die as well as her discovery, through Minnie's encouragement, of reasons to live, to assist in saving herself. When Velma makes that decision and starts back toward complete health, Minnie must deal with her messages as well as the force of Velma's energy. Although there are a couple of points in the narrative in which she seems to question or to appear uncertain about her ability to provide what Velma needs, she is nonetheless successful in playing the role that enables Velma to return to health.[10]

Beyond the messages she receives and the information Old Wife provides, Minnie also draws upon musical energies and rhythms that appear to be initiated by the traditional music provided by the record player in the healing room (which is identified as the "music room") but that branches out into the music of the spheres. Throughout the healing process, Minnie hums "up and down the scale" in rhythm to those pulses, but she also receives—through her whole body but especially through her hands—what can only be described as healing musical pulses. Perhaps inspired by the songs on the record player, or the dancing of the *loa*, or Velma's own dancing rhythms, they are in synch with Minnie's own humming at times and dramatically, strikingly more powerful than her humming at other points. Early on, the narrator observes that Minnie "might strike the very note that could shatter Velma's bones" (4).[11] Minnie is "unconcerned" about that possibility at this point, but mentioning it makes clear the delicate balance she must maintain in controlling her own body as a conduit for powerful forces that make themselves available to her but that are ultimately beyond her control.

Minnie operates in the world that Sula could only glimpse, that Baby Suggs could only contemplate, and that Beloved tried to escape. She adds a dimension to the strong black woman character by being able to go back and forth between those worlds without physical or psychological injury to herself. This occurs in the out-of-body experiences that she undergoes. Minnie anticipates Cooper's Clora by escaping the confines of physicality and temporality. Minnie and Old Wife simply leave their bodies (57, 60–63) for their chapel in the woods and leave others to interpret what they think is happening. The rationalist Dr. Meadows, who has been shushed in the healing room for reciting the Hippocratic oath, observes that it "seemed . . . that the right hand of the healer woman was on its own, that she had gone off somewhere and left it absent-mindedly behind on the patient's shoulder. And it seemed that the patient was elsewhere as well. So like the catatonics he'd observed in psychiatric. The essential self gone off, the shell left behind" (57). Perceiving but not understanding the complexities of what he sees, Dr. Meadows will shortly be as transformed as other residents of Claybourne. Buster, the father of Nadeen's child, will similarly be drawn to the idea of being in two places at once. For him it is as mundane as witnessing the healing as well as attending an interview in another room with Doc Serge. These actions are a small step to his willingness to accept the possibility of out-of-body experiences that Minnie and Old Wife are gleefully executing.

Crisscrossing the barriers between life and death much more freely than Beloved did, Minnie communes and travels with the dead Old Wife. The power and control that enable her to accomplish both feats tie her to Mama Day talking with George after his death and with Clora traveling throughout the world to watch over the branches of her family—though she cannot verbally communicate with them. From the moment Minnie is identified as strange or possessed, she is more tied to otherworldly phenomenon than to matters of her fictional world. While Bambara succeeds in immersing her in the natural (woods, chapel) as well as the supernatural (unexplained powers, talking with Old Wife), she is less successful in claiming for Minnie a place in the routine social world that she inhabits. Her very powers separate her, make her more than normal, and assertions that she is—or can be—"the woman next door" do not ring true.

One site on which such assertions are hinted at is in the realm of the romantic. Evidence suggests that Minnie's gift has effectively superseded any possibility of romantic or sexual liaison. Unlike Gaines's Octavia or the Mama Lena Youngers who at least had sufficient sexual encounters to produce children, Minnie Ransom is not conceived with a sexual side, though it is clear that she has a heightened feminine sense. While Hansberry shuts Mama Lena out of the possibility of continuing romance after Big Walter's death, Bambara claims Minnie for the otherworldly and severs romance completely from her life. However, to listen to Old Wife's perceptions of Minnie, one would think that she is strikingly attractive to men and has a host of them pursuing her in the manner of Eva Peace. I would argue that these are mere assertions unsubstantiated by the narrative. Consider, for example, Minnie's presumed designs upon the young Dr. Meadows. Old Wife maintains that Minnie is anxious to complete Velma's healing process in order to get home and get dressed to receive the young doctor who is attending Velma (50). Later, Minnie herself says to Old Wife, "'let's get on with the business at hand. I want to go home, set my hair and brew some tea. Expecting company tonight,' winking" (62), to which Old Wife responds: "'Minnie Ransom, I'm gonna be right there on the porch with you. So you best be prepared to put aside any hussy notions about messing with that doctor man, you heifer'" (63). However, there is no suggestion that Minnie knows Dr. Meadows or has had any encounter with him before his visit to the healing room (perhaps she plans to achieve the rendezvous through extranatural means?). Doc Serge and Cleotis the hermit, who are contemporaries with Minnie and the men who understand her gift, have no interest in her beyond that understanding. Even a hinted at or manufactured active sexual dimension, however, is far more than most earlier strong black literary women are allowed.

Still, the portrait of Minnie Ransom is limited to her specialness, to the powers that make her an otherworldly and unusually strong black woman character. Her gift effectively isolates her as thoroughly as Mama Lena Younger is isolated. As the character who is at the top of the hierarchy in her world, Minnie, like Mama Lena, has no peers. She also joins Mama Lena and Baby Suggs in having no confidants in this world. Indeed, Old Wife illustrates the extension of the isolation of the strong black woman character, for her only confiders are beyond her immediate fictional realm. Old Wife is in many ways a god substitute for Minnie; she calls upon her in the way that Mama Lena calls upon God. Although the patterns have changed appreciably, therefore, some of the problems inherent with strong black female characterization nonetheless linger.

An additional tie to another strong black woman character comes in one of Minnie Ransom's signature expressions. She advises Old Wife and Velma on several occasions to "Hold that thought." The thoughts to be held refer to the "weight" necessary to choose health over illness (5), to whatever baggage makes Velma "growl" under Minnie's hands (41), to Old Wife's assertion that Velma and Minnie are "cut from the same cloth" (62), to Old Wife's assertion that Minnie might not deserve her gift (63), and to Minnie's suggestion to Velma that she is the key to her own "perfect health" (104). The phrase places Minnie in the advisory position that characterizes all strong black women characters, but it ties her specifically to Morrison's Baby Suggs. Remember that Baby Suggs hobbles out of bed on the last day of her life, makes the pronouncement about there being no bad luck in the world but "whitepeople," and leaves Sethe and Denver to "hold that thought forever" (104). Baby Suggs and Minnie Ransom not only share the same phrasing, but this intertextual echo justifies comparison of their positions as strong black female characters in their respective texts.

Minnie and Baby Suggs are the salt eaters who have learned not to succumb to the bite of the serpent, whether that serpent is a system called slavery or the madness of potential chemical warfare and suicide in the 1960s and 70s. Through powers from within as well as from beyond, these women survive in worlds that did not intend their survival. Baby Suggs survives to choose her own exit and then to return from that escape. Already gifted with the capacity to exit and return, Minnie Ransom survives to assist in the creation of a new breed of survivors and saviors as exemplified in Velma. Like her strong black literary ancestors and descendants, Minnie focuses on her "offspring" in an effort to ensure that they have a future, both in this world and beyond it.

II. Tough Enough to Kill, Tough Enough to Transcend Death: J. California Cooper's Clora

The neo-slave narrative genre that has captured the imaginations of Ishmael Reed and Toni Morrison has also appealed to J. California Cooper. In *Family* (1991), she narrates the history of Clora, a black woman character who finds herself enslaved in the South in the same way that her mother was before her and the same as Clora's children will be. The narrative focuses on the multiple generations of females trapped in these historical circumstances. Attractive women without men who are used for sexual pleasure by "the Masters of the Land,"[12] these women fit into a mythic pattern that Cooper weaves to illustrate the interconnectedness of all humankind. The story begins in Africa before "the slave catchers" come and ends sometime in the twentieth century with Clora's observation that, because of intermarriage and geographical relocations, the branches of her family extend throughout the world. Through the many streams of her blood, she is, indeed, the Mother of all humankind.

In the American historical layer of the story, Clora's mother Fammy commits suicide after she kills the master for whom she has borne nine children (Clora, her firstborn, has a different father).[13] Her breaking point comes at the juncture of two occurrences: her master turns her over to his son for his sexual initiation, and her oldest daughter, Clora, is now 12, an age at which she can be raped and her mother can do nothing about it. This Corregidorian potential drives the mother's murderous actions, but they cannot save Clora, for the master's son immediately rapes and impregnates the 12-year-old. She bears her first child and continues having children for "the Master of the Land" until she has a fateful encounter with his wife. The white woman takes a poker to Clora when she sees how much like her own husband Clora's sixth baby looks. Clora, in a Dessa Rose kind of anger, takes the poker away from the woman. Realizing the probable consequences of her action, Clora decides to take herself and her children out of slavery by poisoning them all. This less bloody deed than Sethe Suggs's only results in Clora "dying." The children are desperately ill, but they survive. So, too, in a way, does Clora. She is dead but not dead, somewhere between here and there, locked in an eternal limbo from which she can watch over her children but cannot communicate with them. It is from this wherever space that she narrates the tale of her family. She can move from state to state and continent to continent to visit her children, but she cannot change her status or end her extranatural condition. Her position enables her to become the ultimate saintly mother by sacrificing a potentially peaceful eternity to engaged worrying.

Clora's strength, therefore, is measured in the human realm as well as in the extranatural realm. On the human side, she, like Baby Suggs, must endure years of seeing children to whom she has given birth either die or exist with the threat of being sold away from her—especially under the eye of the jealous mistress. As an inexperienced adolescent enslaved mother forced back to the fields immediately after childbirth, Clora cannot prevent the consequences to the first two of the six children she bears for her master.

> They wouldn't let us carry our babies on our backs with us, or nothin. We had to lay them down by the side of the field and leave em there for four or five hours til it was time for us to eat somethin, then we could feed our babies. I laid my first one out there, wrapped in a gunnysack. It was a boy, and he kicked that sack off and lay out there in that bakin sun all them hours. His little tender skin was just bout cooked. He died from them burns. I cried, oh how I cried. You don't want them to grow to be slaves, but you do want your children to grow up.
>
> The next one I lost, I put him up high off the ground in a shade tree and he got bit by a scorpion or a snake. Couldn't save him neither. Yes, lost both of em. As they died, I dug their graves, wrapped them in their gunnysack cloth, and covered them with the land that blonged to the Master.[14]

Strikingly here, Clora's strength is exhibited in the very narration of these two deaths. Certainly she has to endure the death of two children when she herself is but a child, but the narrative distancing from the trauma of those

losses ties her to the tradition of "taming all that anger down." Except for referring to her first child's "little tender skin" and mentioning that she cried,
she carefully controls the structure of the narration. Reminiscent of the declarative mode that contains Frederick Douglass' anger, or the poetic structure that Etheridge Knight used to control the chaos of his violent emotions,
Clora similarly distances herself through memory and sentence structure
from the horror of what she narrates. A mother is forced to leave a baby perhaps two weeks old for hours on end. She must surely have been haunted by
the possibilities of what could have happened to it, yet she must endure the
separation or endure the overseer's as well as the master's wrath. She tames
her anger down (as well as her innocence) and suffers the loss of her child.
Indeed, in telling of her second baby's death, there is no register of emotion.
She simply conveys the information. There is none of the anguish that a
mother forced to wrap her dead child in gunnysack and bury it must have
felt. And perhaps it is the bareness of narration that intensifies the horror. It
is also, simultaneously, the control of the form that marks the mother's psychological strength. She endures exceptionally well given the details of what
she relates.

Like Baby Suggs, who can remember only that one of her children liked the
burned bottom of bread, Clora is not allowed to develop any undue motherly
attachment to her first children. She cannot complain that she must dig their
graves or that only a single sentence is recited in the way of obituary. She must
gird her loins and move on with the work that needs to be done. Slavery necessarily makes her strong, but she bears her burdens impressively even considering that externally-imposed need to carry on. It is only when she is no longer
"alive" that she will be able to fulfill the nurturing role of mother—at least in
her mind, through her expressions of concern and obvious love for her children, as well as in the narrative she develops about them—that Sethe and Baby
Suggs are able to fulfill in the free state of Ohio.

Although she does not go into gruesome detail, Clora is also strong in her
ability to withstand sexual exploitation, especially given the circumstances
under which the master takes his pleasure. Her favorite child, Always, the
one for whom she has particular concern throughout the novel, is occasionally in the shack when the master comes to Clora's bed. Clora must endure
the child's awareness of her mother's violation, her helplessness. Always
"would lay under that bed and not make a sound" (26) as the master is rap-
ing her mother on the bed. Throughout these scenes, Clora displaces her
body from the fact of its violation as she shifts her primary concern to her
daughter (think of Sethe having sex with the man who chisels Beloved's
headstone). Her action makes clear that Clora is already in the mode of self-
sacrificing that will define her even more when she attempts to take the children out of their present circumstances. That mode is indicated further in

the risks she takes for Always; her love for Always leads her to challenge slavery in quiet ways to keep the child's "stomach full of all the good food" that she "could steal, beg, or borrow" (27). We need but contemplate the fate of Margaret Walker's Aunt Sally in *Jubilee* (1966) or those of several other literary women to realize the seriousness of these risks.

Her realization that she is the only one to die as a result of the poisonous dinner leads Clora to focus immediately on her children. "I died and left them children and Always in that terrible world, in these bitter times, all alone. Now, I was dead but I could feel my heart still grievin. My soul was not at rest! Was it cause my children was left behind me? Oh Lord!" (35). Clora is driven to the desperate act of attempting to kill her children in an effort to save them, and her anguish upon discovering that she has not places her squarely in the tradition of the strong black self-sacrificing mother. Her conclusion about the state in which she finds herself gives her a supernatural mission: "I blive I was left out here so I could watch over my children, my blood, my Always . . . just for a little while. That is why I am able to tell you this now" (36). Her mission is comparable to Mama Lena's desire to save Beneatha from heathenism as well as to M'Dear Sophie spiritually watching over Velma Henry's healing process.

Clora's contentment in sacrificing a potentially peaceful eternity to be able to watch over her children is at least equivalent to her willingness to kill her children in an effort to place them beyond, save them from, the physical and psychological brutalities of slavery. Clora's actions obviously invite comparison to those of Sethe Suggs, who is similarly inspired to save her children by attempting to kill them. While Sethe acts on a moment's notice, Clora has several hours in which to plan her deed. She moves from cleaning house and the encounter with the white woman, to contemplation of her confrontation and the consequences of it, to going into the woods to pick the poisonous plants, to building a fire, to boiling the weeds, to feeding her children, and to coaxing them to bed and to sleep. Thoughts of her mother killing the master and herself also weigh upon her mind as she plans to kill her children. I emphasize the passage of time and Clora's determined deliberateness to illustrate the unwavering strength of mind that is necessary for her to follow through on the deed. Knowledge of what the Master of the Land will do to her for having challenged his wife (" . . . I would be tied down and beat to the very end of my life" [34]), combined with her knowledge of what is in store for Always (" . . . she was the oldest and I knew her hard times was right on her for soon" [35]), enables Clora to stay her course against morality, against contrary nurturing instincts, against any obstacle.

Like Sethe, she claims the right to mother beyond the mere state of biological delivery. By determining the fates of her children, she thereby appropriates a certain amount of the power that the Master of the Land has held as his exclusive right. This appropriation is far more challenging than stealing food for Always because it seeks to undermine the very system of slavery. Clora truly becomes her own mother, therefore, not only in sexual exploitation (17) but in the destructively drastic response she offers to slavery. Clora, however, runs a risk that her mother did not. By attempting to kill her children instead of her master, her good intention of mothering has embedded in it the problematic possibility of her considering the children her property, objects with which she, like the Master of the Land, can do as she likes. Intention here, as in Sethe's case, is the only thing that separates the mother from the master, what makes one repulsive act understandable and the other merely horrible.

Clora draws strength from the space that she identifies with her mother. Described repeatedly as an old "broke-down chicken house" (9), this is the space to which Fammy takes Clora to spend the last few minutes with her on the night she kills her master and herself. The space is a haven, a pausing place, where the women characters make difficult decisions and renew their strength to carry them out. Although Fammy cries and holds Clora on that fateful night (as Eva Peace does before she burns Plum to death), she does not turn from her murderous resolve. The chicken house is the space to which Clora retreats at 12 to cry and recover when the young Master of the Land rapes her (17). It becomes her haven over the years, including one occasion on which she takes a book from the big house and stares at it in a vain attempt to decipher "all them crooked marks on that white paper" (29). And it is there that, through her tears, she gathers her resolve when she decides to kill herself and her children (33). The "broke-down chicken house" anticipates the "ole chicken house" (112) that Always, a few years later, will ask her new master to give her as her own space. The women characters are thus bound together in a type of space that allows them to claim whatever of themselves they can claim during slavery.[15]

With what Clora and Always claim for themselves, they transcend slavery psychologically and/or physically. When her retreats to the chicken house no longer allow Clora to transcend psychologically, she decides to make the physical leap into another way of being. With its connotations of fertility and rebirth, the chicken house becomes a kind of gateway into another world; it evokes the ritual that Mama Day performs with Bernice and the journey on which she sends George in *Mama Day*. From decisions inspired in this space, the extranatural joins with the natural to enable Clora to become a different kind of strong black woman character. As she watches over the many generations of her family, they become as numerous as the fertility inherent in the chicken house implies.

On the extranatural side, Clora exists—that is the primary cause for her strength—in a place and with powers of movement unknown to her living kin. There may be limitations in her state, but it is first and foremost more than human. Clora is therefore one kind of extension from the type of character that Minnie Ransom is—whereas Minnie makes excursions into the otherworld, Clora "lives" in one manifestation of that otherworld. In this wherever space, she is first and foremost clairvoyant. She sees the end of slavery before it occurs and realizes that if she had held out, "somehow," for another 20 years, she would have been free. While she asserts that hers is a limited clairvoyance (51), it is nonetheless superior even to Minnie Ransom. More often than not, Minnie needs Old Wife to reveal information to her. Clora can see for herself, even though she is unable to do anything about what she witnesses.

Along this line of progression in extranatural strong black women characters, Clora is in a better position on occasions than Minnie Ransom or Mama Day, but she is unable to do what either of them can. Minnie can act, while Clora can only see; Clora can see where Minnie cannot. Mama Day can feel, sense things that Clora would be able to see, whereas Mama Day can cause things to happen that Clora never can. That is painfully clear when Clora watches Always being raped while her youngest daughter, Plum, is slowly dying from being crushed by the gears of the wagon under which she has hidden and on which Always' new owner has taken Always to his plantation: "But, she did not die right away. She was unconscious, near death, when the wagon stopped and the new master got out and pulled Always, on her back, to the ground. God . . . why ain't you helpin them? Helpin me? What good is what you have let me do, if I can't do nothin for nobody? But who can know Your reasons?" (84).

The powers that make all of these characters more than human, therefore, have various kinds of limitations. Recognition of such limitations, however, does not in any way diminish the argument that these women characters are lifted from the ranks of "normal" characters and given special powers and talents. Their powers separate them as effectively as they reconnect them in stronger ways to the characters and places around them, as well as to the histories of which they are a part. Indeed, in every case, those histories provide one of the major reasons the women are endowed with special powers. Minnie is tied to the moment when Karen Wilder (Old Wife) reaches out to recognize her as one of the chosen, and her connection to M'Dear Sophie links her to Velma, whom M'Dear Sophie has delivered and also sensed Velma's gift. Through these women, Velma has to reach backward to claim her heritage before she can move forward with her spiritual work in the community. Mama Day's history, like Velma's, is one of locating and naming the spiritual ancestry that makes the future possible. Extricating Cocoa from Ruby's clutches is equated to lifting family history and future from the curse of slavery and its ugly consequences. For Clora, watching her children forge new futures is a corrective to her grandmother and her mother having killed themselves because they could see no way out of slavery.

In a way, perhaps Clora's extranatural condition makes her even more susceptible to the plights of her children. Her abilities give her a heightened awareness of how they are suffering and brings out even more her nurturing and mothering tendencies. "I watched my children," she says, "always prayin, to keep them from the beatins, punishments, hunger, grief and misery that is soul and core of the life of a slave. To see my, or any child workin, slaving in that hot, heavy sun that falls on your life like a big ole weight" (55). Her powers therefore cause her to suffer spiritually as her children are suffering physically. Ultimately, her special condition makes her realize that there is even suffering that makes it impossible to tolerate death. When she learns that Plum will not be bought by Always' new owner, and because she knows Always has always taken care of the infirm Plum, Clora laments: "Ohhh! Tear my heart up, life. Just tear my heart up! You done always done it! Just keep on, keep on . . . til I can't even stand death" (69). Recognition that there are some things that could make death something other than the peaceful condition it is rumored to be raises questions about Clora's earlier intention to "save" her children by killing them. Unable to save them through death, she can only watch from "death" as they live out a fate worse than death.

Noteworthy in Clora's spiritual being is the fact that, although she is extricated from life and the horror of slavery, she is still bound by one of the primary traits identified with other strong black female characters. She is still bound to God and to a desire to make moral sense of the world that she has left. Given little opportunity to practice Christianity on her master's plantation, Clora nonetheless acquires a rudimentary knowledge of God and His mysterious ways. She calls on God in ways comparable to Mama Lena and Mama Day, though those two characters are poles apart in their actual belief. For Mama Lena Younger, the calls are heartfelt and born out of a tradition of faith. For Mama Day, God is a familiar and comfortable habit—to be respected, of course, but finally not confining when it comes to her performing the conjuring work she needs to do. Clora seems to view God in ways closer—though not exactly comparable—to Mama Lena than to Mama Day. In very traditional approaches, she consigns her dead children to Him, asks Him for mercy, frequently exclaims to Him, credits Him with the beauty of the world, and thanks Him on numerous occasions. Even when He does not immediately offer an explanation for why she is where she is, she nonetheless thanks Him. In the permanent loner state in which she must exist, He becomes her primary confidant.

A refusal—or an inability—to move beyond traditional Christianity even under the special condition in which she exists illustrates the bonds of characterization that tie many of these strong black women to each other as well as to the cultures that formed them. For example, Mama Day's abilities to create lightning storms and to commune with the dead do not lead her to push God completely out of the picture; in fact, she almost apologizes when she helps Bernice become pregnant by insisting that she never tried to go over Nature, the realm of God. Lauren Olamina's creation of a new religion in Butler's *Parable of the Sower* is drawn from a traditional biblical model. In a world in which Cooper uses Clora to forge a new mythology, it begins with Christianity, the familiar mythology. Clora's narrative is finally the sermon that Janie's grandmother, Nanny, could not preach in *Their Eyes Were Watching God*. Clora's sermon is one in which most of her children find happiness; they marry people who truly love them, they prosper financially and educationally, and they live out the dreams that black women characters like Clora could not live. When Clora finally asserts that she is "so happy, so glad, so full up with joy" (218), she could easily be a church sister delivering a testimony on Sunday morning or shouting in ecstasy over the love of Jesus, for the phraseology derives its connotative meanings from that context.

Even as Clora is locked into a recognizable mythology, she is also the center of the new one. As Mother to all humankind and as a clairvoyant receiver in her wherever place, she approaches the status of a goddess. No matter the recurrent horrors of what she witnesses, she is nonetheless able to see. That ability enables the mostly omniscient narrative that comes to us as readers. Clora is able to see into the minds of her children and the people in her children's lives. In thereby duplicating authorial license, she attains a space that no other strong black woman character has achieved in the literature. She reaches the point of being able to become truly reflective. That she does not—preferring instead to focus on her children—keeps her in the tradition identified with Mama Lena Younger. The very assumption of connectedness between the entire human family is predicated upon the model of parents and children, and in this instance, upon the model of *mothers* and children. Clora's omniscience, as far as it goes, is always put in service to her children; she does not exist for any other purpose. Her narrative solidifies a myth of Motherhood, one that is inviolable because the intentions driving it are so thoroughly altruistic.

We readers are the congregation for the sermon and the audience for the myth. Above all else, Clora is aware of weaving a narrative, of addressing an audience, and of having that audience support her emotionally and spiritually. If God is her primary confidant, we are her secondary one. In the voice of intimacy and appeal that she adopts, she plays mother to us as well as to her own family. Indeed, her voice approximates at times the "island voice" that actively engages readers in Naylor's *Mama Day*. Clora explains, directs, cajoles, occasionally pleads, and sometimes seeks critical confirmation of the observations she makes. Throughout these gyrations, the *orality* of her presentation is the prominent feature. She addresses her audience as "you" and cultivates familiarity with it by using such expressions as "you know," "I'm tellin you this," "you see," "bear with me," "chile," and "I'm tellin you." She invites her audience to "see" on several occasions as if she is literally pointing out something or indicating that she is in the colloquial, casual mode of explaining something. The interrogative mode serves to hold readers' attention and invite them more intensely into the narrative, as in "Do you know what happened?" (35) and "You know what I did?" (222). She works the emotional register with questions such as "Ain't that something sad?" (30) when a young man is beaten to death for learning to read and "Oh, do you know a mother's heart?" (43) when she observes the punishment her children receive. Reminiscent of the tactics that William Wells Brown uses in *Clotel* (1853), Clora's strategies are equally designed to encourage her audience to reject slavery and all other forms of humankind's inhumanity to various of its members.

In the critical confirmation strategies she employs, Clora surmises a certain amount of knowledge in members of her audience that would enable them to arrive at the same conclusions she has drawn about slavery and various human interactions. She assumes that her audience knows that a black woman had little redress against the sexual advances of her slave master, so she can assert "Even havin him, I still didn't have nobody. You all know that!" (16), with the implication that the audience knows that voluntary and loving relationships between white masters and enslaved black women were generally not a possibility. She offers comments on human nature and the possibility for conflict no matter what color people are and cajoles: "You hear what I'm tellin you! . . . You see what I mean?" (53). "I don't need to tell you what all went on" (60), she says, when the master discovers that her son has successfully escaped from slavery; she expects the audience to know the system and how it operated to retrieve runaways. When she asks, "Do I need to tell you what she felt?" (155) in response to one of Always' sons being returned to her, again Clora is depending upon basic human emotions to make her case for her.

We are the "children" Clora can reach. Her own children are lost to her forever. Yet Clora gives up everything—even a peaceful eternity (though she does say she is getting tired near the end of the novel)—for those children. Her untainted motives make her as saintly as Mama Lena Younger professes to be. Clora has never been loved romantically; she has never experienced the pleasure of sex; and she has never known any work that was not designed to destroy her very being. Her children have been the only remotely good thing that has happened to her, and even that has not been without a considerable amount of pain. She can only imagine what it would have meant if those children could have been conceived in love. She voices that imaginative conceptualization when Always—after the death of one sibling and the dispersal of the others, and after many other trials and tribulations—finally marries by choice after Emancipation.

> And they came together in marriage. They made a home. And it wasn't too long fore they made a baby, chile.
>
> Oh! My! My! How much we slaves, of all colors, have missed. Oh! My! I never did get to feel nothin like that. There ain't been nothin, NOTHIN, like you wantin somebody and them wantin you. Loving. Lovin somebody! Just really nothin like making love to somebody you love, when you BOTH want to and you together doin it! Oh! My! My! Well, that's what they had, when they was freed. (210–211)

Clora's only consolation for this great sense of loss is the knowledge that her children, yet again, have achieved what was impossible in her lifetime. It seems as if all of her pain is manageable *because* she can see this good result for her children. She thus has the advantage of knowing that her total commitment to and sacrifice for her children has not been in vain. The ultimate jolt would perhaps have been to see them in perpetual slavery without the possibility of change; the many changes she witnesses, though it is difficult for her to keep track of them, nonetheless signal significant progress for those of her blood.

It is perhaps understandable that Clora identifies most frequently with Always, the child whose father she was able to choose. Although the child is considered an enslaved person nonetheless, Clora has at least executed as much freedom in conceiving her as possible under a repressive system. Her choice evokes comparison to Harriet Jacobs in *Incidents in the Life of a Slave Girl* (1861), but departs from that in the deliberate choice of a black father for Always. "My blood" is thus a more meaningful phrase for her in reference to Always. For example, when she follows her son Sun and observes that he marries into a white family and that his children and grandchildren will be more white than black, she remarks, "He would have money. And children. Little African, French and whatever all the Master had been, but, white children, new blood. I went to thinkin on Always. Pretty soon, I went back to Always, my blood" (126).

From her wherever space, Clora has been able to watch Always and all her children. It could reasonably be argued that perhaps some of her energy, her intense *desire* for their safety and happiness, has been subsumed into the plans to make their lives better. If the very air that surrounds them assists in processes that Velma Henry and Minnie Ransom set into motion, then why could not similar energies work for Clora's children? They suffer, as Velma Henry does, but, like her, most of them ultimately triumph. Their mother's desire for their triumph could be as much a part of the actual working out of their fates as are the circumstances that immediately control their lives. Clora's inability to communicate with them, therefore, may finally not be as much of a factor in their lives as it initially seems. Ultimately, Clora, the extranatural strong black woman character, observes the achievement of what every other strong black female character has wanted for her children—a healthy and sufficient space for them to live to their fullest potential and be fulfilled. Who knows but that Clora is a shapeshifter who, in the very shifting of her shape, has enabled energetic possibilities for change in the lives of her children that are unknown even to her?

Chapter 6 ∼

Strength as Disease Bordering on Evil

Dorothy West's Cleo Judson

I f any strong black female character in African American literature lives up to the stereotype of being destructive and domineering, then that character is Cleo Jericho Judson in Dorothy West's *The Living Is Easy* (1948). Not only does Cleo dominate, silence, and emasculate her husband, but she turns her daughter into a mousy, obedient drudge and destroys the marriages of two of her three sisters; the third sister's husband ends up in a mental institution. Throughout all her destructive and psychologically damaging behavior, however, Cleo is never effectively challenged in her position of authority. Her husband, her daughter, and her sisters understand, accept, welcome, and/or tolerate her will to power and her will to be first and foremost in their lives. Her refusal to consider their wishes, combined with her absolute refusal to allow any opposition, makes clearer than any other portrait in the literature the pathological nature of the strength of some strong black women characters. The strength that may be excused or understood in some instances has, with Cleo, metamorphosed into a disease that feeds on the perceived weakness or lack of decision-making ability of those around her. Cleo is an insatiable cancer, and those around her keep willingly giving her new cells on which to feed. She feeds ravenously and is consistently effective in suppressing any tinges of guilt or other expressions of conscience. She masks her emotions by taming down within herself any urge to show sustained affection. She posits such expressions as weakness and as minor battles lost in the war against men and poverty. In fact, she describes getting the money from her husband to rent a ten-room house as a "minor skirmish with her husband."[1] Determined to win at all costs, she refuses to count those costs until it is much, much too late. The implications of what she does as well as a consideration of how she is constructed place Cleo and *The Living Is Easy* into an especially problematic consideration of strong black female character.

The novel is set primarily in Boston in 1914 and the four years following it. It has a brief but important flashback to Cleo's childhood in South Carolina as well as a look at her husband Bart's early days as an entrepreneur in Springfield, Massachusetts, where Cleo was sent to work in service when she was 14. Bart Judson, the "Black Banana King of Boston," marries the beautiful young Cleo Jericho, who is 23 years his junior, in part to save her from the young white man enamored of her in Springfield as well as because he falls desperately in love with her. In Boston, when she is 29 and Bart has cornered the banana market for which he is famed, Cleo schemes to move to a larger house where she can more appropriately raise Judy, her five-year-old daughter, and to which she hopes to bring her three sisters, Lily, Charity, and Serena, each of whom has a child. Lily resides in New York (where she has remained after a planned trip to Boston because she was too frightened to continue on the train and where she has married the porter who took pity on her during that fateful ride); Charity and her husband and child live in South Carolina, a short distance from the family home; and Serena, her husband Robert, and their child live in the family home with the sisters' father following the mother's death. Cleo succeeds in bringing her sisters and each of their children to Boston for an extended period of five months that turns into four years, which effectively means divorce for Charity and Lily, and separation for Serena.

There is also a communal influential dimension to Cleo's character that, with the exception of Baby Suggs, is not apparent in the characters of other strong black women characters. Cleo's scheming has as its base—in part—an effort to move into the best circles of "colored" upper-class Boston Society. She has, prior to the novel's opening, become friends with a white/black woman of substantial family name. This woman, Althea (Thea) Binney, and her brother Simeon provide additional grist to Cleo's strength mill. She intercedes with another society woman on Thea's behalf and schemes to get that woman, known as The Duchess, married to Simeon. She hosts a Christmas party at which persons judged to be most important in colored society show up. They are not bashful about trading on their names for the benefits of Bart Judson's money. As parvenu, Cleo plays her role well and barters lives and fortunes as if they were poker chips. Her ability to effect these communal outcomes lies in large part to the stuffiness that surrounds colored society; few of the people actually talk in great depth to each other. That aura of silence enables Cleo to lie, lie, lie, and if anyone ever finds out, they are all too polite to challenge her.

Cleo's ability to effect these outcomes also resides in how her character is constructed in the novel, and, in terms of the power she holds over her sisters, the position she holds in her family. Within the first few pages of the novel, she is painted unlike any other strong black woman character encountered in the literature. Her fierce mental strength is apparent, as is her physical determination, as she moves her daughter Judy faster than her short legs will take her along a Boston street. Cleo is painted as "hissing" at Judy and as having a "secret life" (3). A variety of words and phrases surrounds her that would be inappropriate for any other strong black woman character in the literature: "prodigal" (3), "aliases" (4), "pawnshop tickets" (4), "unkindly" (5), "irresistible" spending (6), "plotting" (50), "despotic nature" (70), "duplicity" (75), "charming insincerity" (90). West withdraws sympathy from Cleo in direct proportion to her lack of affection for and unkind treatment of her daughter and to her scheming against her husband. Yet readers perhaps find Cleo as fascinating as those around her. We watch in horror to see the extent to which her manipulations will take her and to see whether anyone—within or outside her family—will be able to stand up to her.

A woman without scruples, Cleo shows no reluctance to take whatever she needs to achieve her objectives. She steals from her daughter Judy's piggy bank (4), steals money from her sisters (19), schemes to steal a portion of the rent money by telling Bart that the new house will rent for $50 a month when the landlord agrees to take $25 (54), takes money that Bart has designated for Judy (268), and commits just about every other larcenous act one can imagine connected to money. Cleo is driven by a desire to be a colored, upper-class "Bostonian," to separate herself and her family from the "niggers" migrating from the South. She wants to move so that Judy will not have to go to school with "little knotty-head niggers" (5).[2] As a social climber, Cleo shows none of the Christian basis that other strong black women characters have claimed, though she will claim that she is Christian.

Cleo rejects the nurturing side of mothering, but she retains the controlling side: "To her a child was a projection of its mother, like an arm which functioned in unison with other component parts and had no will that was not controlled by the head of the woman who owned it" (86).[3] It is important to note that she not only "mothers" Judy, but she also mothers her sisters, their children, and, to some extent, her husband. Her brand of mothering revisits in its imperative nature and insistence upon conformity the type apparent in Ernest Gaines's Octavia as well as in Mama Lena Younger. The glaring difference is that positive arguments could be made for Octavia as well as for Mama Lena in terms of their ultimate intent. West paints Cleo's intent as always flawed, thus the continuum between intent and outcome rests upon such faulty premises that the entire house of cards collapses onto itself. If the root of mothering is flawed, then no expected good outcome can result. Though Cleo consistently asserts that she is striving for those untainted outcomes, her methods are so ugly and her character at times so unlikable that readers almost immediately reject her claims.

Whereas other strong black women characters rely on silence as effectively as words to urge those around them to comply with their wishes, Cleo tongue-lashes people. There is no subtlety in her strategies, only deceit. She whips people with her tongue even beyond the pain of Octavia whipping James with a stick or Mama Lena slapping Beneatha or beating Walter Lee with her fists. The psychological damage that Cleo effects is much more destructive. She drowns the spirits of those around her with her ugly words. And even when she knows the power of those words, she does not desist from using them. For example, she calls her husband Bart "Mister Nigger" or refers to him as a "nigger" on several occasions (150, 177, 213, 234, 276). Embarrassed in the face of such intraracial adoption of interracial slurs, Bart merely stands tongue-tied. By using words as a whip, and by not censoring the content of those words, Cleo places herself in a class by herself, one into which her husband and sisters are too ashamed or too afraid to enter. This trait enables her to subdue The Duchess and to put Simeon in his place on a couple of occasions.

And why is Cleo able to get away with such actions? In relation to her sisters, Cleo is able to rule their lives in part because of her position as oldest child and because of her extraordinary beauty. Apparently people have difficulty recognizing and/or responding to evil when it masquerades in a beautiful form. That pattern was set when Cleo was a child. When Cleo, at 12, tied the braids of her sleeping sisters together and turned her youngest sister's pants inside out, her sisters suffered more than she did for the whipping she received, which was made even worse because Cleo lied to her mother and said that she was sleepwalking when the incidents occurred. Her mother could not "beat the truth out of her," which suggests the intensity of commitment to amoral behavior to which she will later adhere.

> Finally Mama had to put away the strap because her other children looked as if they would die if she didn't.
> They couldn't bear to see Cleo beaten. She was their oldest sister, their protector. She wasn't afraid of the biggest boy or the fiercest dog, or the meanest teacher. She could sass back. She could do anything. They accepted her teasing and tormenting as they accepted the terrors of night. Night was always followed by day, and made day seem more wonderful. (15–16)

When Cleo demanded that her father pay her for bringing his lunch bucket to the mill each day, her sisters followed suit, but the unscrupulous Cleo conned them out of their money. They forgave her because they could not imagine the light, the angel of their lives, being angry with them.

When I speak of the circle of acceptability surrounding strong black women characters, nowhere is that more apparent than with Cleo. She knows the position she holds as her father's firstborn, beautiful child, and she trades on that distinction. A brief glimpse from her father's point of view makes his position clear: "Pa couldn't bring himself to tell Mama [about paying the children for bringing his lunch]. She would have wrung out of him that Cleo had been the one started it. And Cleo was his eldest. A man who loved his wife couldn't help loving his first-born best, the child of his fiercest passion. When that first-born was a girl, she could trample on his heart, and he would swear on a stack of Bibles that it didn't hurt" (18). Mr. Jericho becomes good training ground for Cleo's later interactions with Bart Judson, for she tramples Bart's heart just as effectively into the ground. Cleo craves acceptability, and she gets it—from the sisters needing her to do stunts for them in spite of her having taken their money to Bart's desperate love for her, for indeed, her beauty is the cliff from which Bart leaps to his own destruction. Although we get glimpses of the narrative from Bart's point of view, they are not sustained or introspective enough for us to see the full effect of Cleo's destructive nature on Bart. What is clear, however, is that he knows she is greatly flawed, but he is content to have any little piece of her that she allows. He knows that he wants her with him on his deathbed; what she does in between may be difficult for him to accept, but he does so nonetheless because of her incredible beauty. In other words, Bart's love for Cleo is borne of a hunger and desperation not unlike Sethe's pleading for understanding from Beloved. If it means that he will have to give his life to receive acceptance from the beloved, then he will do so.

The age difference between Bart and Cleo is also another factor in her ability to manipulate him. In this May-December union, he is perhaps struck by this prize of a woman he has been able to win. He is older; she is young. He is dark; she is fair. And in those early-twentieth-century color-struck societies about which West writes, her fairness gives her an advantage far beyond the consequences of her ugly behavior. It enables her, in fact, to control the marriage bed as effectively as she controls finances. At the beginning of the novel, Cleo and Bart have been married ten years, and we could reasonably assume that she has permitted him sexual encounters for perhaps the equivalent of two or three months of that period. To Cleo, sex is another way in which men dominate women, and she is determined to remain aloof and contained. This is not a matter of whether or not she likes sex, for she asserts that she is not repugnant to it; this is a matter of control.

In contrast to the literary women who have lost husbands or lovers and are therefore understandably without sexual partners, Cleo is without one in the house in which she resides with her husband. She manipulates sex as a weapon in the war against Bart, which makes his staying with her all the more problematic and which highlights even more the impact of her acceptance by those whom she abuses psychologically. Bart is so in love with Cleo that he will accept being referred to as "Mister Nigger," that he will live as a eunuch in his own house for the sake of his daughter's upbringing and the possibility that his wife will one day become a bit more sexually generous.

Cleo's lack of sexual interest is in direct contrast to the strikingly beautiful appearance she presents to all who bask in the shade of her sunshine. While many can only speculate about her intimate relations with Bart, others know their limits. When her sisters arrive, she consigns Bart to a small bedroom on the second floor of their three-story new house and installs her daughter in her own bed (which mirrors the sleeping arrangements of each sister and her child). When one of her sisters, in expressing a desire to see her own husband, states to Cleo: "You can get in Mr. Judson's bed whenever you've a mind to," Cleo's response is: "I haven't been near that nigger's room since my sisters walked into this house" (177). In the early stages of the marriage, Bart had merely been an unwanted sperm donor but solid material provider (Cleo had hoped he would die early and leave her a rich young widow); now he is a physically unwanted though necessary material provider. His physical positioning in the household at this juncture mirrors the absolute lack of status he holds in Cleo's life. She wants him to hand over his money, be quiet in her presence because she prefers to talk, believe without question whatever she tells him, and be undemanding of conjugal rights. Each day her actions convey to Bart how physically and emotionally complete—if not financially so—she is without him. Cleo's choice not to engage in sex renders her as asexual and unromantic as many other strong black women characters studied thus far.

Cleo's abstinence reflects her generally unhealthy and contained emotions. Certainly other black women characters can refuse to cry or show signs of weakness. Cleo, however, is a model of unhealthy containment of emotion. If she shows her daughter that she loves her, she believes, she will somehow be irrevocably weakened. The same is true with any emotion that she may show with her sisters, so she is about containment. Striking examples occur with her daughter, her husband, and her sisters. On a trip to Bart's place of business (after Cleo has schemed to get the new house), when Bart cannot contain his excitement about showing Judy and Cleo around the store, Cleo initially accepts, then the following scene occurs:

> Suddenly [Bart] swept Judy up in one arm and caught Cleo close to him with the other. His devotion to his wife and child was like an aura around them. Cleo felt her throat contract with a strange compassion, and she could not bear the emotion that made her see his singleness of heart. She tore herself away from him lest she reveal her understanding and return his tenderness.

'You show Judy the store,' she said shakily. 'I'll go ask Miss Muldoon [the accountant] for a piece of paper to write to Lily.' (81)

Cleo is not only at war with Bart; she is at emotional war with herself. While it is never articulated precisely what she feels she would be missing in a clear expression of emotion, she feels/knows that it would be a diminishing of her perception of herself, the power she wields over others, and the position she holds in her family. That is a potential weakness that she cannot allow.

The same kind of containment occurs later in the novel in a scene in which Judy and the other children appear. It is Christmas morning, and the four children, who have risen much earlier than the adults, make a happy picture around the Christmas tree as Cleo later observes them. When they invite her into the room to see what Santa Claus has brought, she "quickly" responds: "'I can see from here' . . . She did not want the children to have a close view of the naked face of her happiness" (221). And, indeed, that naked face of happiness is short-lived. She resorts to lecturing them on how best to escape being black when one of the girls asserts that she wants a "colored doll." Cleo is slightly ashamed, but she does not repent: "If she let her heart go, it would flood with pity because they were little colored children. And what would she use then to bolster their pride? But she could not leave them with that betrayed look" (221–22), so she asks for Christmas kisses, only to escape that ritual when they all declare that they have not yet brushed their teeth—a prerequisite that she has insisted upon before they kiss her.

At a moment when readers would expect Cleo to express some heartfelt emotion—upon learning that the father with whom she has not communicated for ten years has drowned and that Serena's husband Robert has been jailed for killing a man—she even smothers that. She hears this information on the evening of the Christmas party, from which her husband and sisters have absented themselves for fear of embarrassing her class aspirations (she calls them "second-class niggers" for doing so—228). When Bart comes downstairs to find her crying (yes, she does cry this once in the novel), she seems on the verge of melting the ice block that is her heart: "She knew, and could not take time to deny it, that in him was a vital power from which she was renewing her own. His presence was calming her turbulence, restoring her courage, and clearing her mind for furious thinking. If he left her alone, some part of herself that had fastened itself to him with tentacles would be torn from her" (273). He stays, only to have her refer to him as "Mister Nigger" a few pages later (276) when he is hesitant to spend Judy's inheritance on a lawyer for Robert. Notice, too, how she *uses* Bart's presence; his calming effect from the distressing news merely clears her mind for "furious thinking," which will probably be directed in some negative way against him. She gains her strength from parasitic engagement and then turns it against her host. This rise and suppression of emotion, this mixture of suppressed tenderness and concomitant insult, characterizes Cleo throughout the novel.

These traits in Cleo, combined with the inability of those around her to object to them or challenge her, enable her to run roughshod over everyone in her path. The hurricane image is especially appropriate to her, for the amorality inherent in it is comparable to what we witness in Cleo (in spite of her protestations of belief in God). She is constructed as the epitome of a cold-hearted, calculating, manipulative woman who respects only her own will to power. The negative consequences upon the characters around her are apparent throughout the text. She presents the worst example in the literature of the consequences of strength upon other characters, those within her family as well as those outside the family.

Initially, Cleo's husband Bart suffers the negative consequences of Cleo's strength. He experiences a diminished and compartmentalized sense of self because of her constant stripping away of any authority he may accrue and of any healthy sense of self he may have. He is constantly the victim of psychological abuse. Because Cleo does not allow him any power over what happens in his home, he essentially consigns that space to her. His is an exterior life, realized in his business in the Fanueil Market and with the bankers of Boston. Yet his tremendous success (particularly so for a black man in business in the second decade of the twentieth century) makes no mark upon Cleo beyond its money-making results. She does not share the pride he rightfully feels in his accomplishment and readily insults him before his employees and fellow businessmen. On the occasion that she and Judy visit his shop, she accuses Bart of being cheap in the presence of Miss Muldoon, his accountant, and Chris, his Irish assistant: "'You can't bear to let money go, can you, Mr. Judson? You'd use any excuse to get forty-five miserable dollars back'" (76). Her strategy is always to focus attention and faults on others before they can be directed toward herself, for she knows that she has not paid $45 for the rent. She is alternately bored, irritable, and suppressing of emotion in Bart's office, but just as important, she conveys to those who work for Bart the fact that she does not respect him or his work; to her, money is the only thing that matters.

The traditional gender roles as well as the manhood that many black women characters are accused of taking from black men become the sites of several exchanges between Bart and Cleo. He tells her, "paternally," in his office: "You worry your head about woman affairs. I'll do the rest of the worrying" (81). Perhaps Cleo is born "out of time," as Claude McKay would say, for she has no patience with playing a secondary gender role. To her, this war is about men having an unfair advantage, and she will use whatever she can to level the playing field. Unfortunately, the person she perceives as the enemy most of the time is Bart, for "men were her enemies because they were male" (38). She has even resented her mother's tenderness with her father (16), for it suggested the kind of dependency that she despises, and she has early developed a sense that men are celebrated much more than they deserve: "What was there to being a boy? What was there to being a man? Men just worked. That was easier than what women did. It was women who did the lying awake, the planning, the sorrowing, the scheming to stretch a dollar. That was the hard part, the head part. A woman had to think all the time. A woman had to be smart" (21). Cleo reaches these conclusions when she is an adolescent usurped in her trick-performing for her sisters by a boy who in turn earns their admiration.

Her battles with Bart begin at the moment of the "consummation" of their marriage, and they would be particularly troubling to anyone who bares himself in the intimacy of sexual performance: "When Cleo was twenty, their sex battle began. It was not a savage fight. She did not struggle against his superior strength. She found a weapon that would cut him down quickly and cleanly. She was ice. Neither her mouth nor her body moved to meet his. The open eyes were wide with mocking at the busyness below. There was no moment when everything in her was wrenched and she was one with the man who could submerge her in himself" (35). This is all the more awful because Cleo had "no real abhorrence of sex in her, . . . but her *perversity* would not permit her to weaken" (35–36, my emphasis).

Designed to destroy any male ego, such scenes make it all the more noteworthy that Bart remains with Cleo for ten years before her sisters arrive and for another four years after that point. During all those years, at every opportunity, she yells at him because he is frugal, steals shamelessly from him, lies constantly and outrageously to him, denigrates anything he has to say, and has no noticeable respect for him. From Bart's perspective, "Cleo embarrassed his manhood by calling him down before the girls whenever he put a word in" (225). She prefers, in all conversations, to be the one talking. This generalized pattern is also apparent from one of her exchanges with Simeon: "She always heard a man out with impatience. A resentment rose in her. If either was going to do the talking, let her do it. When men spoke, she knew that their worlds were larger than hers, their interests broader. She could not bear knowing that there were many things she didn't know; that a man could introduce a subject, and she would have to be silent. Her defense was to shut out of her mind the didactic sound of their voices" (140). It is a wonder that Bart makes it to the end of the text with any ego intact, for Cleo's harangues are designed to strike at the core of his masculinity. Though he still retains a desire to provide for his family when his store fails and he sets out for New York, in essence his departure, at 56, is the end of his career as well as the end of his relationship with Cleo, for if he cannot make it among bankers and businessmen who know him, how successful will he be in starting over among strangers? He will not be in touch with Cleo until he has money to send, he thinks, for he knows that if he sends a letter without money, "she would tear it up without reading it" (346). Bart has been Cleo's gravy train, a working, bread-winning machine; the brief flashes of his humanity that she recognizes are always submerged under the immediacy of her patholog-ical objectives.

The fact that Cleo refers to Bart as "Mr. Judson" throughout the novel is further evidence of the distance, the lack of intimacy, between them. His-torically, there was a pattern in African American culture in which younger wives referred to older husbands as "Mr.," as Celie does to her husband in Alice Walker's *The Color Purple.* The historical pattern reflected a sense of re-spect, a respect that could never be mirrored in Cleo's use of the title. Every time she uses it, she reminds Bart how much older he is, what she expects of him in terms of "providing," and that he can never be the sexual partner whose first name she would cry out in a moment of ecstasy.

Certainly we can argue that Bart, like Walter Lee, has the option of sim-ply leaving the female-dominated household. No matter how sick that household, however, he has been a necessary part of it. And no matter how sick the woman in it, Bart has loved her. We do not see enough of his psy-chology to know why he would undergo so many extended years of flagella-tion, but he has willingly endured them. Perhaps this is another instance in which West constructs the characters around Cleo in order to reveal Cleo's worst qualities. Bart's weakness is his love for Cleo; by rejecting that and contributing to his financial destruction, she becomes monstrous. Bart is long-suffering, a trait that many of the strong black women characters share and that Cleo is utterly lacking. He is ultimately psychologically martyred to Cleo's warped sense of existence. The fact that he is a martyr by choice only casts more aspersion on Cleo, makes even clearer the diseased nature of the strength that allows her to dominate those around her. Bart has been one way for Cleo to change, to melt her ice-cold heart and become a loving in-dividual; that she does not only indicts her more. Bart's purposes in the nar-rative, therefore, are multiple within the text as well as for readers who evaluate the final intent of the novel.

Whereas Bart exists "un-wifed," Judy grows up "un-mothered" as a neg-ative consequence of Cleo's strength. Judy is "un-mothered" by a woman who ironically maintains that she values family over everything else. How-ever, Cleo's narrow definition of family does not include her husband and only includes her daughter as a piece of property, not as a growing being who needs guidance beyond instruction into the mores of being a little Boston lady. Cleo alternately wonders where Judy came from (44, because she is so unlike Cleo), looks at her coldly (54), or is bored with her (219). She tells herself that she is interested in Judy's education and development, but the text is hard put to provide evidence for that beyond the fact that Judy goes to school and takes piano lessons. To Judy, her mother's face is "shut-away" (53), and she must learn to decipher Cleo's moods—when she should be silent (most of the time), invisible (on command), or unhearing (when the sisters gather in Cleo's room, where Judy now sleeps, for their nightly talks, including reminiscences about "down home"). Cleo's possessive attitude toward the child is always clear, for Cleo muses at one point: "I want her to be a Bostonian, but I want her to be me deep down. Judy, her frightened heart cried, be me as my sisters are Mama. Love me enough to let me live forever" (141), which amounts to the height of selfishness and disregard for anything Judy might want. In an argument with Bart about Judy's inheritance, Cleo asserts in reference to the cost of a lawyer for Robert: "Whatever it costs, it's cheap at the price of *my* child's pride" (275, my emphasis).[4] She uses Judy when she needs her to picture her own longevity or to make a financial argument; otherwise, the child is not very valuable.

There is one instance in the text when Cleo *seems* to feel genuine emotion for Judy, but that is pity, not love. It occurs when they are about to enter the rental house and Cleo inspects Judy to make sure that she is presentable. The pattern of short-circuiting tenderness continues here:

> She scanned the small upturned face, and a rush of protective tenderness flooded her heart. For a moment she thought she had never seen anything as lovely as the deep rich color that warmed Judy's cheeks. She herself had hated being bright-skinned when she was a child. Mama had made her wash her face all day long, and in unfriendly moments her playmates had called her yaller punkins. Now her northern friends had taught her to feel defensive because Judy was the color of her father.
>
> 'Don't speak unless you're spoken to,' Cleo warned Judy, and mounted the steps of the house before which they stood. (42)

As with Bart, Judy can develop little healthy ego under the tutelage of a woman whose major characteristic is her predictable unpredictability.

Judy finally learns to see through her mother, to know that she lies, but such knowledge does not alter the relationship between them. Judy observes at the age of ten: "Her cousins thought Cleo could stand up to anything. But Judy felt secret pity for her where the others felt secret awe. Cleo made a big noise to scare people into letting her be boss. Judy was beginning to see that Cleo was the boss of nothing but the young, the weak, the frightened. She ruled a pygmy kingdom" (308). Such knowledge, however, does not alter Judy's position in relation to her mother. Judy is still silent most of the time,

acquiescent in everything, and one of the young, the weak, and the frightened. Cleo is shaping her to accept her lot in life and perhaps even to make
excuses for it, even as she is trying to force her into class pretensions that
would presumably subsume some of these traits.[5] Expectedly for those class
aspirations—if not for identification with her mother—it is always Judy
who must bring the consciences of the other children into working order.

This shaping is totally Cleo's work, for she selects the tutors and dance
instructors, along with the school and other extracurricular activities. Cleo
plans, in her usual authoritarian way, what the lifecourse will be not only for
Judy, but for her nieces and nephew:

> She wanted Vicky, who was a brilliant first-grader, to be a schoolteacher. Judy,
> who was showing dexterity with her first piano lessons, must be a celebrated
> pianist. Penny, who exhibited no talent for anything except kicking her heels
> when the graphophone whirled, could train for sobering settlement work. . . .
> Tim, poor child, thought Cleo, as slow a walker and talker as he was, he
> would never be the brightest jewel in her crown. He might as well go into
> business. That didn't take brains, not educated brains, anyway. (220)

The jewel and crown imagery is well-placed, for Cleo sees the children as
moldable art objects, *things* that she can shape to her own fancy. They, like
"Mr. Judson" in providing Cleo's financial support, have little to say in the
matter.

In considering Cleo's "un-mothering" of Judy, it is important to note that
Judy calls Cleo by her first name most of the time. When she addresses her
on Christmas morning, she uses the formal "Mother" (220). Both are emotionally distancing; for a child to call a parent by a first name is to erase the
biological fact of a woman having given birth to a child. In some instances,
the first name designation is conceived so that the mother will not feel a
sense of aging. Since Cleo is not particularly concerned about that, perhaps
the first name in this instance merely ties to the distancing. The use of
"Mother" achieves distancing by denying the closeness that "Mama" or
"Mommy" would evoke; the irony is that West asserts that "Mother" is
Judy's "term of endearment" for Cleo. Such a relegation highlights yet
against the abnormality in the mother/daughter relationship, the lack of ease
between Cleo and Judy. It would be difficult to project exactly how Judy will
turn out, but being raised by a mother whom one knows is a constant
schemer and liar cannot be overly healthy in one's emotional growth.

Some of the ugliest consequences of Cleo's strength occur in her interactions with her sisters. Initially, she plans the rental of the larger house with
the intent of bringing them—minus their husbands—to Boston. Upon their
arrival, she makes her home and the surrounding lifestyle so attractive that

these three very poor women are flattered beyond imagination at her paradisiacal existence. But once Cleo offers the temptation of the apple, she controls the bites so that her sisters are very quickly financially dependent upon her. Thus, they cannot leave Boston without her assistance (even if they wanted to do so), and she is prepared to exert all of her persuasive ability to get them to change their minds if they were inclined to leave. When they initially think of returning home—after the two weeks on which they have all agreed to stay—Cleo literally becomes ill. That illness gains her time and sympathy until the visiting children start to school with Judy. After that, Cleo is in complete control.

For Cleo to retain control, her sisters must not only occupy that position of dependency, but they must also have some lack, some tender spot, from which she can shape her vision of the reality that is appropriate for them. In each case, her sisters are weaklings who eventually accept the mothering that Cleo offers them, even when it means giving up (especially for Charity) the men they love. For Lily, the lack is an inability to shape reality without Cleo's influence. She believes anything Cleo tells her (51). Cleo turns Lily against Miss Hattie, the woman their father marries after their mother's death and sends Lily on the escape that gets her to New York (she was on her way to Cleo in Boston but did not have the stamina to continue). It is due to insecurity and inertia that Lily marries the dark-skinned porter who helps her on the train and in New York. Cleo has little difficulty, therefore, in encouraging Lily to believe that her husband Victor is so angry with Lily for coming to Boston and staying so long that he will resort to physical violence against her if she returns. Lily becomes so frightened that she lets Cleo read and "interpret" letters from Victor. Cleo stretches the fragile bond between Lily and Victor until it breaks; by the time Victor comes to Boston to try to reclaim his family, Lily is so brainwashed against him that she claws his face, yells and screams at him, and uses the "Mister Nigger" epithet she has learned from Cleo to destroy her marriage and to shame the man who loves her. She is now ripe for Cleo to try to reshape her into the image she wants. Cleo succeeds almost too well, for Lily is too timid even to join Cleo's Christmas party. Cleo "was struck by the fact that though Lily was pliable, there was nothing really to work on except a mass of fears. Her hand had been largely instrumental in Lily's sorry making, and now she could not remold her into spine and sinew" (218). Nonetheless, Lily and her daughter remain in Boston with Cleo. Lily only thinks of Victor when she is forced to, and Cleo does not feel any guilt about lying to Lily about Victor's intentions or about the heavy hand she has played in destroying the marriage. After all, Victor is a man and therefore Cleo's enemy.

Charity's weakness and lack of self-esteem manifest themselves in food. When her husband, whom she loves deeply, takes up with another woman (as he suggested he would do if she stayed overly long in Boston), Charity stays in Boston and eats. The more she eats, the less value she has in her own as well as her daughter's eyes. She becomes totally dependent upon Cleo's and Bart's largesse. When Charity, after receiving the fateful letter from her husband, asserts that she will get a job, Cleo's response is instantaneous: "'You think I want to see my sister slaving in somebody's kitchen? I'll take care of you and Penny as long as I draw breath'" (178). Cleo wants to be the "man" in the lives of all her sisters, that is, performing the functions for them, through Bart's money, that Bart performs for her. She never examines the logic of this connection; she just accepts the scheming, lying, planning role that she identifies as woman's lot, role, rightful purpose in life.

For four years, Charity does not go outside the Judson house. She is therefore freely available to Cleo's manipulations, and she mainly does as she is told. Not once does she blame Cleo for having a hand in the demise of her marriage, and she does not have the confidence or the money when she receives the letter to return to South Carolina and try to reclaim Ben. Indeed, Cleo advises her to forget about Ben, with the ease with which we might imagine slaveholders trading one black "spouse" for another. Cleo wants Charity to be emotionally as well as financially dependent upon her. Charity makes that objective easy by eating herself into the monstrosity that even Cleo has difficulty accepting. "The weight of her body was vast, and her small feet steadily ached. Her bloated face was beet-red and a little moist from the effort expended on her slightest movement. She had long since given up trying to find a becoming dress. The search was too unrewarding, and her abnormal addition of pounds burst the stoutest seams in a week. She wore Mother Hubbards exclusively, for in her painful consciousness of her obesity she no longer left the house" (211). When poverty replaces plenty, Charity's size becomes a focal point for Cleo's insults when they discuss Easter clothes for the children. "'What do you care about clothes? You haven't put the first foot outside the front door in four years. You've lived for this kitchen. Pretty soon nothing will fit you but a tent. No wonder you're worried about keeping a roof over your head. I'd worry, too, if I thought they'd have to cut a bigger door to get me out'" (290). Another one of Cleo's emotional suppressions emerges as "she longed to tell her sister she was sorry, but she had never been able to master the simple words of apology" (291). Charity laughs the insult away, for, in a rut from which she cannot escape, "she had lamed herself with her gluttony" (292); her only response to Cleo has to be in the blues tradition of laughing to keep from crying.

This formerly beautiful woman is a flower nurtured to spoiling by a woman who may love her but who can never express that love or save the flower. Though Charity shortly takes a job cooking at the barrel house across the street (a sign of the devolution of the neighborhood), it may lift her spirits momentarily, but it cannot transform her situation. Again, we can introduce the idea of choice here. Couldn't Charity have just taken Penny and left Cleo's house? Without resources, that would not have been a particularly viable option for a small town southern woman in big city Boston. Then, too, Cleo's response to that might have been more immediately destructive than what Cleo enables Charity to do over time by living off Bart. As Judy observed, Cleo thrives on the weak, and she always recognizes them: "The power of her personality was like a tongue of fire that ignored locked doors and penetrated whatever reticences might stand in the way of her passion to probe the lives of other women and tell them how to live them" (104). Not only has she invaded Charity's inner life, but she has reshaped Charity's body. Cleo looks absolutely gorgeous beside the bloated Charity, so Charity serves Cleo's ego physically as well as emotionally.

Though Cleo is not finally able to destroy Serena's marriage to Robert, it is not for lack of trying. When the narrator asserts that Serena is "the star" by which Robert's life is guided, and that if he could convince her to marry him, he "would have the world" (161), readers know that Robert will falter without Serena, which is precisely what he does. When he goes to another town looking for work, he is so desperate that he passes for white and gets a job as a policeman. Forced to recall his "blackness" in a difficult set of events, he kills a white policemen who is intent upon killing another black man. The tangled situation gets resolved, but Robert ends up in a mental institution in Boston. Serena hires herself out in order to pay for his keep. Cleo has set into motion the chain of events that led to this disaster by pretending that Serena was needed in Boston to help resolve a family matter and then by keeping her there as Robert grew more and more frantic in her absence. It does not matter that Cleo has convinced Bart to pay for the lawyer who defends Robert; it is her fault that he was imprisoned in the first place. The ugly consequences of events Cleo initiates make her appear demonic.

The question might reasonably be asked, Why does Cleo manipulate her sisters this way? The counterpart question in the strong black woman character scenario is, Who told Cleo that she had to take charge and be in charge of everybody and everybody's life? Who told her to decide that her sisters' lives needed improving, especially when they were all happy, even though poor? Is this an Eva Peace-like aspiration to goddess head? These reflections put her plan into motion: "Victor Bates was no worse than the average second-rate husband, Cleo conceded. But he was a road man. Lily spent half of her nights alone, with only a sleeping child to look to for protection. Victoria was going on seven. It wasn't doing her any good to have a jack rabbit for a mother. She and Lily would be better off in Boston, where Cleo could look after them both, than in New York with one little man who spent most of his time bowing and scraping to white folks" (53). So Cleo proceeds to create what she hopes will be a transplanted southern paradise in Boston. Great ironies abound in this aspiration, because Boston class consciousness automatically minimalizes southernness. Perhaps it is in part to counteract the rules imposed by the Binneys and their friends that Cleo wants her own little paradise at home, one in which she rules and expects her family to be just as deferential as she is to the Binneys. Still, the irony remains that Cleo's southern "paradise" was one in which farm labor dominated and in which she learned early that she was subordinate to her white friend Josie, the one to whom she ran after playing tricks on her sisters. The South is also the place from which her mother extricated her at 14 and sent her to Springfield, Massachusetts, because she recognized the potential sexual misadventures that could occur with a beautiful, young, almost white, black girl among unscrupulous white male employers in the South. What Cleo seeks to recreate, therefore, is only an image in her mind.

The image nonetheless guides her use and abuse of her mental strength against her sisters. "All of her backward looks were toward the spellbinding South. The rich remembering threw a veil of lovely illusion over her childhood. Her sisters, with their look of Mama, would help her keep that illusion alive. She could no longer live without them. They were the veins and sinews of her heart" (53). When Lily arrives in Boston and Cleo embraces her, "she knew that some part of her interrupted childhood was restored" (165). When Charity and Serena arrive, "Cleo's created world was complete" (166), and the women spend their first night reminiscing about the South. "The others listened dreamily to Cleo remembering back in a way that cast a magic spell over the South and their sister" (167). Cleo tries to mirror in this re-creation the power over her sisters that she had when she was 12 and performed cartwheels for them. She works desperately to ensure that her role at center stage in her sisters' lives will never again be usurped by a male—as it was by the boy who performed for her sisters in the South.

Of the many problems with this attempt at re-creation is the fact that the impact of Cleo's actions upon the lives of her sisters have many more serious—and destructive—consequences than her youthful antics. She cannot simply climb a tree and make them forget the presence of a boy. And destroying their marriages is much more morally bankrupt than taking the coppers their father had given them. Reshaping their minds and bodies is even more destructive. It is not until Cleo learns of her father's death that she changes her mind about the "illusion" of the South: "Over all her bright images of the South there must remain this bitterest one. It had broken the chain of enchantment. She would never again feel separate from the harshness of down home" (284). And why should she, for she has recreated emotional distress as powerful as that accompanying a southern lynching in her own little tainted paradise in Boston.

The childish wish implicit in Cleo's re-creation of an imagined southern paradise might place her in the category of Beloved and inspire us to view her as a child with an arrested state of development, which would mean that, instead of considering her strong, we should perhaps consider her merely selfish. That potential argument, however, loses credibility in the face of the number of characters who are kind to Cleo in her formative years, such as her parents, her sisters, Josie, the spinster who hires her in Springfield and other employers there, Bart, and the people she encounters in Boston. Cleo is not the result of someone having done something *to her,* as is the case with Beloved; her personality traits are pretty well formed before any of these encounters. Even Mrs. Jericho sending her daughter off to Springfield is not cruel, for Cleo had already surpassed her mother's influence and looked forward to the change. The childish re-creation thus comes from a fully formed *woman* character's mind, with all the attendant problems and responsibilities. When Cleo elects to play god with her sisters' lives, therefore, she is to be held fully accountable for her actions and their results.

Even as Cleo plays god, she asserts that she believes *in* God. Her actions give lie to that assertion, but her notion of morality—or lack thereof—is nonetheless worthy of note. To Cleo, God is fate, or at least good luck.[6] In spite of her mother's efforts "to bring her up a Christian" (15), Cleo does not evolve. She manifests a "sluggish conscience" (55) even in response to her own daughter. She thinks that she can "sleep away her sins, and rise the next morning, like a child, with a clear conscience" (142). Her relationship to God centers upon her perception of His responses to her pathetic and desperate needs; otherwise, she ignores Him, which makes her a direct contrast to most of the black female characters conceived in her literary generation. Cleo rushes to write to her sisters once Bart agrees to pay their fare, because "things got done if you did them without thinking. If you thought, your scruples stopped you. It was always better to do today what your conscience might not let you do tomorrow" (83). Placing "scruples" and "conscience" in the same sentence with Cleo is itself an incongruity, for she exhibits little of either. She lies to everybody about everything, yet there is one occasion on which she asserts that she "can't bear liars" (289) when she thinks a prospective renter will not show up. Cleo's moral development is almost completely lacking, no matter assertions to the contrary.

When she prays, it is on the occasion when, four years after the arrival of her sisters, she has received a dispossession notice. She must get $80 to the rental office or her family will be evicted. Knowing that she must get the money, or Bart will find out that she has been mismanaging rent monies, she exclaims: "Jesus, what am I going to do? Lord Jesus, help me, help me" (316). Another version of the hip-pocket variety of Christianity, Cleo's plea is pitiful, for she has exhibited no respect for the very source to which she prays. Her pathetic prayers, as in "God, you've got your eyes on your sparrows. Look down on my little ones, too" (319), continue throughout this section, as do her exclamations, as in "by God" (320), "O Lord" (322), "What in the name of God" (333, 337), "My God" (339), and "Lord God" (340); the exclamations are all used in careless instances of disrespect and handy calling out for the sake of calling out. The problem is not so much *what* Cleo prays for in the first instance, for keeping a roof over her family's head is a valid objective; the problem is with Cleo the invincible offering prayer at all. In her mouth, the pleas sound like blasphemies, because we know that she is using the children—yet again—to her own selfish ends and to cover her own devious behavior. Her faulty motives invalidate her supplications. To Cleo, God is a meaningless expletive; her references to Him do not in any way reflect a belief in Him. Indeed, even on the day that she "prays" so fervently, Victor comes to give money to Lily for a divorce, and Cleo says "slowly and venomously" once he has stated his purpose, "Get out of *my* house, Mister Nigger" (336, my emphasis). She also lies and tells Lily that she has sent Charity to work across the street when in fact it was Charity who decided to accept the job.

Cleo's lack of Christian principles, indeed her lack of any visible moral or ethical code, sets her outside the traditional strong black woman character's adherence to Christianity. Ironically, the answer to her desperate prayers finally comes in the form of Bart, to whom she must ultimately appeal for the rent money. To Cleo, religion is a toy, something to be picked up and put down as needed. It does not touch her in any serious, life-altering way. All of her calls upon God can be equated to verbal expressions such as "Gee whiz," "Oh my," or "You don't say," for they have little more substance or serious intent than that. Cleo, finally, is a woman who is not above attempting to toy with God in the way she toys with her family. Her desperation and exasperation come from the fact that He is beyond her control.

In assessing Cleo's actions, it is interesting to engage her creator's attitude toward her. West's construction of Cleo is almost as diseased as Cleo's actions throughout the narrative. West passes judgment on Cleo and leaves her undeveloped throughout the novel. Where Cleo enters the text is where she leaves it. In other words, she remains the same, with no redeeming character traits, for almost 350 pages. West sacrifices complexity of character development to indictment of the social system that inspired her creation and of the woman who represents it. And there is a significant moment near the end of the text when Cleo has an opportunity to grow. Rather than allowing for that possibility, West drops Cleo back into the viciousness—now perhaps tempered with a different kind of desperation—in which we have seen her throughout the novel.

When Bart comes to Cleo, weighed down with groceries, with the loss of his business, and in need of a kind word, Cleo could, even at this late point in the narrative, reach out to him. For once, "she did not want the money" (344) that he passes to her to keep her going until he can send more, and she urges him to take it back and rent another place. In the midst of this crisis, however, and when Cleo is finally willing to pass up money, she is still deceitful. She takes $100 from her bosom that she has stolen from the divorce money Victor has brought to Lily, and says: "Here's more. Lily's husband came and gave it to me for being so good to her and Vicky. There was more besides, and I sent Lily up to pay the rent. All this is clear. I want you to have it. It'll help with your bills. You won't have to leave Boston" (345). Her one moment of almost understanding Bart's plight and her willingness to help are submerged under her incredible lie. The gesture is also much too little, much too late, for it is a mere "drop in the bucket" (345) for what Bart needs. He will try his luck again in New York. Even Cleo's "tender" embrace of Bart and her near tears at this point cannot erase her lies or her destructiveness. She is in a situation where, even an apology for what she has done to Bart—and certainly truthfulness about the money in her bosom—would have been slight gestures toward redeeming her. Instead, West lets her rot in her repulsive personality, for as soon as the door closes her selfish motives emerge. She begins speculating on who will take Bart's place in "loving her best." Without other options, she settles on six-year-old Tim. She will train him to love her best and "try to be the man of the house" (347).

Cleo ends where she begins: self-centered, selfish, plotting, dishonest, but keeping on keeping on. Bart is Cleo's last chance for redemption in the text, but West lets her pass it up. Cleo's heart beats "strongly" as she comes to the course she plots for Tim. By allowing Cleo to continue to wallow in her own dirt, West makes it impossible for readers to forgive or forget the monstrous things she has done. Her sisters only collect bits and pieces of her deceitfulness (Lily learns about her stealing a portion of the rent money, and Charity hears her lie); readers have the whole cloth. In them rests the judgment toward which West has so diligently led Cleo. In making Cleo despicable from her inception, West raises questions about her overall intent in creating the novel and the character of Cleo Jericho Judson.

In creating Cleo Judson, Dorothy West seemingly had an axe to grind against the colorphobia of those identified with "the Negro upper class" and old money in Boston. By stripping representatives of that group down to the runs in their stockings and the frays in their gloves, as she does with Althea Binney, West unmasks the pretentiousness of this class even as she affirms its reputation. Her greatest attack on class status comes in the person of Cleo Judson, who, like Morrison's Pauline Breedlove in her early years, desperately wants to be a part of the movie star existence that she perceives in those who rub elbows with whites, are indistinguishable from whites, or are themselves white. While color, lack of education, and lack of beauty force Pauline out of her aspirations, Cleo is poised to capitalize on opportunities for advancement among the black Bostonians. Her money makes them overlook—at least superficially—her southern roots, and her ability to put on airs with the best of them similarly shows that the puppy has imitated well its master.

Cleo's infatuation with colored upper-class status is the impetus for her silence in one rare instance in the novel. When she visits The Duchess, she rants and raves until she learns that the pale woman before her is not a white woman who has led a black man astray, but a white/black woman legally classified as colored. Cleo's pause before what she perceives as good breeding and unquestionably preferable color indicates how enamored she is of obtaining the snobbiness associated with The Duchess and, more importantly, with the Binneys. For all her hopes, however, Cleo is ultimately coarse, vulgar, and common. None of the polishing she has received, none of her furnishings or elbow rubbings with the formerly rich and famous will be to her avail. When her fortunes take a downward turn, she does not have the good name of an Althea Binney to open doors for her. It appears as if persons of the stature of those who attended her Christmas party simply consign her to her "southern, nigger" state and do not give her further thought. Having once glimpsed the world to which she aspires, however, Cleo does not give up. Her patching and patching of clothing, furniture, and the house near the end of the novel is not simply for survival, but to hold on to the dream of what she wanted. She is not unlike Scarlett O'Hara being forced to dig in the dirt, except that the dirt is where Cleo has originated and where she has always been.

Cleo's ugliness throughout the text is ultimately a reflection on the wrong-headedness of class construction and class divisions. The bite of upward mobility makes Cleo as aggressively evil as the cancer of strength makes her. Indeed, her strength is put in the service of upward mobility more often than not. By portraying the world into which Cleo wants to be accepted as spiritually and financially bankrupt, West damns the trap of separation into which so many persons of African descent of her generation were willingly caught. Cleo believes that isolating herself from the "little knotty-head niggers" will make her better and will provide Judy with whatever is perceived to be more socially desirable. Her mistake here, as with her misconceived notion of mothering, is that the plant is flawed at the roots; therefore, it can produce no healthy fruit. The plant of class division among black people is really a weed that deserves to be plucked out and exposed to the sunlight. West is clearly intent upon indicting Boston's colored upper-class society; unfortunately, she reinscribes its values in the very process of criticizing them.

It seems, however, that more than mere dissatisfaction with class divisions led West to portray Cleo Judson in such a negative way. As scholars have argued, West's own biography helped significantly to shape the novel.[7] The dark daughter of a light mother born into a world not unlike that of *The Living Is Easy,* West was nurtured by a woman similar to Cleo Judson. That troubled relationship finds its way into the text, just as James Baldwin's troubled relationship with his father found its way into many of his essays and novels. Perhaps it could be argued, then, that West's creation of Cleo Judson is a rite of exorcism, one in which she unleashes venom stored up against her own mother. Her prejudice against Cleo Judson is so strong that such an assessment does not seem particularly farfetched or out of place.

Beyond stemming from class considerations and biography, West's portrayal of Cleo seems to suggest some inherent dislike of a certain type of black woman, that is, the strong, outspoken, nonconforming type. West gives Cleo traits that she can then indict; it is a comparable execution to what Ishmael Reed achieves with Mammy Barracuda in *Flight to Canada.* The difference is that Cleo Judson is a much more physically attractive specimen of the type. Finally, however, Cleo is as much a barracuda in this narrative as Mammy Barracuda is in hers. From attempting to destroy black male characters to denigrating other black characters, these women characters, so these authors argue, are so malicious that they disgrace themselves out of the black community. Indeed, their absence of a healthy communal notion of black progress consigns them to ultimate dismissal.

Chapter 7 ∼

The Stubbornness of Tradition

I. Do What Big Mama Sez:
Ernest J. Gaines's *A Lesson Before Dying*

Ernest J. Gaines's *A Lesson Before Dying* (1993) is comparable to several other works referenced in this study in that it presents an extended example of the impact of a strong black woman character upon her offspring. While Grant Wiggins' great-aunt, Tante Lou, has certainly not given birth to him, she is the only mother he has ever known. She is thus as much biologically his mother as Octavia is James's in Gaines's "The Sky is Gray." She has been the rooted part of the family tree since her own sister left, leaving her a baby to raise, and she in turn remained rooted when that child grew up, gave birth to Grant, and left him with her to raise. Through the act of narrating the story, Grant enables us to see the impact of Tante Lou's raising practices upon him, for he is an exemplary manifestation of the offspring affected by the manipulative strong black woman character. The battles he wages for psychological space are perhaps not as dramatic as Walter Lee Younger's in *A Raisin in the Sun,* but they are nonetheless poignant. To the strong black female character who has reared a manchild under especially difficult circumstances, that offspring has one option: to do as he is told. Thus Tante Lou can exert just as much biological tyranny on Grant as her literary ancestors do on their offspring.[1]

Grant is the teacher at the plantation school (which is really held in a church) in St. Raphael Parish, where dirt-poor blacks, his family among them, have lived for generations. His mission in the current action of the narrative is to go to the jail where a young black man, Jefferson, awaits execution after being falsely accused of murdering a white liquor store owner and to instill in this slightly mentally impaired man a sense of his own manhood. The mission is imposed upon a reluctant Grant by his great-aunt and her friend, Miss Emma, both of whom are in their 70s. They make the request after sitting through the trial and listening to the defense attorney's summation speech in which he asks mercy for Jefferson because to put so diminished a human being in the electric chair would be a waste of electricity, for it would be comparable to killing a hog. Knowing that they cannot save Jefferson's life, but determined that Jefferson should die like a man instead of an animal, they pressure Grant to work to achieve the transformation.[2]

Grant's reluctance stems from his own capitulation to the status quo (although he asserts otherwise), to a general inertia on his part, and to his belief that he should be anywhere else, doing any other thing, than on a Louisiana plantation teaching children who will grow up only to harvest the crops for the owner of that plantation. Grant feels weighed down by the racism that still enslaves blacks in 1948 Louisiana, but he has no plan and little measurable desire to effect change. He clearly views himself as different from the masses of black characters around him, but he does little to clarify how that difference in education and self-concept has made a tangible difference in lifestyle or aspiration. He goes through the motions of teaching for the six months of the year the harvesting and planting seasons allow him to do so, and dating Vivian, a fellow teacher in the nearby town of Bayonne, but he is really a man without a cause, one who finds it ultimately easier to do as he is told than to exert the rebellious and potentially dangerous energy necessary to change his circumstances. His overall situation invites questions about how he has been raised and how the values he presumably has have been instilled in him; in other words, it invites questions about how he has been parented/mothered. He complains and is pouty, even childishly so, in his superficial responses to directives, but he finally does what Tante Lou tells him to do.[3]

The power Tante Lou wields over Grant is based in history, absence, guilt, and expectation. Familial and social history initially inform their relationship. The fact that Grant's mother and father have left him with Tante Lou for the migratory patterns that led many blacks out of the deep South and have apparently never returned places its burden of obligation upon him. There is a tie that binds him and Tante Lou in the losses they have incurred and the constant absences they feel. Tante Lou initially lost a sister, then a niece. Grant has lost a grandmother, a mother, and a father. Thus thrown together on a plantation where Tante Lou worked in the Big House and Grant had performed many chores there, they have experienced the dynamics of racist policies and politics in this world. Because she has had to enter the back door of the Big House for her entire working career, Tante Lou has taught Grant to aspire to a different point of entry into the world that would shut him out. Her initial expectation that he would leave the plantation, go to college, and become a teacher has been fulfilled. Now she requests that he enter the Big House through the back door yet again to ask

Henri Pichot, the plantation owner, for help in getting permission to see Jefferson on a regular basis. What Grant sees as regression Tante Lou sees as expedient under the circumstances. She gets him to do what she wants done because she understands the personal and social history of which he is a part much better than he does, and she is willing to manipulate him in whatever ways necessary to achieve her objective.

It is important that we receive the story from Grant's perspective, for in giving in to the manipulations in spite of his awareness of being manipulated, he indicates emphatically the impact of the strong black woman. What is at stake here—teaching Jefferson—is not the issue, for that is an intrinsically noble process. What is at issue is that Grant is given no choice in the matter. Although he is a college-educated working adult, he has no defense against Tante Lou deciding, with Miss Emma, that he will undertake the task they, but especially Tante Lou, have set for him. In achieving their tyranny over Grant, they share with other strong black women characters their large size and, for Tante Lou, a commanding voice. As they sit at Jefferson's trial, Grant observes, "Both are large women, but his godmother is larger. She is of average height, five four, five five, but weighs nearly two hundred pounds. Once she and my aunt had found their places . . . his godmother became as immobile as a great stone or as one of our oak or cypress stumps."[4] This oak or cypress stump can appear to become a weakling at various intervals, however, when Miss Emma pretends, or so Grant believes, to be ill so that Grant will assume responsibility for visiting Jefferson alone. Grant describes the women as filling up the back seat of his car as he drives to Pichot's house, and at various points throughout the narrative he gives the impression that they achieve what they want as much through size as through will.

A lengthy conversation from the text will serve to illustrate how Tante Lou combines her commanding voice with Miss Emma's less forceful one in an orchestrated performance that enables them jointly to achieve their objective; it is an interesting mixture of saintliness and directive. On the evening after the judge pronounces his sentence, the two women gather at Tante Lou's house. Reminiscent of Mama Lena Younger, Tante Lou commands the reluctant Grant to "sit down" and listen to what they have to say:

> 'Sit down for what?' I asked her.
> 'Just sit down,' she said.
> I settled back on the chair, but not all the way back. I was ready to get up at any moment.
> 'He don't have to do it,' Miss Emma said, looking beyond me again.
> 'Do what?' I asked her.
> 'You don't have to do it,' she said again. It was dry, mechanical, unemotional, but I could tell by her face and by my aunt's face that they were not about to give up on what they had in mind.

'What do you want me to do?' I asked her. 'What can I do? It's only a matter of weeks, a couple of months, maybe. What can I do that you haven't done the past twenty-one years?'

'You the teacher,' she said.

'Yes, I'm the teacher,' I said. 'And I teach what the white folks around here tell me to teach—reading, writing, and 'rithmetic. They never told me how to keep a black boy out of a liquor store.'

'You watch your tongue, sir,' my aunt said.

I sat back in the chair and looked at both of them. They sat there like boulders, their bodies, their minds immovable.

'He don't have to,' Miss Emma said again.

'He go'n do it,' my aunt said.

'Oh?' I said.

'You go'n do it,' she said. 'We going up there and talk to Mr. Henri.'

'Talk to Henri Pichot? For what?' I asked her.

'So you have the right to visit Jefferson.'

'What's Henri Pichot got to do with this?'

'His brother-in-law is the sheriff, ain't he?'

I waited for her to say more, but she did not. I got up from the table.

'And where you think you going?' Tante Lou asked me.

'To Bayonne, where I can breathe,' I said. 'I can't breathe here.'

'You ain't going to no Bayonne till you go up the quarter,' she said. 'You go'n see Mr. Henri with me and Emma, there.'

I had walked away, but now I came back and leaned over the table toward both of them.

'Tante Lou, Miss Emma, Jefferson is dead. It is only a matter of weeks, maybe a couple of months—but he's already dead. The past twenty-one years, we've done all we could for Jefferson. He's dead now. And I can't raise the dead. All I can do is try to keep the others from ending up like this—but he's gone from us. There's nothing I can do anymore, nothing any of us can do anymore.'

'You going with us up the quarter,' my aunt said, as though I hadn't said a word. 'You going up there with us, Grant, or you don't sleep in this house tonight.'

I stood back from the table and looked at both of them. I clamped my jaws so tight the veins in my neck felt as if they would burst. I wanted to scream at my aunt; I was screaming inside. I had told her many, many times how much I hated this place and all I wanted to do was get away. I had told her I was no teacher, I hated teaching, and I was just running in place here. But she had not heard me before, and I knew that no matter how loud I screamed, she would not hear me now.

'I'm getting my coat, and I'll be ready to go,' she said. 'Em-ma?' (13–15)

As with Mama Lena, the strong black woman character rides roughshod over the desires and feelings of her offspring because she has concluded that the objective she has chosen is the proper and morally correct one to pursue; she will achieve it by whatever manipulative means necessary. Like Beneatha and Walter Lee, Grant can offer no challenge to the powerful force that shapes his life and directs his actions. His silent scream of frustration is the measure of that inability, and it echoes Walter Lee's "WON'T SOMEBODY PLEASE LISTEN TO ME TODAY?" Yet perhaps some readers will conclude that Grant is the intractable one, that he should simply do what the old ladies want. After all, visiting Jefferson cannot be such a horrific burden. From this perspective, Grant is again placed in a position comparable to that of Beneatha and Walter Lee in relation to Mama Lena; what she wants for them—that Beneatha will believe in God and that Walter will deter his wife from having an abortion—is not objectionable in and of itself. It is the power dynamic—that the offspring of strong black women characters will do as they are told—that is as problematic in the Gaines novel as in the Hansberry play.

The passage quoted makes clear that posture and silence can be just as effective weapons to use against Grant as haranguing him. The "immovable" body language of Tante Lou and Miss Emma conveys to Grant that they will not be deterred from their objective, and their silence at crucial points serves similarly to convey their determination. When they begin the journey to Pichot's house, the women follow Grant out to his car and simply stand, silently, waiting patiently, until he "had opened the door for them" (16). He remarks: "Not only was I going up to Henri Pichot's house against my will, but I had to perform all the courtesies of chauffeur as well." He slams the door and can "feel" his great-aunt's eyes on the back of his neck, a censoring that is just as effective as verbally chastising him. He makes no effort to avoid the ruts made by tractors, wagons, and trucks, and comments: "My aunt never said a thing, but I could feel her eyes on the back of my neck. I was not aiming for the ruts, but I wasn't avoiding them either. I could hear them bouncing on the back seat, but they never said a word" (17). And indeed, why, at this point, should they? So far, the women have gotten Grant to do precisely what they want. Their silence commands his actions—and responses—as counterpart to their verbal cajoling. Their silence also indicates that, in the hierarchy of control within black family structures to which they adhere, they do not need to give Grant any further attention. After all, he is not their age peer, so why should they waste casual words upon him?

The trait of taciturnity identified with strong black women characters is strikingly clear here. Tante Lou does not feel the need to elaborate on her motives or the decision that she has made. She is humorless, distant, and unaffectionate, not appreciably unlike Mrs. MacTeer in Morrison's *The Bluest Eye*. We can measure her love for Grant only through what she does for him (cooking, providing shelter), just as it is clear that Mrs. MacTeer loves her daughter Claudia through the attentiveness she offers when Claudia has a cold. Such strong black women characters, as *Sula*'s Eva Peace maintains, cannot afford the luxuries of jumping around and playing with their children, hugging and kissing them, or reading to them in the great American middle-class expectation, when urgent matters of food, shelter, or illness are pressing. When her daughter Hannah asks Eva if she ever loved her children, she responds:

> 'I'm talkin' 'bout 18 and 95 when I set in that house five days with you and Pearl and Plum and three beets, you snake-eyed ungrateful hussy. What would I look like leapin' 'round that little old room playin' with youngins with three beets to my name?. . . . They wasn't no time. Not none. Soon as I got one day done here come a night. With you all coughin' and me watchin' so TB wouldn't take you off and if you was sleepin' quiet I thought, O Lord, they dead and put my hand over your mouth to feel if the breath was comin' what you talkin' 'bout did I love you girl I stayed alive for you can't you get that through your thick head or what is that between your ears, heifer?'[5]

If such female characters do not follow patterns of loving interactions when their offspring are young, as Eva does not and as Octavia does not in Gaines's "The Sky is Gray," then they certainly do not change as their offspring enter adulthood. They protect themselves from vulnerability, from outward expressions of love that might cause them to make wrong decisions, and the distancing postures are what they continue to rely on. The gaps in expressing affection in these relationships measure again the diminishing of natural emotional responses that mothering should engender. Tante Lou, like so many of the other strong black women characters, thus becomes suprahuman on several occasions in her postures of emotional containment. She operates primarily at the surface level of ordering Grant around.

It is noteworthy throughout these early interchanges that Grant does not have an acceptable, even remotely adult response to the women's directives. He sulks, pouts, slams car doors, and drives over ruts, all of which are childish reactions. At least Walter Lee can go to the Green Hat, get drunk, and listen to jazz. Although Grant will later get drunk and even start a fight at one point, he still seems more childish than Walter Lee, more at sea about how to claim a space to be or to salvage something that he can identify as being separate from the wishes of Tante Lou. A question naturally arises about what there is in this dynamic that causes Grant to be so powerless. Are family history and guilt sufficient to account for his ineptness? How do these strong black women characters manage to wrap themselves in such an aura of respect—superficial though it may be at times—that wards off all challenges?

Inherent in his upbringing, in the biological tyranny to which he subscribes, is a respectful border beyond which Grant will not trespass; he is as much an adherent to the circle of acceptability as his historical and literary forebears. These strong black women characters instill the parameters of that border in their charges, and their charges willingly or reluctantly adhere to them, but adhere they do. Grant not only accompanies the women to Henri Pichot's house, but he will return alone on another occasion, during which he is forced to wait for two and a half hours while Pichot and his guests finish their dinner before Pichot deigns to speak to him. Grant does not want to take Miss Emma to the jail, but he drives her anyway. He can only sulk and maintain silence during the 13-mile drive, but he nonetheless makes the trip. Perhaps Grant's adherence is couched in part in a comment that Miss Emma makes several times during the course of the narrative: "'I want somebody to do something for me one time fore I close my eyes. Somebody got do something for me one time 'fore I close my eyes'" (22). Although she is speaking to Pichot in this instance, Grant is listening. Her sense of something being owed to her (perhaps for her many, many years of hard work and no reward) is the verbalization of one of the forces that guides Tante Lou's actions with Grant; somebody owes her something for having given her life for so little in return, and Grant is the most immediate and likeliest prospect to effect repayment.[6]

In fact, this border of respect, of giving something back, leads Grant to lie to Miss Emma, to save her feelings after he goes alone to visit Jefferson in jail for the first time. Jefferson has quickly internalized the attorney's definition of him as a hog and responds accordingly to food Grant has brought for him:

> He knelt down on the floor and put his head inside the bag and started eating, without using his hands. He even sounded like a hog. . . .
> 'That's how a old hog eat,' he said, raising his head and grinning at me. He got up from his knees and went back to his bunk. 'That's how a old hog eat.'
> 'All right,' I said. 'But when I go back, I'm going to tell her that you and I sat on the bunk and ate, and you said how good the food was. I won't tell her what you did. She is already sick, and that would kill her. So I'm going to lie. I'm going to tell her how much you liked the food. Especially the pralines.' (83–84)

But Grant cannot think of a good lie right away, so he drives to a club for a beer before he can face Miss Emma. He does not need a big lie, he asserts, "just a little lie or a number of little lies, but a lie it had to be" (86). His commitment to lying, to saving the feelings of the elderly Miss Emma, is a reflection of how well Tante Lou has taught him to recognize his place, his duty, and the border of respect in relation to such women. He enters willingly into the realm of relational possibilities that the strong black woman character has created for him. His growth during the course of the novel is as much a testament to Tante Lou's teachings as it is finally to his recognition that he must evolve, even within the closed system of a Louisiana plantation.

During the course of the narrative, however, a series of interactions with his great-aunt alone or with her and Miss Emma makes clear that Grant is relegated to the position of child—or at least to someone whose opinion does not matter overly much, which is a situation he shares with most of his literary counterparts in their encounters with strong black women characters. On the planned fourth visit to see Jefferson, Miss Emma is not ready at the appointed time. After waiting a decent interval, an impatient Grant blows his horn "hard and long enough for everybody in the quarter to hear it" (76).

> Finally, the door did open. My aunt came out on the porch and pushed the door shut behind her. She stood there watching me. I knew that stand, I knew that look. I knew that she was not coming one step farther and that I would have to come to her. She still watched me as I got out of the car and came up the walk. I stopped short of the porch.
>
> 'Something wrong with you?' she asked me.
>
> I wanted to ask that same question about Miss Emma, but I held my tongue.
>
> 'Don't you know if she was able she would be out here?'
>
> 'Then why didn't she tell me she wasn't going?' I could be teaching my class.
>
> 'Nobody said you wasn't going.'
>
> 'You saying I'm supposed to visit him alone? He's no kin—'
>
> 'Come on in here, boy, and get that bag,' my aunt said. [Note the designation "boy."] (76–77)

Grant enters to get the bag of food and to encounter a Miss Emma who coughs "twice—short and dry—to let me know that she was on her deathbed. Then silence again" (77). His great-aunt refuses to join him on the trip, and he finally realizes "that this had been planned from the beginning" (78), that he would eventually be going to the jail alone. When he sarcastically comments that he will dump the food in the river, his great-aunt threatens: "You better get that food and get out of here if you know what's good for you" (79).

From silent waiting to verbal commanding, Tante Lou does not give Grant a minimum of opportunity to divert from the path she and Miss Emma have planned for him. Miss Emma's part in this strategy is to assert again and again of Grant going to the jail that "he don't have to" "if it's a burden," to which Tante Lou invariably conjoins, "He's going." The long-suffering saintliness of Miss Emma's pathetic expressions strike at whatever core of responsibility—or guilt—Grant may have. Miss Emma certainly wants him to visit Jefferson, but it is Tante Lou who issues the commands. She forces Grant to endure the humiliation of being searched at the jail because "they ain't nobody else" (79). And even if there were somebody else, that would not diminish Tante Lou's power to direct Grant's life. His report to Tante Lou, Miss Emma, and Reverend Ambrose after his visit with Jefferson is still marked by a power dynamic that might best be described as antagonistic love.

> 'I'll be in my room,' I said to my aunt.
> 'That's all you got to say?' she snapped at me.
> 'I spoke, Tante Lou.'
> 'You know what I'm talking about.'
> 'He was all right,' I said.
> 'That's all?' my aunt said. 'Or did you forget to go?'
> 'I went, and he was all right,' I said.
> 'You got more than that to say, Mr. Man,' my aunt said. 'Folks been setting here hours, waiting for you.' . . .
> 'Sit down,' my aunt said.
> I went around the table and pulled out the fourth chair.
> 'He was all right,' I said. . . .
> 'That's not what she want to hear,' my aunt said. 'How he was when you got there, how he was when you left?'
> 'He was all right both times,' I said.
> 'You know what I'm talking about,' my aunt said.
> She looked at me the way an inquisitor must have glared at his poor victims. The only reason she didn't put me on the rack was that she didn't have one. (98–99)

Forced to speak when he does not wish to do so, Grant can only approximate the power of silence that Miss Emma and Tante Lou use against him by providing as little information as possible. Since his objective has been to lie rather than hurt Miss Emma's feelings, he cannot possibly elaborate on any of his comments. He does tell Tante Lou that she can check with the jail to see if he actually went, to which she replies "'I didn't ask for none of your uppity, mister'" (100). He may not provide the information they hope for, but he is still subject to their authority.

Tante Lou uses that authority to chasten Grant throughout the text. When he asserts that he is not going to see Jefferson again, she responds, "'You going back up there, Grant'" and "'You ain't going to run away from this, Grant'" (123). When Grant provides Jefferson with a radio that

Reverend Ambrose calls "sin company" and Grant responds that he does not care what Ambrose calls it, Tante Lou is visibly upset: "'Grant!' my aunt said. I could see that she was becoming more and more angry with me. Now she got up from her chair. 'You don't talk like that!' she said. 'Never!'" (181). She forces him to go to the jail on the occasions when Reverend Ambrose accompanies them, which is peculiarly repugnant to Grant because, in the manner of Beneatha Younger, he has rejected the fundamentalist brand of religion that Ambrose and his great-aunt practice. Yet "one look" (187) from his great-aunt guarantees his acquiescence, and he endures their admonitions that he should join in the process of trying to save Jefferson's soul before the execution.

Tante Lou is as concerned about religion as Mama Lena Younger, and it is a particular sore spot for her that Grant has not embraced the spiritual traditions that she upholds. She and Miss Emma join Reverend Ambrose in recognizing the need for Jefferson to convert, or at least become receptive to God, before he dies. Religion is the source of Miss Emma's strength on several occasions, especially at those times when she cannot seem to get through to Jefferson. After her first visit, for example, when Jefferson is distant and only concerned about the switch being pulled at his death, Miss Emma exclaims upon leaving "'Oh, Lord Jesus, . . . Oh, Lord Jesus, stand by, stand by'" (74). Both women are upset that the radio may turn Jefferson away from God, and both are anxious for Reverend Ambrose to be there at the moment of execution. In a world in which they have had no defenders, no supporters, the spiritual strength they embrace comes from beyond their world. They fit the pattern of generations of long-suffering historical black women who take their burdens to the Lord. When they cannot relieve themselves of the burdens, they merely ask for strength to be able to endure them. From Reverend Ambrose's perspective, therefore, the fate that Miss Emma is experiencing with Jefferson is God's way of "testing" (123) her. The implication is that, though she may be crying now, there will be joy in the morning. This position is particularly short-sighted and abhorrent to Grant.

Such a worldview presupposes a minimal expectation that the events of life will ever run smoothly, or perhaps it presupposes a defeatist or tragic approach to life. For these women born in the latter days of Reconstruction, who have experienced the new form of slavery that existed in the plantation Louisiana treated in *The Autobiography of Miss Jane Pittman,* there is little that they hope for in life. At best, they endure the ailments attendant upon bodies worn out by physical labor and no possibility for enlightened mental development; they invest what little hope they have in their children or grandchildren somehow escaping the fates that have befallen them. At worst, they are worried into early graves. Their lives follow the predictable patterns of weekday visits to each other and to church on Sunday, with an occasional school play held at the church providing one of the few diversions. What has happened to Jefferson has severely disrupted their routine, and it causes them to muster what little power they have to use it wherever they can. They can only spend so much of it on Henri Pichot, thus Grant becomes their primary focus.

Tante Lou gives Grant special treatment in spite of her seeming gruffness with him. After all, it is her house in which he lives and her food that he eats. Physical nourishment is important in the text; since Tante Lou has not been able to encourage Grant toward her brand of spiritual nourishment, the physical part becomes even more important. She cooks all his meals, frequently leaving them in the "warmer" of the stove if he comes home late. He notes the rules of their eating rituals when he informs her that he is going to eat "in town" after she has forced him to take them to see Henri Pichot: "I was supposed to eat soon after she had cooked, and if I was not at home I was supposed to eat as soon as I came in" (24); her only response is silence. The next morning, she registers her disapproval at breakfast: "'Food there if you want it. Or you can go back where you had supper last night'" (35). Food is therefore a site on which Grant can register his objections to being manipulated. Disrupting the unity of the eating rituals his great-aunt has established conveys to her his disapproval of her directing his life, but it is ultimately an ineffectual gesture.

Tante Lou is territorial not only about Grant, but about her kitchen. She is annoyed but unable to show it effectively when Grant insists that he and Vivian make more coffee to replace what they have drunk while she was at church. Her reaction is "'You taking over my house?'" (113), and she stands "like a boulder in the road, unmovable." He maneuvers around her to make the coffee, possibly because Vivian is present, since he is seldom able to stand up to his great-aunt on other occasions. She then turns her attention to interrogating Vivian, especially about her religious beliefs. When Vivian serves the coffee, Tante Lou thanks her politely, and Grant comments: "My aunt knew how to make you feel that she was of a lower caste and you were being too kind to her. That was the picture she presented, but not nearly how she felt" (115). The masking is a part of Tante Lou's possessiveness. Grant maintains later that "she really knew how to be polite to people when she felt they were interfering with something that belonged to her" (163). An unwillingness to give up her kitchen to Vivian is a recognition as well that some unwanted change in her relationship with Grant will eventually come. She is holding on to a way of life as well as to a physical space.

For Miss Emma, as well as for Tante Lou, how well the offspring eats the food that has been prepared is a measure of acceptance and of things at least being familiar if not exactly in the same relationship. Every visit to the jail means food Miss Emma prepares specially for Jefferson. Regardless of whether he eats, the ritual means some sense of normalcy in a thoroughly abnormal situation. She considers his rejection of her food a rejection of herself, and she outdoes herself with each new opportunity in an effort to effect positive responses in Jefferson. Readers could reasonably cull menus from the text, for feeding Jefferson is a primary part of the plan to reclaim the best in him. It is also a sad commentary on the level at which the strong black woman character is forced to operate. Lacking education herself, Miss Emma must rely on Grant to "teach" Jefferson. What she can offer him is limited to the definition of herself that has been allowed to a black woman who has prepared meals for decades in the Big House on the plantation: she is a very good cook. Thus she hopes that her one skill, the one arena in which she can please, will indeed be pleasing to Jefferson in the current circumstances.

Less psychologically—and seemingly less physically—strong than Tante Lou, Miss Emma gives in to anger or to temporary despair and slaps Jefferson on one occasion. The incident involves food. She tries repeatedly to coax Jefferson into eating something, until he finally asks if Miss Emma has brought him some "corn for a hog" (122) since he is being "fattened up" for killing. Obviously in pain, she "slaps" him, and this is the point at which she questions what she has done to God to have to bear this burden.[7] That Jefferson would center the district attorney's dehumanizing designation of him on food that Miss Emma brought to him is doubly insulting to her. Not only must she endure her godchild's seeming acceptance of his own dehumanization, but the very rituals to which she and Tante Lou adhere—solidifying relationships through food—have been undermined.[8]

The pathology inherent in the minimally functional family relationship that Grant has with Tante Lou is passed on in his relationships with his students. Hard-core nurturing is what it might best be called. As a child and man who has been ordered around, he orders his students around. As a person whose model for adult-child interaction is based solely on the adult giving commands, so he gives commands to his students. As a person who has not been shown affection, he does not show any toward his students. Thus the chain of dysfunction is renewed with each generation. It is understandable but nonetheless surprising on several occasions to witness Grant's accounts of his interactions with his students. When a child inadvertently counts on his fingers in trying to solve "a simple multiplication problem," Grant "slashe[s] him hard across the butt with the Westcott ruler" (35), then beats him in his palm when the student appears angry. He "jerks" a piece of chalk out of another student's hand and recognizes that still another student is "terrified" by his voice and "fearful" of him, yet he does not alter his tactics with them. Indeed, when he finds one of them playing with a bug a short while later, he brings "the Westcott down on his skull, loud enough to send a sound throughout the church. He jumped, hollered, grabbed at the already swelling knot" (38). Grant thereby goes beyond Tante Lou in being violent with the children, for she only threatens him with violence. He also does not show "any sympathy" (40) when one of his students cries as he relates what will happen to Jefferson, although he knows that she is Jefferson's cousin. He punishes a student for looking out of a window by directing him to "'Get back in that corner and face the wall and stay there. One more word out of you, and you'll spend the rest of the day standing on one leg'" (60). He orders the students onto their knees to await news of Jefferson's death (246, 250), and even at this crucial moment in the text, he threatens to punish those who are disobedient or who have to be excused during the kneeling.

We might speculate that Grant's gruffness with the students is tied in part to the stress he is experiencing because of Jefferson's situation, and indeed he admits to being "irritated" when he strikes the first student. If we offer and accept such an excuse in his case, then we would have to do the same with Tante Lou and Miss Emma. The more likely prospect is that Grant, in interacting with his students, *becomes* Tante Lou—commanding, threatening, punishing. The imperative words and phrases that issue from his mouth could just as well have come from hers. His students are bodies merely waiting for his voice to command them, just as he similarly presents his body to Tante Lou to do her bidding.

The only way Grant can gain a measure of control, to get out from under the influence of Tante Lou, is to banish her and Miss Emma from his narrative. For long stretches when he visits and interacts with Jefferson, there is no mention of the women, and as the execution date nears, they are less and less visible. Though he may have erased their corporeal presence from the narrative, they are still, as in his interaction with the students, present in him. As the narrative develops, Grant's relationship with Tante Lou is deemed not immediately worth salvaging, or at least not worth reconciling in the current action of the text. Or we might conclude that it is so written in stone that it cannot possibly be changed. Or perhaps there is less a need to confront her physically than for Grant to confront, alone, what he has internalized from Tante Lou; in other words, what he carries of her inside him is what he must come to terms with.

The site consequently shifts from the strong black woman character directing the young black male to the young black male bonding with an even younger black male, spiritually and psychologically if not physically. The focal point for change, therefore, becomes the relationship between Jefferson and Grant. But Grant can only execute a change by drawing upon what

Tante Lou has taught him—sacrificing and being concerned for others. He becomes brother, mother, and father figure to Jefferson, finally allowing him to open up a healing space within Grant's own being. It is with Jefferson, after all, that Grant expresses heartfelt emotions to someone in the text besides Vivian—as they walk around the cell when he is trying to persuade Jefferson to eat Miss Emma's gumbo (190–94). At the very end of the text, he stands crying before his students, visibly expressing the emotions that he has contained so frequently in the text. Herman Beavers raises questions about the object of the tears: "Himself? The children in his class? Jefferson? Are his tears indicative of loss? Joy? Relief? Adulation?"[9] The answers might be a combination of these factors. What is important is *the very act of crying.* Grant is finally able to combine his great-aunt's strength with a healthy balance of emotional expressiveness that presages a growth and commitment he has been reluctant to move toward throughout the text. The diminished boy/man grows by assimilating the best of the teachings from the strong black woman character even as he effectively "kills" her by transcending her confining influence.

As the elderly women disappear from the text, Grant interacts more with Vivian, who serves as a "time-out" space, a safe haven from the pressures of Tante Lou and the burden of thinking about Jefferson (although he does talk with her about the case and although she joins Tante Lou in urging him to visit Jefferson). What little softness he has in the text is mainly reserved for her. Vivian represents a space where he can "breathe," presumably with the implication of being less pressured than the environment at Tante Lou's. A part of that desire to breathe is to take charge of his own mind and actions, to operate as a man, yet questions nonetheless arise about the extent to which Grant can be a man with Vivian. Tante Lou and Miss Emma certainly do not allow him the space that manhood would presumably require. Indeed, he makes the traditional accusation against Tante Lou for forcing him to go alone to the jail to visit Jefferson: that she is in league with white men who would emasculate black males.

'Everything you sent me to school for, you're stripping me of it,' I told my aunt. . . . 'The humiliation I had to go through, going into that man's kitchen. The hours I had to wait while they ate and drank and socialized before they would even see me. Now going up to that jail. To watch them put their dirty hands on that food. To search my body each time as if I'm some kind of common criminal. Maybe today they'll want to look into my mouth, or my nostrils, or make me strip. Anything to humiliate me. All the things you wanted me to escape by going to school. Years ago, Professor Antoine told me that if I stayed here, they were going to break me down to the nigger I was born to be. But he didn't tell me that my aunt would help them do it.' (79)

It could be argued that Grant's complaint focuses on the superficial, that there is an essence that cannot be touched by those prying, potentially humiliating hands, a place that could be held inviolate if he were secure in who he is, as Grange Copeland tries to convey to his son Brownfield. Grant's self-centeredness illustrates yet again his need for growth into a community-mindedness, or at least into thinking beyond his own physical comforts and discomforts. Grant's admission that the whites could hurt him in this way might serve to chastise his aunt, to make her feel guilty for sending him on this errand, but it also indicates his own insecurities as a black man in 1940s Louisiana plantation society. He is not yet secure enough in a definition of what it means to be a man to be absolutely certain that someone else cannot take that away from him.

With Vivian, his notion of manhood seems to center upon sex and an unacted-upon dream to escape his condition as a teacher in a church/plantation school. He impulsively—and rather immaturely—offers to take Vivian and her two children (one of whom is only months old) away from Bayonne immediately after Tante Lou forces him to go to Henri Pichot's house. This would mean assuming the financial and other responsibilities he imagines would be attendant upon heading a household. He talks constantly of escape, but he has no realistically conceived plan for executing a departure. Because Vivian is in a compromised situation with the father of her children and dares not be seen publicly with Grant, that circumstance diminishes as well the extent to which he can function as a man who can proudly be seen with the woman he loves. He does introduce Vivian to Tante Lou and other women in the quarters, but he is uncomfortable in this newly constituted group. Indeed, in this instance, he resorts to the directive posture with Vivian that his aunt uses with him. Vivian is clearly reluctant to attempt to make coffee and serve cake with the foreboding Tante Lou standing "like a boulder in the road," so Grant commands her to "Just do what I said" (115). He wants desperately for Tante Lou and the other women to see him in a different, more manly, light, one in which they have not allowed him to exist.

He also centers his notion of manhood upon the barroom brawl in which he takes on two bricklayers who assert that Jefferson is getting what he deserves: "'Should have burned him months ago,' one said. . . . 'That kind of sonofabitch make it hard on everybody, . . . I'd pull the switch myself, they ask me'" (198). Although the violence might be wrongheaded, as is the idea that a *man* cannot allow the talk to continue without making his objection known, it is nonetheless significant that Grant at least takes action, at least exhibits a willingness to fight. The scene is a testing ground for manhood similar to the way that Milkman Dead is tested in Shalimar, Virginia, in Morrison's *Song of Solomon;* Milkman and Grant end up in about the same beaten-up condition. Yet his willingness to fight is a progression; it is more than his many words of opposition to Tante Lou, more than his many words of hollow plans to Vivian. In the male bonding scheme, therefore, he finally shows more commitment to Jefferson than to any of the women in his life. His identification with the confined state in which Jefferson must exist brings home to him his own confined state. Fighting the men is one arena for his little war, his own effort to move from "hog" to man.

Unlike Walter Lee Younger's situation in *A Raisin in the Sun* and Sidney Poitier's fight to get the drama to unfold from Walter's point of view, *A Lesson Before Dying* does unfold from the point of view of the male offspring much put-upon by the strong black woman character. Equally unlike Walter Lee, Grant has been able to attend college, to move beyond the realm of Tante Lou's influence, at least for four years. His inability to stand up to her, to claim his own space to be on the plantation, is thus as much attributable to his own personality quirks, to his own inertia or weak will, as it is to Tante Lou. He has only a half-hearted desire to teach, or to escape from the plantation. And he would rather engage in sex with Vivian at the home of one of their friends than take the necessary steps to carve out a space where they can be together openly. He has grown comfortable in his inertia, in his ability to articulate dreams without the accompanying expectation that they will become reality. It is to Tante Lou's credit that she forces him to visit Jefferson, for that is the one experience in his life that finally moves him toward true self-realization. In this context, one of Tante Lou's comments takes on renewed significance. When Grant balks at returning to the jail to see Jefferson, Tante Lou remarks: "'You ain't going to run away from this, Grant'" (123), which might reflect her awareness of a pattern in his life (after all, he wants to run away with Vivian), or her awareness of the condition of black women and men in the South on which Grant himself expounds: "'We black men have failed to protect our women since the time of slavery. We stay here in the South and are broken, or we run away and leave them alone to look after the children and themselves. So each time a male child is born, they hope he will be the one to change this vicious circle—which he never does. Because even though he wants to change it, and maybe even tries to change it, it is too heavy a burden because of all the others who have run away and left their burdens behind'" (166–67).[10] By insisting that he interact with Jefferson, Tante Lou thus provides Grant with the opportunity not to run away, an opportunity that amounts not only to "saving" Jefferson but to saving himself. Gaines finally and effectively posits, therefore, that the strong black woman character's intentions are inherently good and that there is no need to make alterations to the character type.

II. New Territory, No Change:
Pearl Cleage's *Flyin' West*

A play first produced in 1992, *Flyin' West* (1995) resorts to the strong black woman character but relies more on innuendo and suggestions of her strength than dramatized illustrations of it. Pearl Cleage allows her characters only one major current action in the strength paradigm, but it is powerful enough to give credence to all the innuendoes. Set in 1898 in the small, all black town of Nicodemus, Kansas, the play finds its subject matter in the numbers of black people, especially women, who migrated from Memphis and other southern towns into Kansas. "Exodusters" in the tradition that historian Nell Irvin Painter discusses in her book of the same title,[11] these black pioneers endured the physical hardships of land and weather and the psychological traumas of racism transplanted to frontier soil in order to carve out new spaces, new ways to be in America. Cleage's cast includes Sophie Washington, a 36-six-year-old black woman who has led her two adoptive sisters to Kansas, where they have acquired substantial acreage. One sister, Fannie Dove, has remained on the land while the other, Minnie Dove, has gone off to college, married mulatto Frank Charles, and moved to England. As the current action begins, Sophie and Fannie have invited Miss Leah, an elderly neighbor, to live with them during the harsh winter. Another neighbor, Wil Parish, who is clearly in love with Fannie, has agreed to check on Miss Leah's property. Two events propel the action: Minnie and her husband Frank, who does not disguise his hatred for "colored people," are coming for a visit, and Sophie is scheduled to deliver a speech encouraging fellow blacks in Nicodemus not to sell their land to white speculators; she has a vision of a self-sufficient black town with all the amenities of that designation. Frank's visit is an interlude while he awaits news of his paternity suit in New Orleans following his white father's death; when his white "brothers" disallow his inheritance, he schemes to get money from Minnie's share of the Nicodemus land.

Setting and history contribute to the dominance of strength, asexuality, and lesser femininity that appear to be primary qualities in Sophie and Miss Leah, the characters on whom I focus initially. Sophie, born in slavery, has taken on the Daniel Boone role: driven the wagon full of supplies and two skittish sisters to Kansas, made the arrangements to get the land provided by the Homestead Act of 1860, led the building of the house and the fencing in of the property, shot the game necessary to survival, planted and harvested the crops, and done everything else required of becoming a successful farmer. Cleage does not make clear why Sophie is without a male companion, but she is clearly comfortable in that state. Miss Leah, on the other hand, bore ten sons in slavery, who were all sold away from her. After Emancipation, she tried to make a life with the man who had fathered those children. They hoped to have more children together in freedom, but all five of them died. Since her husband's death, Miss Leah has migrated to Kansas and cultivated her huge farm alone for 20 years. She has grown into a gruff little old lady who provides the interactive sparks to balance Sophie's strong character. The pipe-smoking Miss Leah appears to be more caustic than affectionate, and she has a desperate desire for independence. The strength of her spirit far exceeds the frailty of her body.

Sophie is undoubtedly the sister in charge, and it is upon her that a designation of strong black woman character seems to rest most comfortably from the beginning of the play. Her movements and actions align her with the strength of Mammy Barracuda or with Alice Walker's narrator in "Everyday Use"; overtones of masculinity abound. Sophie enters after a shopping trip to town: "*She has a large bag of flour slung over her shoulder and a canvas shoulder bag full of groceries. She is carrying a shotgun, which she places by the door. She slings the bag of flour carelessly on the table and, coat still on, puts the other bag on a chair.*"[12] She finally locates some black licorice she has purchased, takes a bite, sits down, and props her "*booted feet up on the window sill.*" The image we get is that of a woman who can manage just about anything. It is perhaps unfortunate that the conceptualization of competent women in a frontier environment does not allow for much deviation from a masculine model. Sophie's character is thus saddled with those overtones from the beginning. Indeed, it could be argued that she serves as the "man" who has carved out the space to allow her sisters to flourish in Kansas. In this scenario, she also becomes "husband" to her sister Fannie as well as to Miss Leah. Simultaneously, she is also the strong mother who sacrifices all for her "offspring," whether that offspring is realized in the present scenario as two sisters or a feisty little old lady neighbor.

In her determination and strong-mindedness, Sophie has little patience for the Bakers, a black couple who have returned east to have their child and whose land is in danger of being purchased by speculators, because they are not "strong" enough for frontier life. When the husband of a teacher she has tried to hire balks at coming west, Sophie comments, "What kind of colored men are they raising in the city these days anyway?" (20). To her, people are not afraid of different things, as Fannie maintains. "They're either scared or they're not," and if one is unafraid, the challenges one must face do not matter. For Sophie, it is a simple matter of meeting the challenge of the frontier head on and developing quickly the skills needed to survive there. The text describes her, for example, cleaning and oiling her shotgun by breaking it down "*quickly and efficiently. She has done this a thousand times*" (19). She chops and carries wood with ease and even carries Frank's suitcase when he presumes upon her strength at the train station; she "*looks at the bag, shifts the shotgun easily to the crook of her arm, picks up the bag and exits*" (26). She values practicality over luxury and would easily have left in Memphis the china that Frank admires as reflecting "the ability to adapt to trying circumstances without a lowering of standards" (31). Still, the others tease about Sophie's "bossiness," which is a natural accompaniment to her single-mindedness. She was able to see a home in Kansas when the others were too young even to imagine that a Kansas could exist.

As a brusque, hulking woman who refuses to emphasize her feminine side, Sophie is locked into the type of the extra-female woman.[13] Her actions seldom get softer than the ones in which we see her engage initially, and her conversation is unwaveringly direct. More often than not, there is an implied threat hovering around her, the implication that she will not suffer fools lightly and that she is ready, at a moment's notice, to do violence to anything or anyone who threatens her kingdom. Miss Leah enters as Sophie sits contentedly chewing her licorice, and they engage in what we quickly realize is a familiar exchange: Miss Leah is irritated with just about everything Sophie does, especially her coffee making. More casual and roundabout conversation leads to an indictment of Sophie. Miss Leah is appalled, she says, at new women coming into Nicodemus who are not as competent as she was when she came and had to do "everything." She did so, she says,

> Because I was not prepared to put up with a whole lotta mouth. Colored men always tryin' to tell you how to do somethin' even if you been doin' it longer than they been peein' standin' up. *(A beat.)* They got that in common with you.
> SOPHIE. I don't pee standing up.
> MISS LEAH. You would if you could. . . .
> SOPHIE. You gonna make me wait until I'm old as you are to get my hands on your orchard?
> MISS LEAH. That'll be time enough. If I tell you you can have it any sooner, my life won't be worth two cents!
> SOPHIE. You don't really think I'd murder you for your land, do you? *(Miss Leah looks at Sophie for a beat before drawing deeply on her pipe.)* (9, 10)

And she never answers Sophie's question. The combination of the adoption of masculine habits and the unanswered question cast a pall over Sophie that supports the general idea of her as a threatening personality. This feeling persists even with evidence to the contrary. Miss Leah is obviously living with Sophie and Fannie, and she clearly trusts them. All of Sophie's actions toward Miss Leah are thoughtful and considerate; she treats her as we would imagine she might treat an elderly relative. We could then simply dismiss

Miss Leah's silence as another part of the banter, but the asked question nonetheless serves, especially at this early point in the play, to plant suggestive hints about Sophie in her role as strong black woman character.

A similar hint gets planted later after Minnie and her husband Frank arrive and Sophie gives Minnie the deed to her portion of the land. Frank sees only the value of the land for which the speculators are offering to pay, not the value of a home.

> FRANK. They're offering $500 an acre. . . . You could be a very rich woman.
> SOPHIE. And I'd be standing in the middle of Kansas without any place to call home. You can't grow wheat on an acre of money.
> FRANK. There's plenty of other land around from what I could see. What's the difference?
> SOPHIE. The difference is we own this land. Whether they like it or not, and anybody who tries to say different is going to find himself buried on it.
> FRANK. You wouldn't really kill somebody over a piece of ground out in the middle of nowhere, would you?
> SOPHIE. This land is the center of the world to me as long as we're standing on it.
> FRANK. And how do you think the rest of the world feels about sharing their center with a town full of colored people?
> SOPHIE. I have no idea.
> MINNIE. None of that matters! Can't you see that none of that matters? This is the land that makes us free women, Frank. We can never sell it! Not ever! (54)

Sophie's mental strength is as apparent here as is her potential physical strength. She has worked to carve out a space to call home, while Frank can see only the monetary value of the land. His hatred of "colored people," his hatred of the blackness in himself, has blinded him to the values by which Sophie chooses to live—and die if necessary. Again, Sophie has done nothing to encourage us to see her as a killer, but the hints of mental toughness essential to such action underscore her role as a strong black woman character.

The readiness with which Sophie is capable of using her gun is apparent in what turns out to be an innocent situation. She and Fannie sit talking after Miss Leah has gone to bed when suddenly there is a noise outside. Sophie reacts instantaneously: "(*She motions toward the candle and Fannie blows it out immediately. Sophie clicks the gun quickly into place and loads two shells into place. She goes quickly to the window and peers out. Fannie stands motionless, watching her. . . .*)" (23). The noise turns out to be three deer that the women stand and admire in the moonlight. As protector of her household, Sophie meets challenges directly and forthrightly. She does not hesitate a moment before readying her gun and moving toward the source of the disturbance. That confidence in her ability to act and to deal effectively with whatever necessitates her action will serve her in good stead for the major dramatic moment of the play. For the time being, it marks her as a fearless woman, healthily in charge of her family.

There is a ritual that Sophie and her sisters share that ties them together in their visions of freedom and womanhood. Apparently Sophie instituted the ritual shortly after their arrival in Kansas. She and Fannie eagerly await Minnie's arrival in order to be able to perform it as a group again. The three women go out into the moonlight, stand in a circle, and hold hands:

SOPHIE. Because we are free Negro women . . .
FANNIE and MINNIE. Because we are free Negro women . . .
SOPHIE. Born of free Negro women . . .
FANNIE and MINNIE. Born of free Negro women . . .
ALL. Back as far as time begins . . .
SOPHIE. We choose this day to leave a place where our lives, our honor and our very souls are not our own.
FANNIE. Say, it Sister!
SOPHIE. We choose this day to declare our lives to be our own and no one else's. And we promise to always remember the day we left Memphis and went west together to be free women as a sacred bond between us with all our trust.
FANNIE and MINNIE. With all our trust . . .
SOPHIE. And all our strength . . .
FANNIE and MINNIE. And all our strength. . . .
SOPHIE. And all our courage . . .
FANNIE and MINNIE. And all our courage . . .
SOPHIE. And all our love.
FANNIE and MINNIE. And all our love. *(A beat.)*
SOPHIE. Welcome home, Baby Sister. (38)

The women counteract the effects of slavery by reclaiming themselves, creating a mythic history that sustains them. This bond of sisterhood and free womanhood is also stronger than the potentially unity-disrupting condition of marriage. Reminiscent of Ntozake Shange's colored girls finding God in themselves and loving her and of Elizabeth Alexander's divas nurturing and supporting each other, Cleage's characters forge an unbreakable bond. Although Frank will test it severely, it will remain as unbreakable as Sophie's vision is indestructible.

Like Sophie, Miss Leah's strength can be measured in the physical as well as psychological realm. During slavery, she gave birth to all her sons at night because that was the only time she was allowed to lie down; women who gave birth during the daylight hours had to squat beside the field and drop their babies "like an animal." Miss Leah was strong enough to contain daylight birthing urges: "If I felt 'em tryin' to come early, I'd hold 'em up in there and wouldn't let 'em. Bad enough bein' born a slave without that peckerwood overseer watchin' 'em take the first breath of life before their daddy done seen if they a boy or a girl child" (18). Whether this is one of Miss Leah's stories that Fannie is collecting or the reality of her life, it nonetheless makes clear her preference for strength even during the confining system of slavery.

Her years successfully working alone in Kansas tie Miss Leah to Sophie in her physical abilities. As the action develops, however, it becomes clear that Sophie and Miss Leah, in spite of their superficial disagreements, share similar philosophies about home, family, and race loyalty. Miss Leah could easily have been incorporated into "the ritual" that is so important to the three sisters. She cannot possibly imagine why Frank prefers socializing with whites in England to enjoying the company of colored people in America. In the mothering, nurturing role she plays with Minnie (she was especially drawn to her as a child on the wagon Sophie drove from Memphis, and she enjoys braiding her hair in the present), Miss Leah exhibits a special affection for her. She has no patience for any trifling colored man, but especially not for one who would harm someone she loves. The harm that crystallizes the action and draws all the women into a concerted effort centers upon Frank beating Minnie to force her to sell her land.

Frank is thus the catalyst that coalesces the strength of all the women characters. Minnie was romantically and immaturely attracted to him when he visited her school to read his poetry. She perhaps married him with all the expectations of a young bride, but she soon learned that Frank valued her only to the extent that she did not hinder his desire to live among and socialize with whites. When her dusky hue interfered, his ugly personality emerged.

When they arrive at Sophie's house, he has beaten her sufficiently to leave a bruise, yet Sophie, Fannie, and Miss Leah tacitly agree to be stupid and pretend, for the sake of Minnie's love for Frank, that Minnie has bruised herself on the train. When Frank's white brothers disinherit him, he can no longer contain his true nature or his true feelings about his less-than-light-enough wife. He beats Minnie into adding his name to the deed so that he can sell her share of the property to speculators. She acquiesces for fear that he will hurt the baby she is carrying. The stage is now set for all the hints of murder and the assertions of psychological strength to be truly tested, for Sophie and the others conclude that Frank must be stopped at all costs.

In planning to use violence to retaliate for violence, Cleage introduces another dimension confronting the strong black woman character. Gaines's Octavia and Hansberry's Mama Lena Younger resort to violence to bring their offspring into line. Their offspring might be difficult, but that is all. Given the opportunity, Mama Lena or Walter Lee may well have acted violently with Willy Harris for stealing their family's money, but the intrafa-

milial crisis takes precedence over the extra-family problems. With *Flyin'
West,* a new factor is averaged into the equation. The black villain is not absent; he is on stage, carrying out his ugliness in action and dialogue with the
other characters. He brings physical harm to one family member and threatens the future of them all. Cleage thus introduces the moral issue of black
characters deciding to kill another black character because he has done
something so beyond the bounds of human decency that he deserves to die.
The strength that it takes to reach that decision suggests that it is not just
Sophie and Miss Leah who are strong black women characters, but Fannie
and Minnie qualify as well. Minnie may have had her lapses from the tenets
stated in "the ritual," but she finally stands with her sisters in eliminating
from their fictional society the abomination of Frank Charles. This decision
also mixes the sinning/saving designation that overlaps with Sethe Suggs. In
killing Frank Charles, the women characters sin against a moral code; however, they save Minnie from physical abuse, and they save Nicodemus from
a man unscrupulous enough to destroy it.

In allowing her characters to arrive at the morally acceptable decision to
kill Frank Charles, Cleage prepares the way carefully and persuasively. Initially, she makes clear the sheer physical effort and determination that it has
taken to found Nicodemus, Kansas. She further posits through Sophie, who
is also a mulatto, that mixed race people so "polluted" have alternatives to
defining themselves and to making their way in the world. She then under-
mines sympathy for Frank (*if* we initially have any for him) by creating him
as inconsiderate and thoughtless, a disrespecter of black women, and finally
as downright villainous. He does not respect the effort that Sophie and the
other characters have expended in achieving what they have; to him,
Nicodemus is simply a colored town in the middle of nowhere (he derisively
calls it "Niggerdemus"), far removed in culture from New Orleans and London, a place merely to be tolerated until he can move on to better things.
His attitude of superiority is based exclusively on color, and he never misses
an opportunity to say something ugly to the other characters, whether it is
about their reading material or back-handed compliments about their china.
Totally lacking in black race pride, he stands in opposition to all the other
characters; in fact, he is the only one who *wants* to pass for white. He therefore evokes Mammy Barracuda in working against black community. He
maintains at one point that a black man lynched in New Orleans "pretty
much brought it on himself" (31). When Miss Leah braids Minnie's hair,
Frank demands that Minnie change it back immediately, because she looks
"like a damn picaninny!" (43). As far as he is concerned, even this brief encounter with frontier colored people is making Minnie revert to some negative colored type that he has successfully covered over by his insistence that
she wear large hats and fancy clothing.

Frank continues his downward spiral through more violence and more insults. After a night of gambling and drinking with "white gentlemen" he has met on the train, and losing considerably to them, Frank pushes Minnie down when she questions whether or not he was passing. When Sophie tells him to "get out," he responds: "You're pretty high and mighty for a nigger woman, aren't you?" (48). When he continues to move toward Minnie, "*Sophie raises the shotgun and cocks it*" (48) as the scene ends. Frank falls through the thin ice on which he is skating when he later beats Minnie into adding his name to her deed. This scene is also the one in which he directs his own demise with his insults and threats.

> MINNIE. No, Frank. I can't ask Sister to split up this land.
> FRANK. I'm your husband. Don't you ever tell me no! *(He reaches to grab her arm.)*
> MINNIE. Don't Frank! *(Moving quickly out of reach.)* I don't care what you do to me, but I won't let you hurt our baby!
> FRANK. *(He grabs her arms and brings her up against him sharply.)* Don't you ever threaten me as long as you live, do you understand me? Do you? *(She nods silently.)* I'll kill you right now, Min. I'll break your damn neck before your precious sisters can hear you holler. I'll kill everybody in this house, don't you understand that? You want to know who I told those white men you were, Min? You really want to know? *(She struggles again, but he holds her.)* I told them you were a black whore I won in a card game. *(He laughs and presses his mouth to hers roughly.)* (56–57)

Recognizing that a character has made himself dispensable is one thing; taking the action to dispense with him is another. For Miss Leah, the fact that Frank had endangered the life of Minnie's child is the crucial factor. "We can't let nobody take our babies," she tells Minnie. "We've given up all the babies we can afford to lose. *(A beat.)* Do you understand what I'm sayin' to you?" (61). Implicit in Miss Leah's question is a request for Minnie to agree that Frank has made himself expendable, for even as she is asking the question, she has already sent Sophie to her place for some "things," ostensibly for Minnie; those "things" contain the ingredients for a special recipe that she plans to use. For Wil Parish, it is the fact that Frank hits Minnie. He does not understand, he says to Fannie, "how a colored man can hit a colored woman" (59), and he offers to "take care of it" (60). For Sophie, it is the combination of Frank beating Minnie and planning to sell her portion of the family land. It is instantly clear to her that the deed must be retrieved and Frank must die. She concocts a plan to have Wil go after Frank and tell him to return the following day because Minnie has had a change of heart and wants to go to the recording office with him. Wil is also to say that Sophie will be in town trying to stop the deal. Instead, the plan is for her to be at the farm.

FANNIE. But what are you going to do?

SOPHIE. A colored man who will beat a colored woman doesn't deserve to live.

FANNIE. Just like that?

SOPHIE. No. Just when he tries to kill my sister and her baby before it's even born yet!

FANNIE. Stop it! That's just what I was afraid of!

SOPHIE. What you were afraid of? Me?

FANNIE. Of what you might do.

SOPHIE. What I might do? Why aren't you afraid of what he is already doing?

FANNIE. He's her husband, Sister!

SOPHIE. If he wasn't her husband would you care what I did to him for beating her half to death?

FANNIE. That's different.

SOPHIE. You know as well as I do there are no laws that protect a woman from her husband. Josh beat Belle for years and we all knew it. And because the sheriff didn't do anything, none of us did anything either. It wasn't a crime until he killed her! I'm not going to let that happen to Min. I'm going to watch him prance across this yard and then I'm going to step out on my front porch and blow his brains out. (62–63)

Sophie's response to Wil's reiteration that he can "take care of it" is the epitome of the strong black western woman character's philosophy: "I appreciate the offer, but the day I need somebody else to defend my land and my family is the day *that* somebody's name will be on the deed. I need you to help me do what needs to be done. Not do it for me" (63).

Only Fannie is reluctant at this point. In the schema of the strong black woman character, her reluctance is significant. Next to Minnie, she has been the one Sophie has taken care of. She is allowed the feminine, cultured side denied to Sophie. Just after the first scene in the play, she and Wil enter, with her carrying a basket of flowers. Wil is clearly enamored, and she is perhaps more dense than coquettish, but she nonetheless is aware of his affection for her. She is the one who wears nice dresses and what jewelry there is available, the one who believes in the fun inherent in dances, the one who fought to bring the good china from Memphis. For hearth and home values identified with traditional womanhood, therefore, Fannie is the representative. She is also the advocate for law and marriage. She reminds Minnie that she loves Frank after Frank pushes Minnie down; she tells Minnie that their own father had a bad temper and suggests that even difficult men can be salvaged. She reiterates the "for better and for worse" portion of the marriage vows.

To win Fannie over to the need to eliminate Frank, therefore, is the final challenge and the ultimate marker of strong black women characters in the text. She joins the scheme when Miss Leah comes to Sophie's rescue. She cannot allow Sophie to kill Frank, Miss Leah asserts. Rather, she will use her special apple pie recipe to accomplish the job. In doing so, Miss Leah remembers the unique bond she has established with Minnie from the moment she saw her: "And then here come Min, bouncin' off the back of your wagon, hair all over her head, big ol' eyes and just the sweetest lil' face I ever saw. Didn't even know enough to be scared" (64). Now Miss Leah will help her special "child" by using her special recipe. It was given to her by the cook of a plantation who had used it when a persistent overseer planned to take advantage of the master's absence to press his sexual attentions upon her. The cook, Ella, knew the overseer was coming, so she made an apple pie. He saw it, could not resist her offers of it, and keeled over dead from the poison before he had a chance to assault Ella. Miss Leah relates this story as she prepares her own gorgeously irresistible apple pie.[14]

It is left to Fannie, the closest feminist model on the frontier to Frank's notion of womanhood, to charm Frank into eating the pie. She plays her part admirably and lies convincingly. The image of accommodating domesticity that she presents, combined with Frank's arrogance and his belief that he is smarter than all the others, enables her to achieve her objective without any glitches. She convinces him that she and Sophie will pay him for Minnie's land rather than have him sell it to speculators, that no one is angry, that Sophie will not be returning for hours, and that he might as well be congenial and have a slice of apple pie while he is waiting for Minnie to wake up from her nap and accompany them to town. Fannie even tells him that when Minnie "saw me rolling out the crust for this pie, she told me to make sure you got a piece of it" (67). She also emphasizes "that a wife's first allegiance is to her husband" (67) and that Minnie is doing the right thing in standing by Frank. Frank's notion of culture is finally what leads him to eat the poisonous dessert. The superficial social interaction that Fannie offers him fits perfectly with his sense of culture, good china, and life in London. Just as he expected his brothers to see the surface similarity—that he looked *exactly* like them—and recognize his paternity suit, so he expects nothing but politeness from Fannie. He underestimates her as badly as he underestimated his white brothers. Fannie's ulterior motive and her solidarity with Miss Leah and her sisters become clear when she calmly responds to Frank's request for her to get a glass of water for his burning throat, "No, Frank. I can't do that" (68). And she stands calmly as he slumps over into eternity.

Fannie becomes a master of expediency and finally exhibits allegiance to her sisters and the ritual rather than to an abstract sense of squeamishness about protecting one's family, home, and land. In this moment, she moves firmly into the strength paradigm. Although she may "shudder" at the sight of the fallen Frank, she does not give in to tears or lose her resolve; instead she signals Sophie and Wil that they can enter and remove the body. In her future actions, Fannie may understandably resort to the role she has earlier assumed, but she does what is necessary in this instance. The same is true of Minnie. After all, it is her husband that Miss Leah, with the consent of the others, has poisoned. Minnie finally chooses the life she is carrying over the life that has tried to diminish her own. Stage directions convey the complexity of her reactions:

> *Miss Leah watches Minnie who moves toward the body then stops, looking at Frank with a mixture of regret and relief. She approaches the body slowly, her anger and fear battling her bittersweet memories of the love she once felt for Frank. She reaches out and touches him tentatively, realizing the enormity of what they have done. She draws back, but reaches out again, almost involuntarily, to touch his arm, his hand, his shoulder. We see her move through a complex set of emotions, ending with her knowledge of the monster Frank had become. Her face now shows her resolve and even her body seems to gain* strength. *She* steels *herself and reaches into Frank's pocket to withdraw the deed.* (68, my emphasis)

Minnie's battered and beaten body provides the emotional support for her finally accepting Frank's death. The "safety" of the home with her sisters is more important than the life she led with Frank; after all, it was frequently more uncomfortable for her than not—even when things were going well with them. She can thus gain strength and resolve and steel herself, as Fannie does, to accept expediency over sentiment.

The final scene of the play, which immediately follows the one showing Frank's death, is set in the spring of 1899, sometime after the birth of Minnie's daughter. The scene is important for reestablishing patterns of strength. As the women gather for a dance, with Miss Leah left to tend the child, Sophie is still the strongest, and the others exhibit traits of traditional femininity. Minnie's *"hair is braided with ribbons and she wears bright clothes. She looks calm and healthy"* (69). Fannie is now Wil's fiancé and is *"dressed up,"* while Sophie *"has on a severe dark blue dress"* (70). The younger women generally appear light-hearted while Sophie remains the more serious one; they complain about her "plain" dress and attempt to make it fancier by adding a broach to it. She allows them to leave in advance of her as she stands in her yard in the moonlight, raising her arms in celebration of their land and freedom. Wil, who has brought flowers for Fannie, accompanies them to the dance and will become Fannie's additional source of strength. Minnie, her baby, and the fading but still effervescent Miss Leah will remain the family for whom Sophie will serve as father, husband, nurturer, and protector.

Even as Sophie stands in the moonlight basking in her freedom and the possibilities of the future, Miss Leah is reiterating to her "granddaughter" the strength paradigm to which the play has consistently adhered:

MISS LEAH. Yes, my granddaughter. We got plenty to talk about, me and you. I'm going to tell you about your momma and her momma and her gran'-momma before that one. All those *strong* colored women makin' a way for lit-tle ol' you. Yes, they did! 'Cause they knew you were comin'. And wadn't nobody gonna keep you from us. Not my granddaughter! Yes, yes, yes! All those fine colored women, makin' a place for you. And I'm gonna tell you all about 'em. Yes, I sure am. I surely am . . . (71, my emphasis)

Strong black women characters are thus doubly aligned with the mythic past the sisters reflect in their ritual as well as with the future, one made brighter because these strong colored women all stood together. Neither Frank nor other forces have been allowed to keep the child away from them, for their alignment with life, health, and the future enables these strong black women characters to keep on keeping on.

Inherent in their strength is one of the problems inherent in the strength of most strong black female characters—in order for them to be strong, black men must be absent, expendable, or diminished. They are absent with Sophie and Miss Leah, and expendable with Minnie. And not only is Frank expendable, but he is created primarily as a one-dimensional villain. With Fannie, the male figure is diminished. Undoubtedly Wil Parish is an ad-mirable, respectable, loving, and supportive man, but this is *not* his story, so he is pushed into the background even when he is on stage. His willingness to kill Frank aligns him with the objectives of the women, as does his phi-losophy of black male/female interaction, but he gets sent on errands rather than initiating them. To his credit, he is not at all insulted when Frank teases him about doing the "woman's work" of clearing and washing dishes. He mends fences for Sophie and checks on Miss Leah's farm, but basically he borders on invisibility. He can be an admirable character only as long as he realizes that his role is to support the women, not to be in a position of au-thority over them or to claim equality with them.

A charge could also be leveled against the play that the paradigm of the strong black female character devolves into anti-intellectualism. The fron-tier life makes these women so practical, in other words, that a man who writes poetry has no place in it. The poetry-writing Frank is thus "effemi-nate," too impractical for the harshness of the frontier and thereby needs to have his polluting influence removed from that environment. Farming life is not for black male poets or for those colored men in the cities about whom Sophie complains. The frontier needs *real* men, and Frank does not fit if a physical connotation is assigned to that definition or if it is located in mental toughness and commitment to family.[15] While the women nur-ture and are committed to family, Frank is antifamily, and that condition probably stems in part from his confused sense of what men should do in the world: write poetry rather than work. This potential charge, however, is partly balanced by Fannie's desire to write a book about Nicodemus. She plans to call it *The True History and Life Stories of Nicodemus, Kansas: A Negro Town*. The stories in Fannie's book will be practical, not flights of fanciful imagination, and they will reflect the lives of "real" characters like Miss Leah. Book writing is book writing, but the purposes to which the writing is put are dramatically different in poetry and oral history. The latter is applauded because it celebrates the frontier lifestyle that is the essence of the women's existence in Kansas. It is also noteworthy, in counteracting the anti-intellectual charge, that one of Sophie's dreams is to get a full-time teacher and school for Nicodemus. She has not set any limits on how far educational exploration can go.

As with most portraits of strong black female characters, there is as much to admire about them in *Flyin' West* as there is to complain about. In many instances, the very things that warrant applause are also the things that occasion complaint; that is no less the case for Cleage's portraits of strong black women characters than it is for Gaines's Tante Lou or Hansberry's Mama Lena. Cleage's characters do what they absolutely must do to live and succeed in their environment. Thus the paradox of strong black female characterization continues: strength is undoubtedly a virtue, but it is also frequently violating and destructive.

Chapter 8 ~

Balance?

Octavia E. Butler's *Parable of the Sower*

earl Cleage's *Flyin' West* holds a strategic place in this discussion in that it looks backward to traditional portraits of strong black female characters in its sacrificial components, and it also includes the specific violence of killing that is not complicated by the usual questions of slavery. It serves as a natural transition to Octavia E. Butler's *Parable of the Sower* (1993). A futuristic vision (from 2024 to 2027) of death and destruction throughout the United States, but especially in California, *Parable of the Sower* is the diary narrative of Lauren Olamina between the years of 15 and 18. The daughter of a drug-abusing mother who has caused her to develop hyperempathy syndrome, a condition in which she believes she experiences the pain of others, Lauren is not only unusual biologically but in every other way imaginable. An inhabitant of a walled community designed to keep out huge numbers of the poor and desperate, including drug addicts, the homeless, and wild dogs that prey upon humans, Lauren is mature far beyond any expectations for a 15-year-old. Well read and visionary, she quickly sees the time when the wall enclosing her 11-family community will no longer hold and all the evils that are outside will destroy what her family and their neighbors have tried to keep inviolate. She plans meticulously for the journey she ultimately makes—a trek through abandoned and mostly barren California landscape and freeways to what she hopes will be a haven in slighter greener northern California. The persons she collects along the way to join her in her Earthseed vision are a walking monument to the concept of a melting pot—African American, Hispanic, Asian, European American, and mixtures thereof—ripe for envisioning a more harmonious multiethnic, multiracial future.

Lauren lives in a world in which violence occurs practically every second. It is literally a dog-eat-dog world where characters pack guns in the tradition of the Old West; where target practice is routine; where characters from walled communities must travel in groups; where technology is at a standstill; where bicycles and walking have replaced cars as modes of transportation; where dirt, filth, and thinness are the norm; where eight-year-olds unprotected by walls are routinely raped; where trust does not exist and killing is routine; where a new drug inspires its users to set fire to anything burnable, including other characters, because the sensation they experience from watching the fire is greater than sex; and where life is cheap and the violation of bodies far exceeds the mere act of murder. Severed body parts (arms, legs) abound throughout the text, eyes are gouged out as a special form of punishment, and there is at least one instance of cannibalism. Humankind is reduced to its basic quest for survival: food and shelter. The strong prey on the weak, and everybody scavenges wherever they can, whether it means removing furniture and other usables from a house recently burned or taking clothing from a dead body. This is not a world for the squeamish, and even six- or 86-six year-olds can be just as quick to steal (and thereby possibly endanger another life) as robust teenagers.

Ironies abound in this world, and morality is neutral if not nonexistent. Lauren's father, who is a Baptist minister and professor, teaches his children and his neighbors how to use guns because he knows they will need to kill to survive. Although he insists that Lauren be baptized when she is 15, he can only get her and the other candidates to the baptizing site by leading them in a bike caravan with guns strapped to their bodies through threatening "neighborhood" territory. He and Lauren quote a lot of scripture in the text, but it does not ultimately control their lives. Indeed, Lauren is looking for an alternative to Christianity; she finally finds that new way of relating to creation by concluding that "God is Change."[1] And if change is the only constant in the world, then traditional morality becomes increasingly flexible. Undoubtedly Lauren is a principled and spiritual person, but her world does not allow one to become weakened by adherence to any belief. While one must focus in the here and the now, there is the remote possibility for something more. Lauren conceptualizes this something more as Earthseed, whose ultimate "Destiny" is "to take root among the stars."[2] Short of obtaining that goal, however, Lauren tries to retain a semblance of humanity in a world where human beings increasingly descend to the level of not just animals, but that group's most vicious predators.

What part does spirituality play in such a world? Lauren's developing Earthseed philosophy is ultimately optimistic in this globally warmed and dying world.[3] It posits that humankind is seed to be planted in another galaxy, another universe. People on earth might be mired in current devolution, but somehow, some of them will attain the stars. Lauren teaches her Earthseed philosophy to the group she collects, and she precedes each of her diary entries with Earthseed verses. Her verses, with their underlying suggestion of traditional religion—certainly in their shape—and bracketed with the parable of the sower from the King James Version of the Bible, give hope to her world in spite of the destruction in which it is currently mired. *Earthseed: The Books of the Living,* which is the title of her presentation to us, becomes a testament not only to the human will to survive, but to envision an existence beyond mere survival.

In the world that Butler has created, the formula that guides behavior is simple: be strong or die. Strength assumes multiple dimensions in the text, and it ties Lauren in various ways to her literary predecessors. Initially, as the works in which such characters appear become increasingly contemporary, some of the ages of these strong female characters decrease. We thus have much younger women exhibiting the greatness of wisdom that was previously associated with older, more mature women characters who were often heads of three- or four-generation households. Tante Lou is still the traditional image of the strong black woman character in her seventies in Gaines's 1993 novel, but Cleage's Sophie Washington is only 36. Yet Sophie controls, commands, and manages the lives of those around her as effectively as the older women characters. Butler pushes the envelope even farther by depicting Lauren between the ages of 15 and 18. Yet her common sense, wisdom, and questing after the meaning of life far exceed her chronological age. The flexibility of speculative fiction might be averaged into this equation, for by making Lauren younger Butler also endows her with the tremendous physical strength that she will need to walk from near Los Angeles almost to the Oregon border.[4]

Lauren's physical size, however, matches in implication if not exactness the physical size associated with some of the earlier literary women. The emphasis is upon her tallness, although we never get an exact height. We do know that she is taller than several of the men in the narrative. She sees that as an advantage, for she decides to assume the disguise of a man during the journey north (157–58).[5] She notes as well that her name is "androgynous" in pronunciation ("like the more masculine Loren") and that she almost has the "chest and hips" (195) of a man. Assumed masculinity eliminates her from the prospect of heterosexual rape, for that is the immediate threat to any woman traveling alone or with weak cohorts; indeed, rape is so commonplace in the narrative that it is treated almost as a necessary evil. The masculine disguise also gives Lauren the advantage of authority associated with a strong young man: "'We believed two men and a woman would be more likely to survive than two women and a man'" (195). Her posture signals to would-be predators that they have a challenge on their hands, which might encourage them to move from Lauren to easier pickings. Lauren makes it known constantly that she has a gun and is willing to use it ("'Out here, the trick is to avoid confrontation by looking strong'"). The very arena in which she is forced to travel, therefore, is a testing ground for survival associated with strength. Lauren locates her potential with the masculine gender, which is an understandable practical decision, but also one that inadvertently connects her to the Sophie Washingtons and Mammy Barracudas. She might be infinitely more attractive than Mammy Barracuda, but she can put a hammerlock on someone's neck just as effectively as Reed's character can, and she can handle the physical activities identified with males as efficiently as Walker's Mrs. Johnson in "Everyday Use," who asserts that she "was always better at a man's job" (50). Lauren's neighbor Harry, who is one of two survivors from her walled community to join her on the trek north, comments after an instance in which Lauren refuses to let an old man join their campsite: "You damn sure talk macho enough to be a guy" (168).

A masculine identity as an enhancer of female strength is thus essential for Lauren's conceptualization of herself and prospects for survival in her blighted world. Masculinity stereotypically connotes that one can take care of one's self, or if attacked, is able to give violence for violence. Lauren's masculine guise adds strength to strength, for as a woman, she is already unusually strong, unusually capable of taking care of herself. Her adoption of the masculine guise raises the same issue that I considered with Sophie Washington: superimposing masculinity upon women characters seems to be the only way to enhance their strength, the only model that western civilization has provided for imagining exceptional physical strength.

Since Lauren is a combination of strength and concern, nurturer and killer, the early signs of her nurturing side are worthy of comment. As the only female child in a family of five children, and positioned as the oldest child, Lauren, like many African American girl/women historically, has been given nurturing responsibility. On several occasions, she is specifically assigned care for her brothers, but she also voluntarily and generally assumes that responsibility. Her caring about them is further noteworthy because they are her stepbrothers, born to her father and the Hispanic woman he married after Lauren's mother's death. When we meet Lauren at 15, she is already an accomplished cook who prepares meals for her entire family, and she is already an assistant teacher to her stepmother in the community's small school. She exhibits the traditional traits of concern about home and hearth usually identified with women. When Amy Dunn, a neighboring child neglected by her 13-year-old mother and other members of her family, is cast out even further after starting a fire, Lauren takes the child under her wing. "I've been taking care of little kids," she says, "since I was one" (33). And though she asserts that she is "tired of it," she is nonetheless good at it. When the three-year-old Amy is later killed by a stray bullet that penetrates the door of their walled community, it is fair to say that perhaps only Lauren mourns for her.

Lauren's nurturing side is also visible in her general, altruistic concern for the welfare of her community and in her even more intense concern that the foremost objective of her people should be to survive. Even at 15 Lauren knows that her world is dying and that humankind must contemplate a different future. "'Space could be our future,'" she tells her father. "As far as I'm concerned," she writes further, "space exploration and colonization are among the few things left over from the last century that can help us more than they hurt us. It's hard to get anyone to see that, though, when there's so much suffering going on just outside our walls" (20). Lauren recognizes that the walls will not hold and that some alternative needs to be considered. When Amy Dunn is killed, she comments that her community is "like an island surrounded by sharks—except that sharks don't bother you unless you go in the water. But our land sharks are on their way in. It's just a matter of how long it takes for them to get hungry enough" (48). An attempt to convince her friend Joanne of the need to be prepared when the walls fall only leads to accusations and reprimands from the neighbors and caution from her father. The bleakness that she comments on to Joanne would seem to be enough to warrant action:

'There's cholera spreading in southern Mississippi and Louisiana. . . . There are too many poor people—illiterate, jobless, homeless, without decent sanitation or clean water. They have plenty of water down there, but a lot of it is polluted. And you know that drug that makes people want to set fires? . . . It's spreading again. It was on the east coast. Now it's in Chicago. . . . Tornadoes are smashing hell out of Alabama, Kentucky, Tennessee, and two or three other states. Three hundred people dead so far. And there's a blizzard freezing the northern midwest, killing even more people. In New York and New Jersey, a measles epidemic is killing people. Measles!' (51)

In the face of these cataclysmic events resulting from global warming and the imminent danger to their community, Lauren's response is nurturing, motherly, visionary:

'We can get ready. That's what we've got to do now. Get ready for what's going to happen, get ready to survive it, get ready to make a life afterward. Get focused on arranging to survive so that we can do more than just get batted around by crazy people, desperate people, thugs, and leaders who don't know what they're doing! . . . I'm talking about the day a big gang of those hungry, desperate, crazy people outside decide to come in. I'm talking about what we've got to do before that happens so that we can survive and rebuild—or at least survive and escape to be something other than beggars.' (52)

These impressive words from a 15-year-old are more than the community can take, and while Lauren can only wish for the day when "people are able to pay more attention to what I say than to how old I am" (73), she nonetheless prepares her own survival pack for the day she knows is coming. It is her concern about the end of her community's world that leads Lauren increasingly to her Earthseed philosophy and the vision of space travel; she sees it is as the only way for humankind to survive.

Further preparation for life outside the wall has come in her father's insistence that Lauren and others in the community know how to use guns. It has also come in how guns have had to be put to use *within* the community. Lauren's father insists that she shoot birds, squirrels, and rats that eat their food because it is a necessity and because "moving targets would be good" (36) for her aim. Lauren must reconcile her hyperempathy (feeling the blows the dying animals feel) with the basic need to survive, which she does without hesitation. The animals "had" to be killed because they ate or ruined the food. Her understanding at 15 is appreciably different from James's in Gaines's "The Sky is Gray"; although his mother forces him to kill a redbird for the family dinner, he and Lauren nonetheless share a back-against-the-wall, human need to survive. Lauren wonders if she could actually shoot and kill thieves such as those who have recently robbed and killed a neighbor, but when the attacks intensify and she overhears her father, the minister, asserting that he will protect his family at all costs (65–66), she is certainly influenced by his position. The neighbors patrol their territory and shoot intruders (wounding them) on at least two occasions; by contrast, the intruders kill several of the community members (one instance involves a fire that burns 11 people and their home). What happens inside the wall, therefore, serves as lessons to quell squeamishness once the walls come down.

Perhaps the most significant event that occurs while Lauren is still inside and that will be relevant to her existence outside is her father's disappearance and presumed death. That tragedy catapults her to a position of leadership within her family as well as within the walled community. Her stepmother is devastated, so it is Lauren who keeps the family going from day to day—cooking, taking care of her brothers, helping her stepmother as much as she will allow. She also assumes the responsibility of speaking to her father's congregation on the Sunday following his disappearance. She is wise enough to deliver a sermon laced with hope even as she knows intuitively that her father is probably dead. She sets self aside in an emotional distancing comparable to her literary ancestors and gives the community what it needs—a message on the need for the seemingly weak to persist against the seemingly strong. In the process of providing what her family and neighbors need, she strengthens herself. The void in authority created by her father's death, therefore, enables/forces Lauren to move into a position of clear-sighted leadership that presages her role outside the walls.

A visionary whose prophesying is deadly accurate, Lauren witnesses shortly after she turns 18 the horrible destruction of her walled community, during which (she believes) the remaining members of her family are killed (her 14-year-old brother had been tortured, mutilated, and killed earlier when he tried to live outside the wall, and her father simply disappeared into some unimaginable fate and death in that outside void when she was 17).[6] In the face of this disaster, Lauren becomes a pioneer in the tradition of Sophie Washington, a nurturer comparable to Mama Lena Younger and other strong black women characters, and a killer the likes of whom we have not before encountered in African American literature. Butler manages this striking combination while she simultaneously ensures that we remain engaged with and sympathetic to Lauren.

Butler prepares her readers for what Lauren must do on her journey as effectively as she prepares Lauren for the journey. The question becomes how, as with Naylor's Mama Day, a killer can be made sympathetic. I maintain, as with Mama Day, that the reader's ability to empathize lies in author preparation for what readers need to accept. With Lauren, Butler uses several means to create sympathy that remains with her character. First, there is the factor of age. Although Lauren is older than her chronological years, she is still an adolescent when we meet her. The concern that Butler places in her mind about the state of humankind thus brings with it an acceptable innocence untainted by the politics of the ugly world in which Lauren lives. American readers are trained to be aligned with youth, with the *Bildungsroman* character who tries to make a way for herself in an unfeeling, at times cruel world. Lauren thus appears to us initially as another representative of innocence potentially sacrificed in the face of corporate, governmental, and general human violence and stupidity.

Second, her victimization also leads us to identify with Lauren. Again invoking innocence, she has inherited a disease—no matter its delusional quality—through no fault of her own. In a world in which drugs are an everyday factor to readers, it is understandable that they would sympathize with someone who has been victimized by drugs. Beyond that initial sympathy, the consequences that Lauren must experience every day further evoke sympathy for her. Her brother tricks her into bleeding when they are kids, and her general condition separates her if it does not effectively isolate her. In addition to the usual complications of growing up, therefore, Lauren has an added one. This disease, impairment, or handicap serves as a neutralizing agent in all the killing that Lauren does. Not only does it frequently stop her, but it signals to readers that Lauren is in a "have to kill" position, for no sane character would thoughtlessly bring such needless suffering upon herself.

Stereotypically, the disease also identifies Lauren with another trait associated with strong black women characters, those who claim that the punishment they mete out to their children in fact causes more harm to them than it does to the children receiving the blows.

Lauren's altruistic concern for her community's welfare becomes the third factor in our sympathetic identification with her. Here is this young prophet, seeing clearly into the future, and no one will listen to her. We respond to this "voice crying in the wilderness" phenomenon and easily become the converts to her vision that the people in her community are not. Lauren feels the need for and wants change for them, never exclusively for herself. She tries to share her vision with Joanne, and she is eager to follow her father's advice to prepare people for the end of the walled community in ways that do not frighten them (by having classes on survival and self defense, for example). Instead of balking at requests made of her, she appears frequently to be in the center of things, doing whatever is necessary for the good of the community. That willingness to give, to help others, aligns her again with many of the women characters treated in this study and keeps the focus on the nurturing side of her personality even when she kills.

Any narrative related in the first person has the advantage of drawing readers more closely to the plights of the character doing the narrating. This is the fourth strategy Butler uses to align readers with Lauren. We are locked into Lauren's world, her way of seeing things, and it seems reasonable to us. Although she quotes from conversations she has with other characters, and succeeds well in presenting their points of view, we are still listening primarily to her voice, her vision, her analyses, her way of seeing the world. We see her wrestle with issues of God and existence. There are no barriers between us and her as we see her shape her Earthseed verses, as we see her struggle with her community's lack of response to its impending disaster, as we see her worry over natural disasters, disease, and the lack of love in her world, and as we see her struggle with the more mundane issues of negotiating friendships, growing up, and experiencing sex. Her self-portrait is not that of a selfish, rapacious person. She is amazingly thoughtful, sober, less judgmental than she could be, and incredibly mature. And she is balanced, not only in terms of personality but also in terms of how she negotiates the maddening world in which she lives. The voice she presents is first and foremost a trustworthy voice, because the issues about which it first writes are decidedly removed from personal interest. When it turns to recording more personal information, therefore, it has already earned a measurable degree of trust from us. The voice, therefore, is *the* voice of authority about its world, an authority that additionally aligns Lauren with women characters who assume authority in a number of contexts in works discussed in this study.

Our sympathy thoroughly engaged, we begin the journey outside the wall with Lauren, a journey in which her strength is centered in the combination of killing and leading/nurturing. Each incident has the aura of survival and the greater good surrounding it. The first occurs in the melee of the burning and destruction of the walled community by "paints," drug users who paint their faces. Lauren "dies" as one of her neighbors is shot, recovers briefly from that, then:

> Someone screamed near me, then tackled me, pulled me down. I fired the gun in reflexive terror, and took the terrible impact in my own stomach. A green face hung above mine, mouth open, eyes wide, not yet feeling all his pain. I shot him again, terrified that his pain would immobilize me when he did feel it. It seemed that he took a long time to die.
>
> When I could move again, I pushed his body off me. I got up, still holding the gun, and ran for the wrecked gate. (142)

In this clash between good and evil, with the "paints" setting fires purely for the sexual pleasure of watching them burn and killing anyone not burned, there is no question where our loyalties lie. Lauren is on the side of civilization and sanity, which means that her killing strength serves her in good stead. The sharks have made their way into her space, thus obliterating the distinction between outside and inside.

As will be true with most of her narration of such incidents, Lauren is almost clinically detached in recounting what happened. Primarily declarative sentences. Little emotion. No lingering over blood and yuk that must have been attendant upon the death. No sense of how it felt to lie under the dead body (think of Beloved recounting her experience of dead men lying on her face). All emotional response is contained in the use of multiple forms of the word "terror," but without giving specific, detailed dimensions to that condition. In other words, as Etheridge Knight asserts, writing controls chaos, contains it, makes it manageable. There is thus a strength of control in the writing to go along with the strength that Lauren must have exhibited to shoot and then to endure the consequences of those shots.

Outside her home space and united with Harry and Zahra, the only other two survivors of her community, Lauren immediately assumes a leadership role. She can do that in part because she has food and water while they only have themselves (Harry has a concussion from rescuing Zahra from a potential rapist and Zahra, who originally lived outside, initially seems to be more sex symbol and emotional responder—her daughter and extended family were killed—than potential leader). Zahra immediately turns to Lauren for answers to questions and general direction, although she is presumably the more experienced character on the outside. Perhaps because of Lauren's height, or her determination, or her forethought in preparing her pack, Zahra defers to her in decisionmaking. So does Harry—when he is finally aware enough to understand what has happened to their community and families. He defers to Lauren as the character with a plan, although he is initially skeptical about her actions and wonders how she can condone activities—Zahra's stealing, for example—that are such a contrast to his and Lauren's Christian upbringing.

Harry and Zahra are the first two converts to Lauren's way of seeing the world, but that conversion comes with the price of another killing. On their first night camping on the trail north, they are attacked by human predators, one of whom Lauren hits over the head with a boulder. Realizing that he is not dead, she asks Harry, who had been standing watch with the gun when the trouble started, to give it to her so she can shoot the unconscious intruder. Although Harry has just killed a man, he is still squeamish:

> 'Give me the gun.' I repeated, and held out a bloody hand for it. 'Unless you want to do it yourself.'
>
> 'You can't shoot him. You can't just. . . .'
>
> 'I hope you'd find the courage to shoot me if I were like that, and out here with no medical care to be had. We shoot him, or leave him here alive. How long do you think it will take him to die?'
>
> 'Maybe he won't die.'
>
> I went to my pack, struggling to navigate without throwing up. I pulled it away from the dead man, groped within it, and found my knife. It was a good knife, sharp and strong. I flicked it open and cut the unconscious man's throat with it. (174)

Lauren effects a clinical narration in the last paragraph that evokes Clora's description of her burying her second child in Cooper's *Family;* she does simply and efficiently what must be done. Since neither of Lauren's companions knows that she is empathetic, a "sharer" of pain, they—especially Harry—can perhaps only view her action as being too efficient and practical, not as the necessity she judges it to be before the man "could regain consciousness and involve [her] in his agony." Her decision to tell them about her history does not immediately bring Harry to acceptance of her action, but he does not depart from the group when she gives him the opportunity to do so. Instead, he calls her a "manipulative bitch" (178) for effectively tying him to her and demands to see some of her journal, perhaps as a sign of good faith on her part.

Butler does a better job on the continuum between intent and outcome in getting readers to approve of the means Lauren uses to achieve her ends. It should be noted, however, that the difference in part lies in the mode of literary expression. We are locked into Lauren's head in the novel and are thereby privy to her most thoroughly examined thoughts, while we can only observe Mama Lena's actions. Also, Lauren's opponents are consistently strangers who are one-dimensionally villainous and, we conclude, deserve their fateful ends, whereas Mama Lena's "opposition" comes primarily from her own flesh and blood.

The time period in which the novel is set is also relevant to a more tolerant response to Lauren's actions. The 1990s saw more black people out of the church and less influenced by religion than in 1959. Gang violence and the Rodney King-inspired era of social unrest that inspired Butler's creation would have been a factor in reader reaction as well. In other words, Butler published her novel in a period when actual events, news coverage, gang warfare, and wars on various sites throughout the world made human violation of human beings almost routine. In such a world, Lauren appears not only as a savior but with the acceptable aura of a Superman or Batman.

Lauren's direct command to Harry, "Give me the gun," positions her farther in power and authority. Although his sense of morality precludes him from responding to that request, after she cuts the man's throat and commands, "Strip the bodies," both Harry and Zahra join in immediately. She directs them to "take what they have, then we'll put them in the scrub oaks down the hill where we gathered wood" (174). And when she says to Harry, "Give Zahra the gun. She can guard us" (175) as they move the bodies, Harry hands the gun to Zahra. Lauren is what we might reasonably call a natural leader, a person who takes charge when circumstances demand or when a vacuum presents itself. Quietly, and without much challenge beyond Harry's short-lived moralistic disapproval, Lauren assumes command of the group; her leadership role will become increasingly solidified as she collects more fellow travelers on the journey north. The pilgrimage essentially becomes *hers;* anyone joining with her must agree to operate by the rules she has set—or the implied rules that have fallen into place through her behavior with Harry and Zahra (think of her journey as Mama Lena's house, where the children who enter must abide by the rules). Where previous strong black female characters may have had authority without power in the real world, Lauren has both. She is the only person in the group initially who has a gun, and she has a plan, supplies, and old maps of the freeways going north. She also has the energy and the stature—and the implied competence therein—that draw people to her.

Given Lauren's position of leadership, it is important that Harry is a white male; thus, Butler introduces some intriguing revisionist considerations of persons usually expected to be in charge. The circumstances she creates are ones in which the usual frequently does not hold sway, and neither Harry nor Lauren expects that. Harry's initial objections to Lauren are based on morality, not on color or gender. Lauren, Harry, and Zahra are all aware of prejudices against persons of color, especially if they are in a mixed couple, so Butler certainly does not intend to suggest that all the usual patterns of racial interaction in America have been eliminated. However, with the variety upon variety of racial and ethnic mixes of the characters who lived in Lauren's community and those now trekking north, she does make clear that factors of survival perhaps transcend most basic racial prejudices. Anyone prepared to deal with the current circumstances, and to deal with them *well,* can be elevated—or elevate herself—to a leadership role in spite of what history and custom might suggest.

Through her Earthseed verses, Lauren enhances her position of leadership. They become as effective as Mama Lena quoting the Bible. In her selection of which verses to show to Harry, she selects ones that are seemingly innocuous, "brief verses that might take hold of him without his realizing it and live in his memory without his intending that they should" (183), as Bible verses did with her. She is consciously controlling her potential converts to Earthseed and is as deliberate and as clear in what she is doing as she was about the wall coming down. "I gave to Harry," she writes, "and through him to Zahra, thoughts I wanted them to keep" (184). Perhaps these thoughts will override Harry's "distrust" of her for having cut the man's throat, but they will assuredly keep Harry and Zahra thinking about Lauren's vision of a future. The idea that Lauren sees herself in a position to "give" thoughts to others indicates that there is little doubt in her mind about who is in charge and why. Her belief that she can convert them is a measure of her strength of mind and the strength of her vision. Her desire may be well intentioned, even altruistic, but it still reflects her notion that her way of seeing the world is superior, the only thing that can save humankind. Other women characters might have focused on their families, as with Mama Lena or Sethe, or their communities, as with Velma Henry and Minnie Ransom; Lauren joins Clora in focusing on humankind.

As the journey continues, Lauren gathers a community. She becomes a futuristic Noah on an arkful journey to a new way of being in the world. Although a couple of characters wander into her vision, she selects most of them carefully. That selection process begins with a young mixed couple, a black man and a Hispanic woman, who are trudging northward with their baby. Lauren interacts with them from a position of what might best be described as nurturing superiority. She determines that the couple should be a part of her group, and she sets out to effect that result. In other words, she acts unhesitatingly as if she *knows* what is best for them. In the hostile environment of the freeway, where predatory opportunity rules most interactions, the couple invites attention because of their huge packs and baby carriage. Although Lauren herself has concluded not to have children, she is attracted to them because of the baby, perhaps another signal in her schema that Earthseed must take root among the stars. When a young human "coyote" grabs the couple's newly replenished water supply, Lauren trips him as he attempts to get away. She suffers the jarring pain of his fall, but she earns the gratitude of Travis, the black husband and father. The couple does not join Lauren's group immediately, but they stay near them. Lauren concludes that they are "potential allies" and invites them to join her campsite the following evening. "We're natural allies," she tells the doubting Travis, "the mixed couple and the mixed group" (191). While that may be true, it is equally true that Lauren has concluded that "they need us more than we need them." She is consciously selecting allies, therefore, whose dependency will not challenge her position of leadership and who may be moldable into her vision of Earthseed. Lauren selects her people as much on intuition as practicality (she "reads" Travis well enough to know that he will eventually join her group). After all, in the open world in which they live, everyone is potential prey, whether dependent or not.

Her physical strength and shooting ability finally endear Lauren to the couple, for she protects their baby by shooting a wild dog that tries to drag it from the couple's camp. When Harry comments that Lauren has "adopted those damned people" (193), Lauren concludes that she has "pretty much adopted him and Zahra, too." The point of view from which she evaluates other characters and her world continues to indicate where authority and power are located in the text—Lauren is center and central; others are drawn to her. Lauren is the nest builder, gathering her small birds to be nurtured, first into acceptance of her as leader, and secondly into her vision of Earthseed. Travis and his wife Natividad become part of the group, and Lauren begins to share her verses with them. Less than two weeks later, she believes that Travis is her "first convert" (205), followed by Zahra, to Earthseed, for she had determined that she would "like to draw them all in" (203). In her vision of Earthseed, therefore, Lauren becomes a fisher of humankind, and no matter the nonbiblical basis of Earthseed, the biblical parallels to Jesus and His disciples are nonetheless evoked. Of California's Highway 101, Lauren asserts that it is "a river flooding north. I've come to think that I should be fishing that river even as I follow its current. I should watch people not only to spot those who might be dangerous to us, but to find those few like Travis and Natividad who would join us and be welcome" (205).[7]

Although she remains cautionary and suspicious, ever capable of killing, Lauren also retains much of the altruistic spirit her father instilled in her. After a slight earthquake, she helps an old man who has fallen, and she leads the effort to rescue two white women from a caved-in shack in which they have taken refuge. While the incorporation of the latter two into the group is not as planned as with Travis and Natividad, Lauren nonetheless takes constructive advantage of opportunity—and she pays a price for it. Immediately upon rescuing Jill and Allison (Allie), human predators attack her group of seven. She stabs to death—and suffers the attendant hyperempathetic pain—the man who attacks her, and her companions kill three more predators. This attack serves to solidify the group and to incorporate Jill and Allie even before they are officially informed of what is required for entry. It also aligns the 57-year-old Taylor Franklin Bankole, who will become Lauren's lover, with Lauren and her people. The renewed community to which Lauren aspires is thus shaping itself along the freeway; where it will end up becomes almost secondary.

Lauren uses whatever strategies necessary to ensure that her group will survive and grow. She resorts to implied obligation when she says to the dismissive Allie, "We risked ourselves for you today. . . . You don't owe us anything for that. It isn't something you could buy from us. But if you travel with us, and there's trouble, you stand by us, stand with us. Now will you do that or not?" (218). Allie's roundabout response amounts to consent, and Lauren welcomes the two women into the group. As effectively as Lauren convinces newcomers to abide by the implied rules of grouphood, so she talks the group into accepting newcomers. In spite of their best efforts, a woman and a child find their way into camp one night and fall asleep among Lauren's group. The group must decide the next morning whether to expel them or allow them to join—even though they know both will probably steal initially. Lauren clearly wants—and expects—that the discussion she ostensibly orchestrates will have only one outcome: Emery Solis and her daughter Tori will become members of the Earthseed caravan. Lauren ensures that result even more by inviting the malnourished woman and her child to eat with them before the discussion takes place. That action binds Emery and Tori to the group and appeals to the group's humanitarian instincts not to cast them out once they have tasted the fruits of paradise, so to speak. Lauren argues that "for the little kid's sake, I wanted to help them at least with a meal" (260), but her larger strategy of incorporation is never far in the back of her mind. Since the group also gives Emery and Tori food before they are scheduled to depart, that makes it additionally difficult for them to leave, or for the group to vote against them not remaining. Through these actions, Lauren encourages the reassertion of traditional humanitarian values, the reclaiming of humankind from the lowest depths of its animal kinship. Numerous rebirths, or conversions, take place along the road to the haven in northern California where Bankole has land sufficient to accommodate the group.

By the time her group solidifies, Lauren has also collected Justin, a child orphaned when his mother was killed in one of the many sporadic gun battles that occur along the freeway, and two additional characters, Grayson Mora and his daughter Doe, who escaped from slavery in southern California. Lauren finally gets unexpected company in the fact that Emery and Tori, as well as Mora and Doe, are all sharers, all victims of hyperempathy syndrome. The last of its members, especially Mora, may remain skeptical of Lauren's group for awhile, but no one wants to depart from the sanctuary of safety in numbers. And new allegiances are formed: Zahra and Harry become a couple, then Lauren and Bankole, and finally Mora and Emery. Justin adopts Allie as his "mother," and Tori and Doe become fast friends. In these new family formations, individuals fight for each other. Gunfights swirl around them and occasionally are directed toward them. One challenge to the group—during which the girls and Emery have to be rescued from "paints"—results in Lauren being wounded by gunfire and Jill being killed, and it is Lauren who comforts Jill's sister Allie. Like many of those traditional strong mother figures, Lauren wraps the defiant Allie in her arms and lets her wail out her grief.

Another challenge comes, perhaps unexpectedly, from within the group. Mora asks for a gun to stand watch with the wounded Lauren, but Lauren refuses because he cannot shoot. When Bankole similarly refuses, Mora asserts: "Shit, . . . Shiiit. First time I saw her, I knew she was a man. Just didn't know she was the only man here" (283). After a tense moment diffused by Zahra, Lauren explains: "'Everyone's tired and everyone's hurting, . . . Everyone, not just you. But we've managed to keep ourselves alive by working together and by not doing or saying stupid things'" (283), to which Bankole adds: "'And if that's not good enough for you, . . . tomorrow you can go out and find yourself a different kind of group to travel with—a group too goddamn macho to waste its time saving your child's life twice in one day'" (283–84). Detained by self-interest (where else, Lauren questions her diary, can he go?) if not outright conversion, Mora remains with the group. And in the schema that Butler has created, Lauren is indeed stronger than he is. His attempt to insult her and the men in the group is yet another of those sites on which the strength of the black female character is laid to be measured. His challenge finally locks Lauren securely into the circle of acceptability that surrounds other strong black women characters; she will not experience further objections from members of her group.

Lauren is overall an altruistic, generous leader, one thoroughly committed to protecting "her people." But her character is not one-dimensional; she is not merely the strong woman character capable of gathering her flock and dispatching any enemy. There is an additional dimension to her that few of the earlier strong black female characters have had. She is impressively, healthily sexually active—without the guilty conscience of passing a moral judgment on her behavior and without the emotional detachment that more frequently characterized strong black women characters. As early as 15, Lauren shares the sexual pleasure that is the counterpart to her ability to share pain. In the world in which she lives, obviously, she has many more opportunities to experience the pain than the pleasure. Yet she and Curtis Talcott, her teenage partner, manage to find a quiet place even in their crowded, walled community—and they even manage to use condoms. Their relationship is short-lived when the walls are torn down and Curtis disappears; like Lauren's father, he is probably killed.

The romantic relationship Lauren develops with Bankole reflects her position in the group. As the mature leader of her people, she selects an older, mature man as her lover although she briefly wishes he "were younger so he would live longer" (211). They both supply condoms for their first lovemaking session, a thoughtfulness that illustrates again the maturity on both sides. Shocked at learning that Lauren is only 18, Bankole exclaims: "'You're a baby! I'm a child molester!'" (245) and finally settles into acceptance with "'You look and act years older'" (246). Lauren's maturity enables her to smile at Bankole when he first smiles at her, although that might initially appear to be a risk in the freeway predatory culture. She is instantly, almost intuitively, attracted to him (perhaps her romantic side operates in a way comparable to her intuitive selection of people). There is no coyness in her about that attraction, no set of religiously imposed rules hanging over her shoulder to prevent her from acting freely and pleasurably, no aura of shame surrounding the need to find privacy some distance from the camping group—only a full-fledged recognition of the need to have someone on watch as the various couples exit to make love.

Lauren's behavior represents a dramatic progression in black women characters' attitudes toward sex, marriage, and family. Baldwin's Elizabeth Grimes is saturated with guilt for having had a child out of wedlock, and Christianity becomes the yardstick by which she measures herself to have fallen short. Sex is something that happened in the past for Sethe Suggs (she does have sex with Paul D, but that's after an 18-year hiatus), Eva Peace, Mama Lena Younger, and Tante Lou. It is barely hinted at with Mammy Barracuda. And while Minnie Ransom talks about it, there is no evidence in the text that she actually participates in it. For Clora and Baby Suggs, slavery makes sex an ordeal to be endured; it is not possible for either to take pleasure in it. Sophie Washington is without a romantic partner and there are no prospects in sight. Only Lauren seems to have balanced strength and sexuality, but this balance has come at a price. Lauren has concluded that the world in which she lives is not one in which she could, in good conscience, give birth to a child. When she is only 16, Lauren comments: "My point is—my question is—how in the world can anyone get married and make babies with things the way they are now. . . . I like Curtis Talcott a lot. Maybe I love him. Sometimes I think I do. He says he loves me. But if all I had to look forward to was marriage to him and babies and poverty that just keeps getting worse, I think I'd kill myself" (80). Her attitude does not change appreciably beyond this observation during the two years we are allowed into her world. Her position immediately evokes comparison to that of Ruth Younger. Pregnant Ruth must contemplate bringing a child into poverty, and all the familial and moral forces around her are arrayed to encourage her to have the child no matter what. It is considered synonymous with being black and female, with being human. In Hansberry's world and the worlds of so many of her literary counterparts, decisions not to have children are antithetical to black existence. Black women characters, especially strong black women characters, have babies, so the logic goes, no matter their economic conditions or their potential for nurturing the children.

The choice not to have children removes Lauren from the biological nurturing and the potential biological tyranny that defines so many of the other literary women, but it does not remove her, as has been illustrated, from general nurturing tendencies. She nurtures adults, and she nurtures children; the latter are an important part of her vision for Earthseed. Remember that it was Travis and Natividad's child Dominic that first attracted Lauren to the couple. She takes young Justin immediately into the group, and she realizes the value of having Tori and Doe among them. As a fisher of humankind, she salvages the children of other characters. Lauren is perhaps more superficially comparable to Mary Rambo in the position she holds in relation to children—adopting them and wishing them well. Indeed, it could be argued in several instances that her attitude toward children is one that she also has toward a couple of adults in her group.

Her opposition to marriage under certain conditions is not a permanent one, however. She agrees to marry Bankole, but the ceremony does not take place within the current action of the text.[8] In her own actions as well as in her support of the various couples around her, Lauren exhibits an enlightened (or perhaps merely different) attitude toward partnering. It is legitimate if the couples commit themselves voluntarily to each other; sanction by legal or religious authorities is irrelevant.

The *pleasure* Lauren takes in sex and her nonjudgmental attitude toward marriage are the clearest signals that a different morality is at work in this text than in those previously examined. "I am Earthseed. Anyone can be" (72), Lauren declares early in the text. She is thus *not* made in the traditional image of God that readers might bring to the text or that into which her father tried to baptize her. She chastises herself, perhaps unfairly so, for being a "coward" (7) in not resisting the baptism because her father's God is not her God. Her God is capsulized in her essential Earthseed verse:

> All that you touch
> You Change.

All that you Change
Changes you.
The only lasting truth
Is Change.
God
is Change. (3)

In Lauren's world, only those persons who can embrace change will be likely to survive. Instead of trying to hold on to the stasis of tradition as reflected in her father's God and the God of Mama Lena Younger, Lauren turns to a different concept of religion and spirituality. There is no church to attend in her belief system. No obedience is required. No impossible set of rules by which to live. The basic tenet is the recognition that humankind, not particularly special in itself, is part of a large natural system in a reciprocal set of never-ending interactions. From this perspective, religion is as much chemical and physical as it is intangible and spiritual. Indeed, Lauren resists calling Earthseed a religion; it is simply what she believes. There are many verses in her *Earthseed: The Books of the Living,* but the one above is the key.

Far from being as restrictive as traditional Christianity, Earthseed allows humankind to make more choices in how it executes its own destiny. Lauren is certainly determined that Earthseed should take root among the stars, but the day-to-day path by which people prepare for that objective or how long it takes can be acted out in a range of possibilities. The best ones apparently are contained in Lauren's Earthseed caravan, where people recommit themselves to altruistic interactions among themselves and joint protection against predators. There can be no judgment passed on killing because that is a necessary evil in Lauren's world. It would have been blasphemous to Mama Lena, but she would not have survived a day outside Lauren's walled community. Earthseed argues for a flexibility that is antithetical to Mama Lena's very existence. Her children could only mold themselves into her belief system, not shape one of their own. And while Lauren shares with Mama Lena the desire to convert people to her kind of spirituality, there is much more leeway in that conversion process and far less stricture in the system to which they are being asked to convert.

Instead of accepting a belief system, as Mama Lena and so many of her counterparts do, Lauren dares to envision something else. That something else is initially contained in her persistent, recurring dream of flying and reiterated in several references she makes to a space station and to new worlds being discovered. Lauren's heaven is thus literally, physically reachable. She has but to look up at the stars and see a part of where she wants to be. Taking root among the stars may seem as farfetched as going to heaven, since Lauren's world is so destitute of the resources that enable space travel, but the important thing is that it is *her* vision, not one imposed upon her by tradition and birth. Lauren's escape from Christianity parallels her escape from important other ties to traditional strong black female characters.

A question to ask, then, is, How successful is Butler in balancing the limitations of strong black female characterization with Lauren? She seems to succeed well, for Lauren is healthy in her size, her strength, her authority, her masculine traits, her sexuality, and her spirituality. Yet Lauren lives in a world that none of the other strong black female characters could reasonably inhabit, except perhaps Clora. In order to judge Lauren's balanced character, therefore, we are asked to mix apples and oranges, to evaluate realistic texts with the same criteria as fantastic texts. This potential problem, however, is mitigated by the direction in which black women's fictional texts have moved over the past couple of decades: the fanciful exists side by side with the realistic, the otherworldly takes up residence in this world, and the dead speak about as well as directly to the living. Barriers within genre have been crossed as effectively as barriers between worlds. Sethe, Baby Suggs, and Beloved can thus exist in the same sphere, the living Cocoa can speak to the dead George in Naylor's *Mama Day*, and the "dead" Clora can witness her family's growth for generations.

It is thus less problematic to consider Mama Lena Younger and Lauren Olamina in the same contextual frames of reference than it might initially appear. Also, serious contemplation of the current state of realistic affairs in America, as Butler herself avows, will make clear that events she portrays in *Parable of the Sower* do not relegate themselves as easily to the realm of the fantastic as we might suspect. Yet we do live in a world where morality presumably reigns, and from that perspective Lauren Olamina's superstrength, both physical and mental, is not appreciably less questionable than that of her predecessors. That she is as likable as Pilate Dead in Morrison's *Song of Solomon,* or as charming as Minnie Ransom does not alter the fact that she makes choices for other characters, imposes her will subtly at times and directly at other times, kills without conscience, and has eliminated any sense of guilt from her personality. Likable or not, a series of final questions remains. Can these tangled traits in strong black female characters ever be untangled? Will there always be easily approvable features interwoven with ones that can be strongly rejected? Will such characters always be wrapped primarily in auras of external necessity that shape their interactions instead of having such interactions shaped from their internal wants, needs, desires?

Chapter 9 ~

Conclusion

Can this Mold be Broken?

Angelina woke up feeling just a little bit tired. It was always difficult managing the lives of her people. What with disentangling three sets of bad marriages, deciding on punishments for the kids who had stolen the keys to the space ship's orbiting controls, and formulating new laws for treatment of the elderly, she hadn't gotten to bed until three a.m. And without a proper dinner at that. A measly little snack of half a cow, eight loaves of bread, and a cake or two were just not enough for a two-thousand year-old, seven-foot tall, four hundred pound, strong black woman. She would have to speak to her cook about having more food available when she returned from her duties as leader of this clan of settlers. Even immortals had to eat. She needed her strength to fight off galactic invaders and to continue to have four babies a year. And she really needed to be well nourished when she returned to tackling the problem of how to realign the planets.

Obviously this little scenario did not come from any African American fictional text currently in existence. Its *probable* appearance is not farfetched, however, when we consider the path on which twentieth-century depictions of African American female character traveled. When I concocted this scenario to introduce my presentation at the "Body Politics" conference hosted by Karla F. C. Holloway at Duke University in November 1996, I had not yet seen anything comparable to what I playfully described. Imagine my surprise, therefore, when three years later I read Paula Woods's *Inner City Blues* (1999) and discovered that her protagonist twice makes references to realigning planets as descriptive of the superhuman feats black women routinely perform. The black female detective Charlotte Justice, in introducing herself to her audience and situating herself within a family context, comments: "My youngest sister, Rhodesia, the psychology student, keeps telling me I suffer from the Supersister Syndrome, while my Grandmama Cile says I'm just like every other black woman she knows—trying to keep the solar system in order by juggling the planets herself."[1] A few pages later, in referring to the man we later learn killed her husband and young daughter, Charlotte exclaims: "Getting on with my life meant I rarely discussed Cinque Lewis with anyone or acknowledged the void he'd caused in my life. I didn't discuss it on my job, didn't discuss it with my friends, and, above all, I didn't discuss it with my family. To talk about it now, after all those years of silence and evasion as if it were nothing, was inconceivable, like trying to change the planets in their orbits. Not even Supersister could pull that one off" (pp. 43–44). The reference to planets is a metaphorical limitation when she needs it to be, but a compliment when her grandmother utters it in referring to Charlotte's abilities. It is noteworthy that Charlotte's silences echo Mama Lena Younger's and other strong black women characters who find no confidants in their fictional worlds.

It is also noteworthy that Woods moves references to her character to the interplanetary realm, for that direction has certainly been hinted at with the development of many of these characters as they have progressed along a seemingly never-ending path of strength. Black female characters are so dominant in many of the works in which they appear, so morally and physically strong, so otherworldly at times, that such repeated representations raise questions about the direction in which the literature is going, the authors' conscious or inadvertent complicity in that single-mindedness, and whether change can be effected even if such change were recognized as desirable.

A literature, or a portion thereof, can be stifled or contained in many ways. It can labor under the burden of advocacy, as was the case with many of the African American literary works of the nineteenth and early twentieth centuries. Many writers were determined that their works be used to the larger good of incorporating black people into the great American democratic experiment. One of the most famous examples is Charles Waddell Chesnutt, whose diary entry for May 29, 1880 made clear his intent to use literature to advocate acceptance for black people, to lead the public on, "imperceptibly, unconsciously step by step to the desired state of feeling."[2] He vowed to "gladly devote" his life to this missionary endeavor. His artistry is apparent, but so is his advocacy. More recently, we see examples of the literature being so specifically encased in the historical, literary moment that they become timebound, as has proven true with some of the poetry of the Black Arts and Black Aesthetic movements of the 1960s. Consider the example of Don L. Lee (now known as Haki Madhubuti) and this little expression:

wallace for president
his momma for vice-president
    was scribbled
    on the men's room wall
    on
    over
    the toilet
where
it's
    supposed to be.[3]

Students reading the poem in the first decade of the twenty-first century do not have access to the immediacy of the circumstances that enabled Lee to play the dozens with a southern white racist governor; at the moment of its composition, however, Lee was thoroughly engaged with the social movements and civil rights activities of his day. While the politics of these situations might have been apparent and aboveboard, the politics that stifled the development of black female character as presented in this study were more subtle. It might even be argued that many of the writers presenting images of strong black women characters could assert that they were not adhering to any political stance, just representing black women as they imaginatively conceived them.

It is this gap between public intention and private wish that warrants the exploration here. Lorraine Hansberry would assuredly have argued that she was accurate in merely representing a certain type of black female character in her portrayal of Mama Lena Younger. The same would perhaps be true of Pearl Cleage and her portrait of Sophie Washington, as it would for most of the other writers treated here. The so-called truth of representation has overshadowed the problem of duplication and stifling. Few stopped to consider, it seems, that they were re-presenting variations of the same type, no matter how thoroughly engaging the individual portraits might be. A set of circumstances perhaps innocently set into motion nonetheless has led to a dominant pattern of development for black female character, one that has seemed to overshadow all others.

After a couple of years of working on this project, I was not optimistic that significant deviations from the pattern would ever occur. I was more inclined to believe that strong black women characters would continue to dominate the literature. They might acquire dimensions relevant to contemporary issues in African American literature—just as Cleage sets her character on the frontier with the increasing discoveries of black women's movement westward—but the basic pattern would remain. In the late 1980s and early 1990s, especially, it seemed as if the pattern on which this book focuses was so well established in African American literature that it would not soon be broken. Strong black women characters paraded in various guises, but their strength was still the primary feature. I read Shay Youngblood's *The Big Mama Stories* (1989), for example, and found—with a few twisting variations—several Mama Lena Youngers.[4] I read Michelle Parkerson's "Odds and Ends (A New Amazon Fable)" (1983), the story of a strong young black woman, Loz Wayward, fighting against hostile forces on an interplanetary outpost. Set in 2086, the story is overlaid with a lesbian theme, in that Loz has to deal with the death of her lover, Sephra, but the strength motif is still dominant.[5]

Many times in making presentations on what I initially titled "this disease called strength," I was asked to offer examples of healthy portraits of black women characters currently available in the literature, characters whose primary raison d'être is not from a strong base. The first couple of times, I had to scratch my head for a response, then I began consciously to gather a few references in anticipation of future questions. Would Alice Walker's Celie fit? She certainly does not control anyone's life in *The Color Purple* (1982), not even her own in the early stages of her existence, and she certainly does not have the kind of power of voice or action that defines strong black women characters. But is it necessary to trade strength for victimization? Would Carlene Hatcher Polite's Ideal in *The Flagellants* (1976) fit? She, like Celie, is not particularly strong physically or psychologically, but she is also not healthy; not only does she use drugs and alcohol, but she also seems to exist on a mental edge.[6] While Ideal and Celie begin to find different ways of conceptualizing themselves near the ends of the novels in which they appear, they do not serve as particularly hopeful counterparts to the strong black female characters.

Would a character such as Paule Marshall's Avey Johnson in *Praisesong for the Widow* (1983) suffice as a counterpoint to the strong black female character? She definitely undergoes a process of trying to become healthy. Her quest for self moves her from being victimized by her own desire for materialism to embracing the value of heritage and African roots. She and Celie are more balanced by the ends of their texts than is Ideal, and perhaps that is worthy of accolades. Perhaps, too, accolades should be bestowed upon Jessie Foster in Marita Golden's *and do remember me* (1992). Like Celie, she is sexually abused, but unlike Celie, her abuse occurs at two very distinct points in her life—once when she is young and repeatedly raped by her father and a second time when she is an established singer and is raped by a friend of her estranged husband. She deserves respect for surviving, but the state of her mental health remains questionable.

But where are the more recent cracks in the mold? There certainly is no single line of them, but perhaps there are tiny fissures here and there and perhaps in places we have not previously considered. For example, do we need to turn to popular fiction to find black female characters who are self-sufficient without diminishing anyone else, who are secure in their own identities, who are sexual and spiritual beings who appear to continue to live in this world instead of escaping into immortality or purgatory? There are such portraits, including characters in Connie Briscoe's *Sister and Lovers* (1994) and *Big Girls Don't Cry* (1996), as well as those in Terry McMillan's *Waiting to Exhale* (1991) and *How Stella Got Her Groove Back* (1996). But is popular fiction a new kind of fantasy, a new kind of escapism from the realities of black women's lives? Few black women live in the exorbitant manners in which McMillan's characters exist, although some of Briscoe's probably intersect more realistically. Yet these are not the works frequently taught in African American literature courses in American colleges and universities. Planners of such courses continue to look for the portraits in works identified with the accepted *belles lettres* tradition.

Recent works by authors recognized in that tradition, however, showcase women characters who may not be exclusively strong, but their health is questionable. Consider, for example, Toni Morrison's *Paradise* (1998), a novel in which black women characters, among others, have their strengths and their limitations. The characters here are closer in conception to Pauline Breedlove and Mrs. MacTeer than to Sethe and Baby Suggs, closer to Hannah Peace than to Eva Peace. They suffer loss, as Mavis does with the deaths of her toddler twins, and they stumble and err much more than the likes of Mama Lena Younger. All of their domestic situations have been ones from which they sought escape. The haven they find in the Convent, with its history of drugs and religious imperialism, is a tainted domestic space. Their "leader," Connie, has made a serious error in judgment by engaging in an affair with one of the powerful Morgan twins. In other words, these women are not in control of very much at all, even though they have a space that is presumably theirs. Their social and mental problems place them more in need of psychiatrists than capable of managing themselves or others. Combinations of determination and faltering, they are more complexly portrayed than some of the women characters treated in this study, though Connie presumably has extranatural healing skills, among others. The aura of the novel is finally otherworldly, but the lives the characters have led prior to their arrival at the Convent have been rather mundane.

One of the latest takes on the strong black woman character is Gayl Jones's *The Healing* (1998). It intersects with the otherworldliness of Toni Cade Bambara's, Gloria Naylor's, and J. California Cooper's novels, but retains the dimension of sexuality found in Octavia Butler's *Parable of the Sower* and Parkerson's "Odds and Ends (A New Amazon Fable)." Harlan Jane Eagleton, Jones's central character, is a drifting faith healer who has acquired her power through suspect circumstances. Caught in the act of having sex with the ex-husband of Joan Savage, the rock star she manages, Harlan later learns that her employer did not consider the state of things as "ex" as Harlan thought. When Joan eventually stabs Harlan in the chest, the knife miraculously bends and the wound heals immediately. The one observer (who becomes the testifying witness preceding all of Harlan's future healings) concludes that Harlan heals herself, which he considers her prelude to healing others. Harlan's gift, like Minnie Ransom's, derives from the mysterious forces of the universe. She has the ability to simply touch—lay hands on—people, and their physical and psychological problems are solved. Her cures range from the relatively minor (sinus problems) to the major (insanity). Harlan treats her gift lightly, and she has no entourage surrounding her as Minnie Ransom does. She travels by bus from one small "tank" town to another and tries to keep her activities as inconspicuous as possible. In her casual dress (she wears bomber jackets and blue jeans) and attitudes, she is curiously detached from the very miracles she effects. Perhaps her sexuality somehow makes that gift appear mundane, for a healer who at a point in her life casually picked up men at race tracks and who betted religiously on horses is somehow seemingly more in the world than separated from it.

While that apparent immersion in sexuality separates Harlan from most other strong black women characters, her ability to heal puts her squarely back in the paradigm of extranatural characteristics that define so many of her literary sisters. Yet Jones is able to imbue Harlan with moments of vulnerability that other strong women characters do not experience. For example, Harlan is nervous and suspicious when Joan uncovers her sexual involvement with Jamey, Joan's ex-husband. She is almost afraid of what Joan will do. There are other moments when Harlan appears shy or uncertain about how to proceed in a given situation. This is especially true in her dealings with the African German horse buyer, Josef Ehelich von Fremd, whom she picks up at a race track. She becomes his lover for a summer, which makes her vulnerable to his suspicions about her being a spy for other horse dealers. In interacting with him and his bodyguards, she places herself in a precarious situation, one in which she is obviously not in control. This potential for physical or psychological harm is alien to most strong black women characters and thus expands Harlan's character even as it intersects with the common elements in previous characters. By giving her a realm beyond her own domestic space in which to operate, Jones enables Harlan to move into arenas not usually allowed many other strong black women characters.[7]

In considering how the portrayal of strong black women characters in African American literature is evolving or where it is going, therefore, it is clear that African American writers—male and female, but especially female—are *not* willing to give up the type. They may place her in a detective role in the midst of gunfire in south central Los Angeles, or in a race war in an intergalactic realm, but they basically love what the characters give to the literature. And what, exactly, do they give to the literature? They suggest that the worlds—fictional and historical—in which black women live and operate do not ultimately subdue them. The bodies that were contained by slavery, segregation, popular media, and public opinion cannot finally be contained by black squiggles on white pages. In spite of the troubled history surrounding the portrayal of strong black women characters and in spite of the toe stubbing in the literature, the writers apparently prefer the possibility inherent in portraying such characters. Even with their limitations, strong black women characters are preferable to characters like Frankie Mae in Jean Wheeler Smith's short story, "Frankie Mae,"[8] or to Pecola Breedlove in Toni Morrison's *The Bluest Eye,* or to Adrienne Kennedy's Sarah in *Funnyhouse of a Negro,*[9] all of whom are characters beaten down by the circumstances of their lives. Perhaps strength, with all its ambiguous dimensions, remains a metaphor for the possibility of autonomy, the possibility of a literature and a people writing and working against the odds to overcome those odds—if not on earth, then, as Lauren Olamina asserts, perhaps among the stars. The question, finally, is not so much "*Can* this mold be broken?" as "Do the writers want to break this mold?" The answer to the latter question is an emphatic "No."

Notes

Chapter 1

1. My generalities refer to stereotypical patterns in represented images of black women. There are certainly alternative, though not as prominent, images of black women in popular culture as well as in literature.

   I recognize problems inherent in categorizing women as "large" or "fat." A woman who wears a dress size 12 or 14 in one culture may be perceived as large or fat, whereas she may be perceived as skinny or at least slender in another. Since I am dealing primarily with black and white conceptions of size in the United States, I would posit that a white woman who wears a size 14 or 16 is generally considered fat whereas a black woman may not be labeled as such until her dress size reaches 22 or 24. Please keep in mind that large size as I will later use it to refer to some African American women does not mean that the women are perceived as unattractive.

   Keep in mind as well generational consideration in terms of size among black women. Primarily as a result of education and upward mobility, many African American women under 30 are often just as conscious about containing their size through diet and exercise as are their European American counterparts.

2. Such depictions occur in autobiography and fiction. For representative examples, see Frederick Douglass's account of the whipping his Aunt Harriet receives in *Narrative of the Life of Frederick Douglass* (1845) and Margaret Walker's account of Lucy and Vyry being whipped in *Jubilee* (1966). For a theoretical discussion of black women's bodies during slavery, see Hortense J. Spillers' 1987 essay, "Mama's Baby, Papa's Maybe: An American Grammar Book," in *Within the Circle: An Anthology of African American Literary Criticism from the Harlem Renaissance to the Present*, ed. Angelyn Mitchell (Durham: Duke University Press, 1994), pp. 454–481.

3. Saidiya Hartman, "Seduction and the Ruses of Power." Special Issue—Emerging Women Writers, *Callaloo* 19:2 (Spring 1996): 537–560.

4. For a discussion of these images in selected European American literary texts published by women writers of the nineteenth and twentieth centuries, see Diane Roberts's *The Myth of Aunt Jemima: Representations of Race and Region* (London and New York: Routledge, 1994).

5. See M. M. Manring, *Slave in a Box: The Strange Career of Aunt Jemima* (Charlottesville: University of Virginia Press, 1998); Marilyn Kern-Foxworth, *Aunt Jemima, Uncle Ben, and Rastus* (Westport, Conn.: Greenwood Press, 1994); Roberts, *The Myth of Aunt Jemima: Representations of Race and Region;* and Patricia A. Turner, *Ceramic Uncles & Celluloid Mammies: Black Images and Their Influence on Culture* (New York: Anchor Books, 1994).

6. Lisa M. Anderson mentions this pattern in *Mammies No More: The Changing Image of Black Women on Stage and Screen* (Lanham, MD: Rowman & Littlefield, 1994), p. 6. See Donald Bogle, *Toms, Coons, Mulattoes, Mammies, and Bucks: An Interpretive History of Blacks in American Films* (rev. ed. New York: Continuum, 1994), p. 11 for a still shot of the mammy from *Birth of a Nation*. Anderson includes the same still shot following p. 86.

7. Distributed by California Newsreel, 149 Ninth Street/420, San Francisco, CA 94103.

8. One of the ironies of the contrasts in *Cabin in the Sky* is that sleek, beautiful Lena Horne plays opposite Ethel Waters, who by this time is the stereotypically large, spiritual singing, matronly black woman. Photographs of Waters from the 1920s reveal her as the sleek, beautiful, *thin,* black woman. This is perhaps another indication of the comforting girth into which black women grow and the perceived "rightness" of that size in particular for casting in certain visual roles. Horne, as the jezebel, fits into another stereotype of black women.

9. Compare the transformed images in Kern-Foxworth, photo essay following chapter 4. See also the images in Phil Patton's "Mammy: Her Life and Times," *American Heritage* (September 1993): 78–87.

10. For a discussion of this phenomenon, where the emphasis is obviously on European American women, see Kim Chernin, *The Obsession: Reflections on the Tyranny of Slenderness* (1981; New York: HarperPerennial, 1994).

11. Donald Bogle asserts that, although Hattie McDaniel (who played the mammy role in *Gone With the Wind*) "weighed close to three hundred pounds" (p. 83), Louise Beavers (who starred in several movies, including *Imitation of Life*), had to overeat substantially to maintain the required large size in the roles she played. "She was heavy and hearty," Bogle writes, "but not heavy and hearty enough. Thereafter [after she was relegated to the role of cook instead of mammy in her debut appearance in *Uncle Tom's Cabin*] she went on force-feed diets, compelling herself to eat beyond her normal appetite. Generally, she weighed close to two hundred pounds, but it was a steady battle for her to stay overweight. During filming, due to pressures, she often lost weight and then had to be padded to look more like a full-bosomed domestic who was capable of carrying the world on her shoulders" (p. 63).

12. Although Hansberry had a hand in the casting for this role, I would maintain that my argument still holds. As Ossie Davis points out, McNeil in the role of Mama Lena became everybody's "great American Mama." In her emphasis on the type in American culture, Hansberry was surely aware of the

comforting implications of such casting. See Davis's "The Significance of Lorraine Hansberry," *Freedomways* 5:3 (1965): 399.

13. Donald Bogle heads the caption for a still of Ethel Waters in *Pinky* (1949) with "Black shoulders were made to cry on," as he pictures her with the young, white Jeanne Crain leaning against her; Crain apparently "learns" the lesson well. Bogle may as well have asserted, "Black female bosoms were made to cry on." See *Toms, Coons, Mulattoes, Mammies, and Bucks,* p. 153. Another still—of an older Waters comforting an even younger white person in *The Member of the Wedding* (1952)—appears on p. 163 in Bogle.

14. See, for example, Herbert Aptheker's *American Negro Slave Revolts* (New York: Columbia University Press, 1943) and Gary Y. Okihiro, ed., *In Resistance: Studies in African, Caribbean, and Afro-American History* (Amherst: University of Massachusetts Press, 1943).

15. Toni Morrison represents this phenomenon in *Jazz* (New York: Knopf, 1992), where hips become *the* site for desire. However, there is a generational gap here as some African American men prefer smaller hips. I thank Lovalerie King of the University of Massachusetts, Boston, for pointing out Eddie Murphy's condemnation of "large asses" in *The Nutty Professor* and the revelation during O. J. Simpson's trial of Simpson's "disdain" for his wife Nicole's "nigger butt" during her pregnancy.

16. The best visual representation I have seen of this phenomenon is in the movie *Soul Food* (1997), in the scene in which Vanessa L. Williams and her screen sisters engage in a love affair with the preparation of a Sunday dinner—in memory of the deceased strong mother/grandmother of the family (who ironically died from diabetes probably induced by these very foods).

17. I made this discovery in 1995, when I was in the process of locating a hotel for my own family reunion, which was held in July.

18. This is another point at which it is important to point out that, in the 1990s, some younger black women preferred skinny legs. Of historical note is the fact that in various black communities throughout the country night clubs held "big leg" contests for black women—well into the 1960s.

19. This pattern influences the literature in several works. There is "Big Sweet," whose adeptness with a knife protects Zora Neale Hurston in *Mules and Men* (1935—the character also appears in other Hurston works) and "Big Laura," in Ernest Gaines's *The Autobiography of Miss Jane Pittman* (1971). Shay Youngblood entitles her 1989 collection *The Big Mama Stories.* Two contemporary film presentations of the powerful Big Mama are *Soul Food* (1997), in which Vanessa L. Williams plays an important part, and *Nothing to Lose* (1997), in which Martin Lawrence and Tim Robbins encounter the wrath of Lawrence's on-screen mother, who admonishes him for coming in late because it sets a bad example for his children, who are more importantly *her* grandchildren. When he tries to talk back, she slaps him, then slaps the Robbins character when he butts in to offer further explanation. This is perhaps one of the few times that a character resembling a screen mammy, here played by Irma P. Hall, could get away with slapping a white character.

20. Toni Morrison, "What the Black Woman Thinks about Women's Lib," *New York Times Magazine,* August 22, 1971, 63.

21. In the article I published on this topic in 1995, I identify several characters and works that fit into the paradigm outlined in the preceding few paragraphs. They include, in earlier, less developed manifestations, Elizabeth Grimes in James Baldwin's *Go Tell It on the Mountain* (New York: Dial, 1953) and Mary Rambo in Ralph Ellison's *Invisible Man* (New York: Vintage, 1952). An early strict manifestation of the type is Aunt Hagar Williams in Langston Hughes's *Not Without Laughter* (New York: A. A. Knopf, 1930; rpt. Collier Macmillan, 1969). Other characters who fit the paradigm are Hansberry's Mama Lena Younger and Morrison's Sethe Suggs, who will be treated in later chapters, Morrison's Eva Peace in *Sula* (New York: Knopf, 1974) and Mrs. MacTeer in *The Bluest Eye* (New York: Holt, Rinehart, and Winston, 1970), Ernest Gaines's Octavia in "The Sky is Gray" in *Bloodline* (New York: Dial, 1968), and several of Gloria Naylor's characters, including Mattie Michael in *The Women of Brewster Place* and the women in *Bailey's Café* (New York: Harcourt Brace Jovanovich, 1992). "The Sky is Gray" is particularly insightful in showing the impact of the unemotional, uncommunicative strong black female character on an offspring. Octavia beats her *eight-year-old* son James into killing redbirds for a family dinner without explaining to him the necessity for such action, and she refuses to allow him to express affection for her by hugging her or saying, "I love you," because "that's crybaby stuff," and he is a "man." Morrison's *Song of Solomon* is equally powerful in showing the consequences to offspring of the strong black female character. Pilate Dead may be admirable for her strength and knife-wielding abilities, but she ultimately cannot—and does not show any inclination to—pass on her survival skills to her feeble-minded daughter or her misguided granddaughter. See my "This Disease Called Strength: Some Observations on the Compensating Construction of Black Female Character," *Literature and Medicine* 14 (Spring 1995): 109–126.

22. Toni Cade Bambara, *The Salt Eaters* (New York: Vintage, 1980); and Gloria Naylor, *Mama Day* (New York: Ticknor and Fields, 1988).

23. Tina McElroy Ansa, "Mudear," *Ugly Ways* (New York: Harcourt Brace and Company, 1993). In *Baby of the Family* (New York: Harcourt Brace Jovanovich, 1989), her first novel, Ansa introduces us to Lena, who is privileged to commune with the dead because she has been born with a caul, that is, her birth sac, over her face. Though younger than the other women, Lena nonetheless reflects the mythical, though she has not used her otherworldly strength to the detriment of others.

24. Alice Walker, *The Temple of My Familiar* (New York: Harcourt Brace Jovanovich, 1983).

25. J. California Cooper, *Family* (New York: Doubleday, 1991).

26. See, for example, James Baldwin's *The Amen Corner* (New York: Dial Press, 1968).

27. This visual history is traceable in images of black women in film, sketches, and photographs, in late-nineteenth-century popular magazines (such as

Ladies Home Journal, The Saturday Evening Post, and *Good Housekeeping*), on television (especially in the 1970s and 1980s), and on the stage. For discussions of representational images of black women in these various media, see Roberts, *The Myth of Aunt Jemima;* Manring, *Slave in a Box;* Kern-Foxworth, *Aunt Jemima, Uncle Ben, and Rastus;* Turner, *Ceramic Uncles & Celluloid Mammies;* Anderson, *Mammies No More;* and Bogle, *Toms, Coons, Mulattoes, Mammies, and Bucks.* See also *Birth of a Nation* and the video documentary, *Ethnic Notions.*

28. In "This Disease Called Strength," I identify the biographies of Zora Neale Hurston and Richard Wright as having direct influences upon their creations of strong black women. In *Black Boy* (1945), Wright recounts how his mother would not let him into the house when boys in their neighborhood took the family's grocery money from him. He paints his mother as being unsympathetic to his plight, generally unemotional, and so strong that she could whip him into a fever without it having any impact upon her. Wright paints black women characters such as Mrs. Thomas in *Native Son* (1940) and Sarah in "Long Black Song" as being in league with whites who keep black men in their place. In *Dust Tracks on a Road* (1942), Hurston recounts how she was so insulted by her stepmother's alienation of her father's affection from his children that she beat the woman unmercifully. In that epic battle, Hurston depicts herself as having almost superhuman physical, emotional, and moral strength. She was still unrepentant about her act many years later. In several of her fictional and cultural works, the character Big Sweet appears as the quintessential strong black woman with an impressive knife-wielding ability. Maya Angelou approximates Wright's depiction of his mother in her representation of Momma Henderson in *I Know Why the Caged Bird Sings* (1970). In one instance, Momma Henderson whips Maya for saying "by the way," because, to her mind, it is blasphemous; it parodies the biblical teaching that Jesus is "the way, the truth, and the life."

29. Alice Childress has drawn upon this mythical relationship in her play, *Wine in the Wilderness,* where a black man wants to paint a triptych of black women, one of whom will be "Mother Africa, regal, black womanhood in her noblest form," an "African queen" (9). Shirley Williams draws upon this relationship in a negative way when she has a black man seduce and financially abuse a black woman in "Tell Martha Not to Moan" by calling her his "Black queen."

30. Alice Walker, "Everyday Use," in *In Love and Trouble: Stories of Black Women* (New York: Harcourt Brace Jovanovich, 1973). Subsequent references are to this edition and will be cited in the text.

31. Nickolas Ashford and Valarie Simpson, "I'm Every Woman," *The Bodyguard Original Soundtrack Album* (New York: Arista Records, Inc., 1992).

32. Maya Angelou, *And Still I Rise* (New York: Bantam, 1978).

33. Nikki Giovanni, "Ego Tripping," in *The Women and the Men: Poems* (New York: Morrow, 1975).

34. In ascribing goddess-like qualities to her persona, Giovanni anticipates literary characters in the 1980s and 1990s who routinely exceed the bounds of human limitations.

35. Zora Neale Hurston, *Their Eyes Were Watching God* (1937; New York: Harper & Row, 1990), pp. 140–41.

36. Alice Walker, *The Color Purple* (New York: Harcourt Brace Jovanovich, 1982), p. 44.

37. Lisa M. Anderson makes passing reference to this phenomenon in *Mammies No More*, p. 41, but it is implicit in numerous discussions of the era. Michele Wallace discusses it in great detail in *Black Macho and the Myth of the Superwoman* (New York: Warner, 1978).

38. Ruby Sanders, "HUSH, HONEY." Unpublished manuscript provided in 2001.

39. Alice Walker, "Women," in *Her Blue Body Everything We Know: Earthling Poems 1965–1990 Complete* (Harcourt Brace Jovanovich, 1991), pp. 159–160.

40. Octavia Butler, *Wild Seed* (Garden City, N.Y.: Doubleday, 1980).

41. See Spillers, "Mama's Baby, Papa's Maybe: An American Grammar Book," in Mitchell, pp. 454–81.

42. For a discussion of the dozens, see Roger Abrahams, *Deep Down in the Jungle: Negro Narrative Folklore from the Streets of Philadelphia* (Chicago: Aldine, 1970); John Dollard, "The Dozens: Dialectic of Insult," in Alan Dundes, *Mother Wit from the Laughing Barrel: Readings in the Interpretation of Afro-American Folklore* (rev. ed. Jackson: University of Mississippi Press, 1991), pp. 277–294; and Abrahams, "Playing the Dozens," in Dundes, pp. 295–309.

43. Daniel Patrick Moynihan's "The Negro Family: The Case for National Action" (Washington, D.C.: U.S. Department of Labor, 1965), in which he argued that the central problem in African American families was matriarchal, emasculating black women, created quite a stir when it appeared, especially in its implications for public policy. Michele Wallace's *Black Macho and the Myth of the Superwoman* (1978) was also controversial in its exploration of strong black women, particularly in their political and interracial relationships, as well as in their romantic relationships (or lack thereof) with black men. Many of the women I treat do not have the public power traditionally expected of matriarchs, and only one of them is sexually active.

Chapter 2

1. I selected the word "tyrant" to describe Mama Lena before I discovered that Hansberry also uses the term to refer to her. In focusing on Mama Lena's absolute control of her household, neither of us intends the despotic or evil connotations frequently associated with this word. I especially want to emphasize that Mama Lena's role and position within her family can rarely—if ever—be challenged.

2. "Lorraine Hansberry," *Dictionary of Literary Biography*, 38 (Detroit: Gale Research Company, 1985), p. 127. Carter also considers the play "less a work of protest than a celebration of the multigenerational black struggle for progress" (126) and notes Hansberry's "emphasis on black social conditions, black strength, black struggle, and Pan-Africanism."

3. James Baldwin, "Introduction," in *To Be Young, Gifted and Black,* ed. Robert Nemiroff (New York: Signet, 1969), pp. xii-xiii.

4. The play boasted the first black director, Lloyd Richards, on Broadway, the first starring role for Sidney Poitier, the first success for its producers, and, most important, the first play to reach Broadway by a black woman playwright. *Raisin* won the New York Drama Critics Circle award for Best Play of the Year in 1959, thereby making Hansberry the youngest American, the first African American, and the first woman to win the award.

5. "Thoughts on 'A Raisin in the Sun'," *Commentary* (June 1959): 529.

6. "Ireland and Points West," *New Yorker* 35 (21 March 1959): 101.

7. "*A Raisin in the Sun*," *New Republic,* 13 April 1959, p. 21. For other contemporary reviews, see Nan Robertson, "Dramatist Against Odds," *New York Times,* 8 March 1959, p. X3; Brooks Atkinson, "The Theatre: 'A Raisin in the Sun,'" *New York Times,* 12 March 1959, p. L27; Harold Clurman, "Theatre," *The Nation,* 4 April 1959, pp. 301–302; Henry Hewes, "A Plant Grows in Chicago," *Saturday Review,* 4 April 1959, p. 28; and Max Lerner, "A Dream Deferred," *New York Post,* 5 April 1959, p. xx.

8. Ossie Davis, "The Significance of Lorraine Hansberry," *Freedomways* 5:3 (1965): 399, 400.

9. Quoted in Steven R. Carter, *Hansberry's Drama: Commitment amid Complexity* (Urbana and Chicago: University of Illinois Press, 1991), pp. 52–53.

10. Quoted in Carter, *Hansberry's Drama,* p. 53.

11. Doris E. Abramson, *Negro Playwrights in the American Theatre 1925–1959* (New York and London: Columbia University Press, 1969), p. 254. Less generous in his assessment of characters and play is Harold Cruse, who dubbed *Raisin* a "glorified soap opera" in which Hansberry forcibly ascribes middle-class values to a lower-working-class family to make them acceptable as integrationists. See *The Crisis of the Negro Intellectual* (New York: Morrow, 1967), pp. 267–284.

12. "*A Raisin in the Sun* Revisited," *Black American Literature Forum* 22:1 (Spring 1988): 110–111.

13. "The Sighted Eyes and Feeling Heart of Lorraine Hansberry," *Black American Literature Forum* 17:1 (Spring 1983): 10.

14. Mama Lena's deceased husband is occasionally referred to as "Big Walter," a distinction designed to separate him from "little" Walter Lee and not necessarily one that designates authority in relation to his wife or other family members.

15. "The Mama" designation is also visible in Mama Lena insinuating herself into a motherly role to Asagai. She immediately assumes that, with him being so far away from home, he needs a nurturing surrogate mother's love:

"I bet you don't half look after yourself, being away from your mama either. I spec you better come 'round here from time to time and get yourself some decent homecooked meals . . ." (52). Historical mamas are noted for playing this role, but even Mama Lena lays it on thick for a first encounter with Asagai.

16. Other members of the cast appearing on stage and in the film included Sidney Poitier (Walter Lee), Diana Sands (Beneatha), Ruby Dee (Ruth), Glynn Turman (Travis), Louis Gossett (George Murchison), and Ivan Dixon (Asagai). Although Hansberry wrote two screenplays and new and substantially different scenes for the film, none of the new material was used. Carter points out that the film "was basically a shortened version of the play." Still, "the final product was good enough to earn a nomination for Best Screenplay of the Year from the Screenwriters Guild and a Special award at the Cannes Film Festival, both in 1961" ("Hansberry," p. 128). A second film version of the play, produced for television in 1989, featured Esther Rolle as Mama Lena Younger and Danny Glover as Walter Lee Younger; other cast members included Kim Yancy (Beneatha), Starletta DuPois (Ruth), and Kimble Joyner (Travis). The play was also transformed into a musical, *Raisin,* that appeared on Broadway in 1973 and has had many reprisals since then.

17. Lorraine Hansberry, *A Raisin in the Sun* (New York: Signet, 1966), p. 27, my emphasis. Notice that, although Hansberry emphasizes Mama Lena's beauty as much as she does her strength (in the sentences quoted and those immediately following), Mama Lena's beauty is never a factor in the play, while her physical and moral strength undergird most of the action.

18. "*A Raisin in the Sun* Revisited," 111.

19. Ferguson argues that Mama Lena's violence should "lead to an examination of African American views on corporal punishment—where such practice is not viewed as abusive and tyrannical but corrective and loving. It's in the Christian tradition of violence as redemption. (Jesus hangs to save mankind.) Ruth uses the threat of a beating to keep Travis in line, too." Personal communication to the author, January 1997. From a different perspective than my own, therefore, Ferguson's comment connects nicely to the Christian basis for the actions of strong black women characters.

20. While it could be argued that the parent/child dynamic is reflective of 1950s historical black reality, in which children were expected to be "seen and not heard," that argument is flawed by the fact that, though she may treat them otherwise, both of Mama Lena's "children" are biologically—if not emotionally or economically—adults.

21. As many scholars have noted, Beneatha's very name places her in a lesser position, "beneath her," to Mama Lena.

22. In Raymond Andrews' *Rosiebelle Lee Wildcat Tennessee* (Athens: University of Georgia Press, 1980), the title character earns the appellation "the Momma" because of a comparable ability to meddle in everybody's business even as she cares for and nurtures them.

23. When Travis balks at going next door to borrow cleanser from a neighbor, for example, Mama Lena simply responds: "Do as you told" (53), which might be an acceptable directive to a child, but she treats the adults in her household the same way. When Ruth rises too soon from resting because of her pregnancy, Mama Lena asserts: "Who told you to get up" (54).

24. Particularly informative in this context are Sidney Poitier's comments on his discussions with Hansberry and Lloyd Richards about how the Walter Lee character should be played. Claudia McNeil was so strong as Mama, Poitier asserted, that unless the Walter Lee character were allowed to play directly against her, the play ran the risk of making "a negative comment on the black male"—presumably because he would appear weak. Poitier argued—and lost—that the play should unfold from Walter Lee's point of view, not Mama's. See Poitier, *This Life* (New York: Alfred A Knopf, 1980), Chapter 17, "A Raisin in the Sun."

25. Ruth might not object overly much to Lena's actions because she has precious few other models for considering mature black womanhood. Remember that she threatens to beat Travis on a couple of occasions, an indication that she has perhaps been inadvertently influenced by Mama Lena. Keep in mind as well that she calls Mama Lena "Lena" or "Miss Lena." Is this an effort to identify, a desire to emulate—even though such aspirations might seem beyond the character traits we see in her?

26. Octavia beats her son James; however, Eva Peace burns her son Plum to death when he develops a drug habit from which he does not seem to be able to extricate himself.

27. Walter Lee even refers to himself at one point as "Walter Lee"—on the occasion when he is trying to persuade Ruth to present his case for the liquor store to Mama Lena (21); thus he is picturing himself in the role of the little boy seeking approval from a parent.

28. Comparison to Eva Peace in Toni Morrison's *Sula* (1974) comes immediately to mind, for Eva, in the role of strong black woman, creates reality through the assigning of names to "Tar Baby" (a white man) as well as to the three "Deweys" (three distinctly different boys she adopts and to whom she gives the same name).

29. Carter, in *Hansberry's Drama,* offers a position directly opposite to my own. He asserts that Walter Lee, by using black folk speech to present the family's position to Lindner, is impressively militant: " . . . In context, Walter is saying that he refuses to be bought off, that he knows he is preparing to do something that will anger a lot of whites, and that how he acts in the future will depend on how the whites act. If they agree to be friendly, so will he; if they want to fight, so will he, and they will have the responsibility for any blood shed then.) Walter's way of speaking in this moment is as much an act of defiance as what he says because Lindner has told him that he and the other whites in Clybourne Park want a neighborhood in which everyone talks and acts the same way" (p. 28).

30. Abramson briefly points out other comparisons to *Native Son;* see *Negro Playwrights,* p. 242.

31. J. Charles Washington asserts that "Lena Younger gives manual labor a kind of mythical, almost Biblical meaning: As Jesus gave his life for man, Big Walter gave his life for her and his family. In other words, work itself, as well as the sacrifice of the worker, is given a higher meaning than the financial and material rewards it was intended to bring." "*A Raisin in the Sun* Revisited," 116.

32. A flaw in the play is the uncertainty about how much time has elapsed since Big Walter's death. The family seems ensconced and comfortable in its current relational and sleeping arrangements. Where, for example, did Beneatha sleep before Big Walter died, since she is now in his place in bed with Mama Lena? Did Travis sleep in the room with his parents before Big Walter's death and Beneatha on the couch? How long did it take for the insurance check to be processed? Except for Mama Lena's acute memories of Big Walter at the moment of receiving the check, the family's grieving for its patriarch seems to be over. Clarity about these issues would enable more accurate interpretations of the impact of Mama Lena's sole influence on her family (e.g., how long she shaped Walter Lee by herself as opposed to raising him *with* Big Walter) as well as her obvious lack of interest in men.

Chapter 3

1. See, for example, Ishmael Reed, *Flight to Canada* (New York: Random House, 1976); Sherley Anne Williams, *Dessa Rose* (New York: W. Morrow, 1986); J. California Cooper, *Family* (New York: Doubleday, 1991); Charles Johnson, *Oxherding Tale* (Bloomington: Indiana University Press, 1982) and *Middle Passage* (New York: Atheneum, 1990); Toni Morrison, *Beloved* (New York: Knopf, 1987).

2. Addison Gayle specifically labels Mammy Barracuda a "man eater" in relation to black males in developing his argument that Reed is too intent on trying to prove collusion between black women and white men. See Gayle, "Black Women and Black Men: The Literature of Catharsis," *Black Books Bulletin* 4 (1976): 49.

3. Gayle discusses Mammy Barracuda in his review of the novel, but it is surprising in critical treatments of *Flight to Canada* and of Reed's work in general that so few critics offer commentary on Mammy Barracuda. Reginald Martin does not mention her in his book-length study, *Ishmael Reed and the New Black Aesthetic Critics* (New York: St. Martin's Press, 1988), and Joyce A. Joyce only alludes to criticism of Reed's portrayal of black women in "Falling Through the Minefield of Black Feminist Criticism: Ishmael Reed, A Case in Point," in her *Warriors, Conjurers and Priests: Defining African-centered Literary Criticism* (Chicago: Third World Press, 1994). While Mammy Barracuda loomed large for Reed, she is mostly invisible in criticism about his work. The absence is especially noteworthy in articles devoted exclusively to *Flight to Canada,* such as Ashraf H. A. Rushdy's "Ishmael Reed's Neo-

HooDoo Slave Narrative," *Narrative* 2:2 (May 1994): 112–39, and Joseph C. Schopp's "'Riding Bareback, Backwards Through a Wood of Words': Ishmael Reed's Revision of the Slave Narrative," in *Historiographic Metafiction in Modern American and Canadian Literature,* ed. Bernd Engler and Kurt Muller (Paderborn: Ferdinand Schoningh, 1994), pp. 267–278.

4. Reed, *Flight to Canada,* p. 57. Subsequent references to the novel are taken from this edition and will be cited in parentheses in the text.

5. Implied or actual catechisms in which white masters try to instill a master text into enslaved blacks appear in various African American literary works. William Wells Brown's *Clotel; Or, the President's Daughter* (1853; New York: Collier, 1972) is perhaps the earliest one, but the pattern also appears in Toni Morrison's *Beloved* (New York: Knopf, 1987) in exchanges between Baby Suggs and Mr. Garner as well as between Sixo and schoolteacher. Again using reversal as a primary textual strategy, Reed incorporates the form of the genre into a modified call and response formula in which Mammy Barracuda reifies black power—sanctioned by whites—over other blacks.

6. By contrast, that mask-wearing trait is a staple of Uncle Robin's character. When Massa Swille calls upon him to testify to his satisfaction as an enslaved person, he says, "Canada. I do admit I have heard about the place from time to time, Mr. Swille, but I loves it here so much that . . . that I would never think of leaving here. These rolling hills. Mammy singing spirituals in the morning before them good old biscuits" (19—ellipses in original)—even as he is slowly poisoning Swille and altering Swille's will to his own gain. Given her tendency to sing "Dixie," it seems an egregiously incongruous mix to have Mammy Barracuda sing spirituals as well. Some spirituals imply support for the status quo, but others advocate battle in this world rather than longing for heaven. For development of this latter argument, see John W. Roberts, *From Trickster to Badman: The Black Folk Hero in Slavery and Freedom* (Philadelphia: University of Pennsylvania Press, 1989).

7. As an illustration of her class consciousness, consider this passage: "Massa Swille, there's some poor-white trash down in the kitchen walking on my kitchen flo. I told them to get out my kitchen and smacked one of them on the ear with my broom" (38).

8. Sondra A. O'Neale shares this evaluation when she asserts that "Reed's own whipping post is the black woman and the persistent theme of his personal philosophy that she joins the white power structure to castigate the black man. But Reed has never created a character so purposed to have his audience join his disdain than the demonic Mammy Barracuda." See "Ishmael Reed's Fitful Flight to Canada: Liberation for Some, Good Reading for All," *Callaloo* 1:4 (October 1978): 177. In reviewing the novel, Gayle comments on this historical perception and asserts: "This is not history, but anti-history, a grotesque distortion to be sure; yet, the theme of collusion, though minus the power implications suggested by Reed, is one in which a great many Black males believe. Such collusions, if such they are, more often than not, are unconscious and designed to serve noble ends. Certainly, those

thousands of mothers, like Wright's mother in *Black Boy,* who punish and abuse their sons for standing their ground against whites, are seeking to save their children, not to affect an alliance with white men. Likewise, those female writers—Lorraine Hansberry and Alice Walker are examples—who in their works, depict Black males as helpless victims, overwhelmed by an all-powerful male dominated white society, are not guilty of collusion—in the sense that Reed suggests" (p. 49). Nonetheless, Gayle concludes that forces are at work generally in the society "to keep Black men in their places." Gayle's comments should perhaps be read in the context of his extreme ideological differences with Reed.

9. O'Neale explicitly posits sexual relations between the two by asserting that "Mammy Barracuda is solely submissive to her master-lover white Swille." O'Neale is also explicit in assigning a lesbian component to Mammy Barracuda's character and comparing her to other of Reed's black heroines. See "Ishmael Reed's Fitful Flight to Canada," 177.

10. Her jewelry is another instance of the status she holds with Arthur Swille, for he has apparently bought several pieces for her. On one occasion when he is particularly enamored of an apple pie she has made, he says: "Pompey . . . go and have them order Mammy Barracuda a ruby ring from Cartier's" (130).

11. In commenting briefly on Mammy Barracuda's diamond crucifix, Hortense J. Spillers remarks that Mammy Barracuda, "in her brilliant captivity, embodies an entirely oxymoronic notion—at the crossroads of wealth and exchange, she is a major player, though not a beneficiary. Wearing wealth's symptoms on her magnanimous bosom and around her neck, she is made to throw a reflection that *shatters* the sight, instead of *healing* it." Spillers, "Changing the Letter: The Yokes, the Jokes of Discourse, or, Mrs. Stowe, Mr. Reed," in *Slavery and the Literary Imagination,* ed. Deborah E. McDowell and Arnold Rampersad (Baltimore, MD: The Johns Hopkins University Press, 1989), p. 31.

12. The notion of Etheric Double is evoked to describe the relationships Ms. Swille and her incestuous sister-in-law Vivian have to Arthur Swille.

13. See, for example, Catherine Clinton, *The Plantation Mistress: Woman's World in the Old South* (New York: Pantheon, 1982).

14. To illustrate the extent to which Mammy Barracuda far exceeds permissible limits, consider, by comparison, William Faulkner's "A Rose for Emily," in which the townspeople ponder tragically long on what to do about Miss Emily because they cannot "accuse a lady to her face of smelling bad." See *Studies in Fiction,* ed. Blaze O. Bonazza and Emil Roy (New York: Harper and Row, 1965), p. 65.

15. In the Neo-HooDoo philosophy he has developed, Reed finds major problems with Christianity. However, he does use it to suggest acquiescence to the status quo. Cato explains to Swille that, by forcing enslaved blacks to follow "only the Jesus cult," the women have become particularly docile: "The women especially be thrilled with the Jesus cult. They don't ask no questions any more. They's accepted their lot" (53).

Chapter 4

1. Gwendolyn Brooks, *Annie Allen,* in *Blacks* (Chicago: The David Company, 1987), p. 100.
2. Toni Morrison, *Beloved* (New York: Knopf, 1987), p. 140. Subsequent references to this novel appear in parentheses in the text.
3. Charles W. Chesnutt, "The Wife of His Youth," in *The Collected Stories of Charles W. Chesnutt,* ed. William L. Andrews (New York: Mentor, 1992), pp. 102–113.
4. While readers generally recognize an otherworldliness in Beloved, they seldom assign such a characteristic to Baby Suggs. In assuming a status larger than the confinement of the human, Baby Suggs shares kinship with Beloved and literary relatives such as Bambara's Minnie Ransom, Naylor's Mama Day, and Cooper's Clora.
5. Another strong black woman in the role of preacher, James Baldwin's Sister Margaret in *The Amen Corner* (New York: Dial, 1968) also has difficulty living as she advises others to live.
6. Alice Walker, *The Third Life of Grange Copeland* (1970; New York: Avon, 1971), p. 216. Italics in original.
7. This reinvention motif recurs in Morrison's work. It is in essence what Sula Peace does as well as what Pilate Dead does on her many adventures and travels. Both women make adjustments necessitated by the circumstances in which they find themselves.
8. This is the strategy that frames Gayl Jones's *Corredigora* (1975), a story of slavery and incest in Brazil and their consequences to the third generation of women fathered by the same Brazilian slaveholder.
9. As this discussion illustrates, black women's strength can be a virtue or a hindrance. For my unqualified appreciation of Baby Suggs's and Sethe's healthy qualities, see my *Fiction and Folklore: The Novels of Toni Morrison* (Knoxville: University of Tennessee Press, 1991).
10. Schoolteacher and the nephew who arrives in Ohio with him to return Sethe and her children to slavery are equally struck by her eyes: "But the worst ones [eyes] were those of the nigger woman who looked like she didn't have any. Since the whites in them had disappeared and since they were as black as her skin, she looked blind" (150).
11. Like many strong black women characters, Sethe has no friends, and she is not involved in any of the institutions (community, church) that Morrison posits would perhaps have saved Hagar in *Song of Solomon.* While a portion of this absence might be voluntary in Sethe's life, it is also because of what her neighbors perceive as her haughtiness, her strength.
12. On several occasions, Baby Suggs exhibits the same directive posture toward Sethe. For example, when Sethe tries to feed Denver after having killed Beloved, Baby Suggs orders, "Clean up! Clean yourself up!" (152).
13. Noticeably, romantic possibility enters Sethe's life when she is at a low point, literally in bed and depressed, in other words, again weakened in comparison

to her previous state. In this condition, she is allowed to be receptive to Paul D, whereas that option failed when she was mentally and physically stronger. Since the impression is clearly that she will be strong again, it remains to be seen in the literature when an unusually strong black woman character and a black male character engage in a healthy romantic relationship.

Chapter 5

1. I focus in this chapter on *The Salt Eaters* and *Family* as examples of strong black women with extranatural powers. For my discussion of Mama Day in a comparable connection, see my 1996 volume, *The Power of the Porch* (Athens: University of Georgia Press), Chapter 2.

2. I trace this pattern in my discussion of conjure women and their powers in *Fiction and Folklore: The Novels of Toni Morrison* (Tennessee, 1991).

3. Toni Cade Bambara, *The Salt Eaters* (1980; New York: Vintage, 1992), p. 1. Subsequent references to this novel appear in parentheses in the text.

4. Mama Mae's absence through a connection to a traditional church might be another way for Bambara to indicate that more than Christianity is needed in the lives of these women. M'Dear Sophie, while absent from the healing room, nonetheless has Velma's best interests at heart. Indeed, it could be argued that she is another strong black woman character who seems to have unusual connections to the forces of the universe. She plays a significant role in turning healing energies toward Velma, a role that increases when it is clear that Velma is indeed coming through her crisis (217ff). Through the power of silence—perhaps akin to that of Baby Suggs—she aids the process of Velma's healing. More attention could be devoted to her as a strong black woman character, but my primary focus here is Minnie Ransom. Similar attention could be—and has been—devoted to Velma, who has received quite a bit of critical attention, including coverage in theses and dissertations.

5. While Bambara has not claimed Johnson's novel as a direct line of influence, she does recount being present at a "passionate" dinner conversation about the novel. See "What It Is I Think I'm Doing Anyhow," in *The Writer on Her Work,* ed. Janet Sternburg (New York: Norton, 1980), pp. 162–63. In that same essay, Bambara refers to Minnie as "a swamphag healer" (p. 165).

6. Because Velma is destined to take Minnie's place as healer, and perhaps even to exceed her, she is intimately identified with the health of the larger community. Bambara makes clear that Velma serves a microcosmic role and that the community cannot be healthy unless she is. Several characters, therefore, experience epiphanic transformations or moments of enlightenment during the thundering interlude that presages Velma's return to complete consciousness and health. It is noteworthy that the thunder is probably identified with the *loa*, which signals again the multidimensional level of Velma's healing.

7. Elliott Butler-Evans goes slightly further in this interpretation by asserting that, for Nadeen, "Velma's healing becomes a rite of passage" and that

"Nadeen's initiation into womanhood and a community of Black women occurs when she experiences in Velma's healing 'a kinship with the woman she did not know,' which enables her to transcend her devalued status and affirm an identity." See *Race, Gender, and Desire: Narrative Strategies in the Fiction of Toni Cade Bambara, Toni Morrison, and Alice Walker* (Philadelphia: Temple University Press, 1989), p. 183.

8. This unusual measurement of time and Minnie's age come together in another reference that Minnie herself makes. When Velma "growls" in anger about things that have brought her to the Infirmary, Minnie asserts: "'I haven't heard a growl like that since Venus moved between the sun and the earth, mmm, not since the coming of the Lord of the Flames. Yes, sweetheart, I haven't heard a good ole deep kneebend from-the-source growl such as that in some nineteen million years. Growl on. You gonna be all right . . . after while. It's all a matter of time. The law of time'" (41). While Minnie may be measuring time metaphorically, she nonetheless indicates a different perception from usual Western traditions even as she causes speculation about her own chronological age.

9. Oshun is a riverain goddess in Yoruba tradition, identified primarily by the metal brass and a mixture of traits, including witchcraft, that are warring and loving. Oya(e), goddess of the Whirlwind, is also known for her witchcraft. See Robert Farris Thompson, *Flash of the Spirit: African & Afro-American Art & Philosophy* (New York: Vintage, 1984), pp. 79–83 and 167. People of African descent in the new world, especially in countries like Brazil, pay regular homage to Oshun. Oya(e), who does not have a counterpart in the new world, shows Bambara's concern with mixing original African and new world African traditions.

10. Janelle Collins provides a possible explanation for Minnie's seeming lapses: "Velma resists Minnie's energy; the destructive energy released by Velma's fragmentation causes interference in the healing forces of Minnie's power." See "Generating Power: Fission, Fusion, and Postmodern Politics in Bambara's *The Salt Eaters*," *MELUS* 21:2 (Summer 1996): 41. Such an explanation suggests further that Velma, once she attains wholeness and accepts her gift, has the capacity to replace Minnie Ransom and indeed to accomplish even greater good.

11. This evokes comparison to the group of 30 women who exorcise Beloved from Sethe's house by the murmurings they make, which are designed to "[break] the back of words." See Morrison, *Beloved*, p. 261.

12. This phrase is used for all the white slave owners and violators of black women's bodies in the narrative. It is thus a significant shaper of black women's strength, for the psychological and/or physical power these women are able to garner usually comes in direct reaction to one of "the Masters of the Land."

13. Fammy, like some of her enslaved literary ancestors, decides to have a child by a dark man so that it will be brown and she will have a better chance of keeping it with her—given the white woman's jealousy; Clora is that brown

child (4–5). Sethe's mother adopted the same strategy, and Ella, also in *Beloved,* simply lets her white child die because it resulted from her being raped repeatedly by two white men.

14. J. California Cooper, *Family* (New York: Doubleday, 1991), pp. 24–25. Subsequent references to this novel appear in parentheses in the text.

15. Always, another strong black woman character, uses that space to plan her physical triumph over slavery. It is there that she exchanges her own son for the Butler baby and sets in process the plot that will enable her to get a plantation after slavery. The lowly, stable-like space, with its biblical connotations, therefore becomes a central triumphant image in the final generations of this much exploited family.

Chapter 6

1. Dorothy West, *The Living Is Easy* (1948; Rpt. New York: The Feminist Press, 1982), p. 4. Subsequent references to the novel appear in parentheses in the text.

2. In her attitude toward southern blacks, Cleo anticipates the Harlem woman in Ralph Ellison's *Invisible Man* who blames southern blacks for preventing northern blacks from progressing faster, as well as Toni Morrison's Geraldine in *The Bluest Eye,* who sees in Pecola Breedlove the epitome of everything she has tried to escape by coming from the South to the North.

3. Her attitude here is not unlike Sethe Suggs's in Toni Morrison's *Beloved.* Sethe can kill Beloved in part because she "owns" her, has claimed the right to Beloved's body and to motherhood that the slaveholder would deny.

4. Obviously, Cleo has no genuine concern for Robert. She is more conscious of winning an argument with Bart and of getting her way as far as dominating over her sisters is concerned.

5. One of the burdens Cleo forces upon Judy is an attempted alteration of her Negroid features. She insists that Judy "pinch her nose" in a nightly ritual designed to reshape it, as much as self-imposed violence can, into a more acceptable Nordic-looking nose. Judy's nose, therefore, becomes the visible marker of Cleo's failed aspirations to upward mobility.

6. By contrast, Bart fervently believes in God. He feels so close to Him in fact that he experiences visions that have guided him over the years in his business success (see pp. 63, 66–67). Bart does not, however, comment upon how—or whether—God guides his relationship with Cleo.

7. Adelaide M. Cromwell, who wrote the Afterword to the Feminist Press edition of the novel and who was a close friend of West's for more than 40 years, comments that West's upper-class characters in the novel "are all based on real people" (359) and that West's father, Isaac Christopher West, served as the model for Bart Judson. She further comments that "The West family home on Brookline Avenue at one time included thirteen persons, all relatives of Rachel West [Dorothy's mother], who was one of twenty-two children" (360).

Chapter 7

1. Another striking literary example of a strong black female character and her impact upon her offspring is Paule Marshall's *Brown Girl, Brownstones* (1959), in which the mother, Silla Boyce, wages psychological war against her husband and her two daughters for mastery of her household. At one point, when her younger daughter Selina calls her Hitler and strikes her mother with her fists, Silla endures the blows, then wraps her daughter in an embrace that is all possessive, all claiming, as the crying daughter gives way to an exhausted sleep in her mother's arms. Marshall's characters are drawn from Bajan culture, which suggests that tenets of the strong woman of African ancestry transcend national borders in the New World.

2. In the 1999 HBO television movie of *A Lesson Before Dying*, Irma P. Hall plays the role of Miss Emma. She is the same actress who plays Martin Lawrence's strongly violent mother in *Nothing to Lose* (1997) as well as the Big Mama who dies in *Soul Food* (1997). By size contrast, Cecily Tyson plays the role of Tante Lou (in the novel Gaines describes her as being very large). What Tyson lacks in physical size, she makes up in power of performance, as the movie has been universally praised. Its power to evoke viewer response is certified in the numbers of my colleagues who found themselves in tears while watching the movie. One reviewer comments that Tyson and Hall "are amazing and moving as two women whose strength, love and dignity guide through the pain." See the http://www.us.imdb.com website.

3. Note that Grant refers to his aunt by the respectful title of "Tante"; it is comparable to calling her Big Mama. In her role as godmother to Jefferson, Miss Emma is called "Nannan," another of those respectful titles that fit into the Big Mama category.

4. Ernest J. Gaines, *A Lesson Before Dying* (New York: Knopf, 1993), p. 3. I will place further references to this novel in parenthesis in the text.

   The image of the women being as immobile as oak or cypress stumps evokes Christian song imagery. "I shall not be moved; just like a tree, planted by the waters, I shall not be moved." Keep in mind that one of the stories in Gaines's *Bloodline* (1968), which portrays a strong black woman character, is entitled "Just Like a Tree."

5. Toni Morrison, *Sula* (New York: Knopf, 1974), p. 69.

6. The strong black woman character usually serves her charges without expectations of reward. It is noteworthy, therefore, to reiterate that Miss Emma is confronting the white plantation owner when she asserts that something is owed to her. Obligation might be implicit in interactions between strong black women characters and their offspring, but it is never stated explicitly.

7. As with Mama Lena slapping Beneatha, perhaps most readers would find this an understandable or acceptable instance of violence. Nonetheless, it *is* violence, and it grows out of the strong black woman character's desire to reinstate a way of life, a pattern of seeing, that existed before the offspring verbalized the disruption that brought on the violence.

8. For an extended discussion of food and its production as indicative of relationships in the novel, see Courtney Ramsay, "Louisiana Foodways in Ernest Gaines's *A Lesson Before Dying*," *Louisiana Folklore Miscellany* 10 (1995): 46–58. Ramsay contends that "food in its acquisition and its preparation not only provides nourishment and a means by which love is expressed but also serves as a medium to exert power, to express other emotions of acceptance or rejection, and to communicate these feelings to others" (46).

9. Herman Beavers, *Wrestling Angels Into Song: The Fictions of Ernest J. Gaines and James Alan McPherson* (Philadelphia: University of Pennsylvania Press, 1995), pp. 229–30.

10. Gaines reiterates the philosophy of a black male savior here that he articulates in *The Autobiography of Miss Jane Pittman* (New York: Dial Press, 1971), where on several occasions the people ask of a newborn black male, "Is you the one?"

11. Nell Irvin Painter, *Exodusters: Black Migration to Kansas After Reconstruction* (New York: Knopf, 1976).

12. Pearl Cleage, *Flyin' West* (New York: Dramatists Play Service, 1995), p. 7. Subsequent references to this source appear in parentheses in the text.

13. In May 1994, I was invited to the Long Wharf Theatre in New Haven, Connecticut, to lead the after-play discussion of *Flyin' West*. I observed that the largest female in the cast had the role of Sophie, even though she was dark-skinned and Sophie is mulatto. The smaller, lighter-skinned black woman who played the role of Fannie maintained that she had never thought in those terms. I found the casting and comment interesting for how we invariably typecast large black women as strong, even though a single instance of casting may go against type in another trait (color in this instance).

14. Of course this scenario evokes Ted Shine's Mrs. Grace Love, who poisons the racist white southerners for whom she works as her "contribution" to the Civil Rights movement. See Shine's one-act play, "Contribution," in *The Literature of the American South: A Norton Anthology*, ed. William L. Andrews, et al. (New York: Norton, 1998), pp. 858–68.

15. The only *real* "man" in the play, it could be argued, is Sophie.

Chapter 8

1. Lauren's active seeking of an alternative to Christianity differs from Beneatha Younger's resistance to her mother's brand of religion as well as to Grant Wiggins' frustration with his great-aunt's belief system, for Beneatha and Grant do not move far beyond mouthing dissatisfaction with the status quo.

2. Octavia E. Butler, *Parable of the Sower* (New York: Four Walls Eight Windows, 1993), p. 71. Subsequent references are to this edition and will be cited in the text. The "seed" idea is one that Butler has explored before, especially in *Wild Seed* (1980), in which the supernatural Doro seeks subjects (seeds) for his envisioned psionic garden of superior human beings.

3. Jim Miller discusses Butler's turning of a dystopian universe into a utopian one in "Post-Apocalyptic Hoping: Octavia Butler's Dystopian/Utopian Vision," *Science Fiction Studies* 25:2 (July 1998): 336–60.

4. Butler continues her portrayal of the strong Lauren Olamina in *Parable of the Talents* (1998), in which Lauren suffers the loss of her husband (through murder), daughter (through kidnapping for reindoctrination from Lauren's system of belief), and the idealic retreat she succeeds in establishing (the dominant cult in America takes over for purposes of retraining Lauren and her followers. They end up as prisoners who are routinely raped and forced to suffer other indignities). Lauren survives into her eighties, never once losing faith in her convictions and never once wavering from her strong leadership role.

5. We are instantly reminded of characters such as Clotel assuming such disguises in their attempts to escape from slavery. This is not the only tie to the slave narrative tradition and to slavery in Butler's novel. Several families apply to move from the walled community in which Lauren lives to the twenty-first century equivalent of a company town, which Lauren's father interprets as a new form of slavery. Four of the people who join Lauren's group going north have been "wage slaves," held in bondage for food and shelter and because they are hyperempathetic, which presumably makes them more docile. The idea of traveling north also echoes the slave narrative tradition and the mythic connotations associated with that space. While California is not the usual site for historical representations of slavery in the literature, it is easily imbued with those connections in Butler's narrative.

6. One brother will reappear in a significant role in *Parable of the Talents*.

7. The name "Natividad," with its close resemblance to "nativity," invites focus on the mother, father, and child who presage a new religion and a new world order. It reflects another way in which Christianity continues to influence such texts, even when the authors and characters are consciously trying to create an alternative belief system.

8. Bankole will indeed become Lauren's husband and the father of her child in *Parable of the Talents*.

Chapter 9

1. Paula Woods, *Inner City Blues* (New York: Norton, 1999), p. 38. Subsequent references to this source appear in parentheses in the text.

2. Richard Brodhead, ed., *The Journals of Charles W. Chesnutt* (Durham: Duke University Press, 1993), p. 140.

3. Don L. Lee, "From a Black Perspective," in *Don't Cry, Scream* (Detroit: Broadside Press, 1969), p. 34.

4. Shay Youngblood, *The Big Mama Stories* (Ithaca, N.Y.: Firebrand Books, 1989). The two elderly women who care for the child in *Soul Kiss* (1996), Youngblood's first novel, also exhibit some of these traditional traits.

5. Michelle Parkerson, "Odds and Ends (A New Amazon Fable)," in *Afrekete: An Anthology of Black Lesbian Writing,* ed. Catherine E. McKinley and L. Joyce DeLaney (New York: Doubleday, 1995), pp. 89–95. Several things are going on in this story, including parodic social, historical, and linguistic references. For example, the men who kill her refer to Sephra as "jemimma" in part because of what they perceive as her audacity in making weapons and in part because of her lesbianism. The fact that Parkerson couches her fable to center upon suprahuman black female characters—with a sexual dimension comparable to Lauren Olamina's—is nonetheless the important point.

6. Ideal also suffers the mental abuse of Jimson, her lover, who, during one long tirade about black women being "holdovers" from slavery in their "mammy-made" tradition of domination, includes this accusation: "Although you are educated, intelligent, some of you black bitches cannot overcome the stamp of matriarchy." See Polite, *The Flagellants* (Boston: Beacon Press, 1987), p. 180.

7. It is worth noting that many of the strong black women characters portrayed in works in the 1990s, including Loz Wayward, Charlotte Justice, and Harlan Jane Eagleton, do not have children. That is a significant departure from their literary sisters prior to the 1990s.

8. Jean Wheeler Smith, "Frankie Mae," in *Black-Eyed Susans: Classic Stories by and about Black Women,* ed. Mary Helen Washington (New York: Anchor, 1975), pp. 3–18.

9. Adrienne Kennedy, *Funnyhouse of a Negro,* in *Contemporary Black Drama,* ed. Clinton F. Oliver and Stephanie Sills (New York: Scribner's, 1971), pp. 187–205.

Works Cited or Consulted

Abrahams, Roger. *Deep Down in the Jungle: Negro Narrative Folklore from the Streets of Philadelphia.* Chicago: Aldine, 1970.

———. "Playing the Dozens." In *Mother Wit from the Laughing Barrel: Readings in the Interpretation of Afro-American Folklore.* Ed. Alan Dundes. Jackson: University of Mississippi Press, 1991, pp. 295–309.

Abramson, Doris E. *Negro Playwrights in the American Theatre 1925–1959.* New York and London: Columbia University Press, 1969.

Alexander, Elizabeth. "From *Diva Studies, drama.*" *Callaloo* 19:2 (Spring 1996): 474–492.

Anderson, Lisa M. *Mammies No More: The Changing Image of Black Women on Stage and Screen.* Lanham, MD: Rowman & Littlefield, 1997.

Anderson, Mary Louise. "Black Matriarchy: Portrayal of Women in Three Plays." *Negro American Literature Forum* 10 (1976): 93–95.

Andrews, Raymond. *Rosiebelle Lee Wildcat Tennessee.* Athens: University of Georgia Press, 1980.

Angelou, Maya. *I Know Why the Caged Bird Sings.* New York: Random House, 1970.

———. *And Still I Rise.* New York: Bantam, 1978.

Ansa, Tina McElroy. *Baby of the Family.* New York: Harcourt Brace Jovanovich, 1989.

———. *Ugly Ways.* New York: Harcourt Brace & Company, 1993.

Aptheker, Herbert. *American Negro Slave Revolts.* New York: Columbia University Press, 1943.

Ashford, Nickolas and Valarie Simpson. "I'm Every Woman." *The Bodyguard Original Soundtrack Album.* New York: Arista Records, Inc., 1992.

Atkinson, Brooks. "The Theatre: 'A Raisin in the Sun'." *New York Times,* 12 March 1959, L27.

Augler, Philip. "A Lesson About Manhood: Appropriating 'The Word' in Ernest Gaines's *A Lesson Before Dying.*" *Southern Literary Journal* 27:2 (Spring 1995): 74–85.

Baldwin, James. *Go Tell It on the Mountain.* New York: Dell, 1953.

———. *The Amen Corner.* New York: Dial, 1968.

———. "Introduction." In *To Be Young, Gifted and Black.* Ed. Robert Nemiroff. New York: Signet, 1969, pp. xi-xv.

Bambara, Toni Cade. *The Salt Eaters.* New York: Vintage, 1980.

————. "What It Is I'm Doing Anyhow." In *The Writer On Her Work*. Ed. Janet Sternberg. New York and London: W. W. Norton, 1980, pp. 153–68.

————. "Salvation Is the Issue." In *Black Women Writers (1950–1980): A Critical Evaluation*. Ed. Mari Evans. Garden City, N.Y.: Doubleday/Anchor, 1984, pp. 41–47.

Beavers, Herman. *Wrestling Angels Into Song: The Fictions of Ernest J. Gaines and James Alan McPherson*. Philadelphia: University of Pennsylvania Press, 1995.

Bogle, Donald. *Toms, Coons, Mulattoes, Mammies, and Bucks: An Interpretive History of Blacks in American Films*. Rev. ed. New York: Continuum, 1994.

Boskin, Joseph. *Sambo: The Rise & Demise of An American Jester*. New York: Oxford University Press, 1986.

Boyd, Julia A. *Can I Get a Witness? For Sisters, When the Blues Is More Than a Song*. New York: Dutton, 1998.

Briscoe, Connie. *Sisters and Lovers*. New York: HarperCollins, 1994.

————. *Big Girls Don't Cry*. New York: HarperCollins, 1996.

Brodhead, Richard, ed. *The Journals of Charles W. Chesnutt*. Durham: Duke University Press, 1993.

Brooks, Gwendolyn. *Annie Allen*. In *Blacks*. Chicago: The David Company, 1987.

Brown-Guillory, Elizabeth. "Black Women Playwrights: Exorcising Myths." *Phylon* 48:3 (Fall 1987): 229–39.

Brown, William Wells. *Clotel; Or, the President's Daughter*. 1853; New York: Collier, 1972.

Butler, Octavia. *Wild Seed*. New York: Doubleday, 1980.

————. *Parable of the Sower*. New York: Four Walls, Eight Windows, 1993.

————. *Parable of the Talents*. New York: Seven Stories Press, 1998.

Butler-Evans, Elliott. *Race, Gender, and Desire: Narrative Strategies in the Fiction of Toni Cade Bambara, Toni Morrison, and Alice Walker*. Philadelphia: Temple University Press, 1989.

Carter, Steven R. *Hansberry's Drama: Commitment amid Complexity*. Urbana and Chicago: University of Illinois Press, 1991.

————. "Lorraine Hansberry." *Dictionary of Literary Biography* 38. Ed. Thadious M. Davis and Trudier Harris. Detroit: Gale Research Company, 1985, pp. 120–34.

Cheney, Anne. *Lorraine Hansberry*. Boston: Twayne, 1984.

Chernin, Kim. *The Obsession: Reflections on the Tyranny of Slenderness*. 1981; New York, HarperPerennial, 1994.

Chesnutt, Charles W. "The Wife of His Youth." In *The Collected Stories of Charles W. Chesnutt*. Ed. William L. Andrews. New York: Mentor, 1992, pp. 102–113.

Childress, Alice. *Wine in the Wilderness*. New York: Dramatists Play Service, Inc., 1969.

Christian, Barbara. *Black Women Novelists: The Development of a Tradition, 1892–1976*. Westport, CT: Greenwood Press, 1980.

Cleage, Pearl. *Flyin' West*. New York: Dramatists Play Service, 1995.

Clinton, Catherine. *The Plantation Mistress: Woman's World in the Old South*. New York: Pantheon, 1982.

Clurman, Harold. "Theatre." *The Nation*, 4 April 1959, pp. 301–302.

Collins, Janelle. "Generating Power: Fission, Fusion, and Postmodern Politics in Bambara's *The Salt Eaters*." *MELUS* 21:2 (Summer 1996): 35–47.

Cooper, J. California. *Family.* New York: Doubleday, 1991.

———. Personal essay. In *I Know What the Red Clay Looks Like*. Ed. Carol Aisha Blackshire-Belay. New York: Carol Southern Books, 1994, pp. 63–73.

Cromwell, Adelaide M. "Afterword." In Dorothy West, *The Living Is Easy.* New York: The Feminist Press, 1982.

Cruse, Harold. *The Crisis of the Negro Intellectual.* New York: Morrow, 1967.

Dance, Daryl C. "Black Eve or Madonna? A Study of the Antithetical Views of the Mother in Black American Literature." In *Sturdy Black Bridges: Visions of Black Women in Literature.* Ed Roseann P. Bell, Bettye J. Parker, and Beverly Guy-Sheftall. Garden City, N.Y.: Anchor Press/Doubleday, 1979, pp. 123–132.

———. "Go Eena Kumbla: A Comparison of Erna Brodber's *Jane and Louisa Will Soon Come Home* and Toni Cade Bambara's *The Salt Eaters*." In *Caribbean Women Writers.* Ed. Selwyn R. Cudjoe. Amherst: University of Massachusetts Press, 1990, pp. 169–84.

Danquah, Meri NanaAma. *Weep for Me: A Black Woman's Journey Through Depression: A Memoir.* New York: One World, 1999.

Davis, Ossie. "The Significance of Lorraine Hansberry." *Freedomways* 5:3 (1965): 396–402.

Dollard, John. "The Dozens: Dialectic of Insult." In *Mother Wit from the Laughing Barrel: Readings in the Interpretation of Afro-American Folklore.* Ed. Alan Dundes. Rev. Ed. Jackson: University of Mississippi Press, 1991, pp. 277–294.

Douglass, Frederick. *Narrative of the Life of Frederick Douglass* (1845; rpt. Cambridge: Harvard Belknap Press, 1960).

Driver, Tom F. "A Raisin in the Sun." *The New Republic,* 13 April 1959, p. 21.

Ellison, Ralph. *Invisible Man.* New York: Vintage, 1952.

Estes, David, ed. *Critical Reflections on the Fiction of Ernest Gaines.* Athens: University of Georgia Press, 1994.

Ethnic Notions. Distributed by California Newsreel, 149 Ninth Street/420, San Francisco, CA 94103.

Fabre, Genevieve. *Drumbeats, Masks, and Metaphors: Contemporary Afro-American Theatre.* Cambridge: Harvard University Press, 1983.

Faulkner, William. "A Rose for Emily." In *Studies in Fiction.* Ed. Blaze O. Bonazza and Emil Roy. New York: Harper and Row, 1965, pp. 62–70.

Freedomways 19:4 (1979). Special issue on Lorraine Hansberry.

Gaines, Ernest. *Bloodline.* New York: Dial, 1968.

———. *The Autobiography of Miss Jane Pittman.* New York: Dial, 1971.

———. *A Lesson Before Dying.* New York: Knopf, 1993.

Gayle, Addison. "Black Women and Black Men: The Literature of Catharsis." *Black Books Bulletin* 4 (1976): 48–52.

Gilman, Sander. "Black Bodies, White Bodies." *Critical Inquiry* (Autumn 1985): 204–42.

Giovanni, Nikki. *The Women and the Men: Poems.* New York: Morrow, 1975.

Golden, Marita. *and do remember me.* New York: Ballantine, 1994.

Gray, Lynn. "Interview with J. California Cooper." *Fm. Five* 3:2 (November-December 1985): 1, 12.

Griffith, D. W. *The Birth of a Nation.* 1915.

Hansberry, Lorraine. *A Raisin in the Sun.* New York: Signet, 1959, 1966.

———. "An Author's Reflections." *Village Voice,* 12 August 1959, pp. 7–8.

———. "Village Intellect Revealed." *New York Times,* 11 October 1964, pp. X 1, X 3.

Harper, Frances. *Iola Leroy.* 1892; Rpt. New York: Oxford, 1988.

Harris, Norman. "The Gods Must be Angry: *Flight to Canada* as Political History." *Modern Fiction Studies* 34:1 (Spring 1988): 111–23.

Harris, Trudier. "From Exile to Asylum: Religion and Community in the Writings of Contemporary Black Women." In *Women's Writing in Exile.* Ed. Mary Lynn Broe and Angela Ingram. Chapel Hill: University of North Carolina Press, 1989, pp. 151–69.

——————. *Fiction and Folklore: The Novels of Toni Morrison.* Knoxville: University of Tennessee Press, 1991.

———. "This Disease Called Strength: Some Observations on the Compensating Construction of Black Female Character." *Literature and Medicine* 14 (Spring 1995): 109–126.

———. *The Power of the Porch: The Storyteller's Craft in Zora Neale Hurston, Gloria Naylor, and Randall Kenan.* Athens: University of Georgia Press, 1996.

Hartman, Saidiya. "Seduction and the Ruses of Power." In Emerging Women Writers, special issue. *Callaloo* 19:2 (Spring 1996): 537–60.

Heglar, Charles. "Survival With Dignity." *Cross Roads* 3:1 (Fall 1994-Winter 1995): 57–68.

Hewes, Henry. "A Plant Grows in Chicago." *Saturday Review,* 4 April 1959, p. 28.

Holloway, Karla. *Moorings and Metaphor: Figures of Culture and Gender in Black Women's Literature.* New Brunswick, N.J.: Rutgers University Press, 1992.

Hopkins, Pauline. *Contending Forces: A Romance Illustrative of Negro Life North and South.* 1900; Rpt. New York: Oxford, 1988.

Houston, Whitney. Soundtrack to *The Bodyguard.* New York: Arista Records, Inc., 1992.

Hughes, Langston. *Not Without Laughter.* 1930; New York: Macmillan, 1969.

Hull, Gloria T. "'What It Is I Think She's Doing Anyhow': A Reading of Toni Cade Bambara's *The Salt Eaters.*" In *Conjuring: Black Women, Fiction, and Literary Tradition.* Ed. Marjorie Pryse and Hortense J. Spillers. Bloomington: Indiana University Press, 1985, pp. 216–32.

Hurston, Zora Neale. *Mules and Men.* Philadelphia: Lippincott, 1935.

———. *Their Eyes Were Watching God.* Philadelphia: Lippincott, 1937.

———. *Dust Tracks On a Road.* Philadelphia: Lippincott, 1942.

Jacobs, Harriet. *Incidents in the Life of a Slave Girl.* Boston: The Author, 1861.

"Jennifer Holliday: Out of the Dark." *Essence* 30:2 (June 1999): 92–94, 96, 152–155.

Johnson, Charles R. *Oxherding Tale.* Bloomington: Indiana University Press, 1982.

———. *Middle Passage.* New York: Atheneum, 1990.

Jones, Gayl. *Corregidora.* New York: Random House, 1975.

————. *The Healing.* Boston: Beacon Press, 1998.

Jones, Leroi. *Dutchman and The Slave.* New York: Morrow, 1964.

Jones, Suzanne W. "Reconstructing Manhood: Race, Masculinity, and Narrative Closure in Ernest Gaines's *A Gathering of Old Men* and *A Lesson Before Dying.*" *Masculinities* 3:2 (Summer 1995): 43–66.

Joyce, Joyce A. "Falling Through the Minefield of Black Feminist Criticism: Ishmael Reed, A Case in Point," in *Warriors, Conjurers and Priests: Defining African-centered Literary Criticism.* Chicago: Third World Press, 1994.

Kelley, Margot Anne. "'Damballah is the First Law of Thermodynamics': Modes of Access to Toni Cade Bambara's *The Salt Eaters.*" *African American Review* 27:3 (Fall 1993): 479–93.

Kenan, Randall. "An Interview with Octavia E. Butler." *Callaloo* 14:2 (Spring 1991): 495–504.

Kennedy, Adrienne. "Funnyhouse of a Negro." In *Contemporary Black Drama.* Ed. Clinton F. Oliver and Stephanie Sills. New York: Scribner's, 1971, pp. 187–205.

Kennedy, John Pendleton. *Swallow Barn, or, A Sojourn in the Old Dominion.* Philadelphia: Carey & Lea, 1832.

Kern-Foxworth, Marilyn. *Aunt Jemima, Uncle Ben, and Rastus: Blacks in Advertising, Yesterday, Today, and Tomorrow.* Foreword by Alex Haley. Westport, CT: Greenwood Press, 1994.

Kolmar, Wendy K. "'Dialectics of Connectedness': Supernatural Elements in Novels by Bambara, Cisneros, Grahn, and Erdrich." In *Haunting the House of Fiction: Feminist Perspectives on Ghost Stories by American Women.* Ed. Lynette Carpenter and Wendy K. Kolmar. Knoxville: University of Tennessee Press, 1991, pp. 236–49.

Lee, Don L. *Don't Cry, Scream.* Detroit: Broadside Press, 1969.

Lerner, Max. "A Dream Deferred." *New York Post,* 5 April 1959, p. xx.

Lohmann, Jeanne. "Lady on a Bus." In *Cries of the Spirit: A Celebration of Women's Spirituality.* Ed. Marilyn Sewell. Boston: Beacon Press, 1991, pp. 143–44.

Lowe, John, ed. *Conversations with Ernest Gaines.* Jackson: University of Mississippi Press, 1995.

Manring, M. M. *Slave in a Box: The Strange Career of Aunt Jemima.* Charlottesville: University of Virginia Press, 1998.

Marshall, Barbara J. "Kitchen Table Talk: J. California Cooper's Use of Nommo." In *Language and Literature in the African American Imagination.* Ed. Carol Aisha Blackshire-Belay. Wesport, CT: Greenwood Press. Pp. 91–102. 1992.

Marshall, Paule. *Praisesong for the Widow.* New York: Putnam's, 1983.

Martin, Reginald. *Ishmael Reed and the New Black Aesthetic Critics.* New York: St. Martin's Press, 1988.

McMillan, Terry. *Waiting to Exhale.* New York: Viking, 1992.

————. *How Stella Got Her Groove Back.* New York: Viking, 1996.

Miller, Jim. "Post-Apocalyptic Hoping: Octavia Butler's Dystopian/Utopian Vision." *Science Fiction Studies.* 25:2 (July 1998): 336–60.

Mitchell, Loften. *Black Drama: The Story of the American Negro in the Theatre.* New York: Hawthorn Books, 1967.

Morrison, Toni. *The Bluest Eye.* Holt, Rinehart, and Winston, 1970.

———. "What the Black Woman Thinks about Women's Lib." *New York Times Magazine,* 22 August 1971, 63.

———. *Sula.* New York: Knopf, 1974.

———. *Song of Solomon.* New York: Knopf: 1977.

———. *Beloved.* New York: Knopf, 1987.

———. *Jazz.* New York: Knopf, 1992.

———. *Paradise.* New York: Knopf, 1998.

Moynihan, Daniel Patrick. "The Negro Family: The Case for National Action." Washington, D.C.: U.S. Department of Labor, 1965.

Naylor, Gloria. *The Women of Brewster Place.* New York: Penguin, 1982.

———. *Mama Day.* New York: Ticknor and Fields, 1988.

———. *Bailey's Cafe.* New York: Harcourt Brace Jovanovich, 1992.

Nazareth, Peter. "An Interview with Ishmael Reed." *Iowa Review* 13:2 (1982): 117–31.

Ochiai, Akiko. "So Far Apart: African American Men in *A Lesson Before Dying.*" *Griot* 16:1 (Spring 1997): 39–47.

Okihiro, Gary H. ed. *In Resistance: Studies in African, Caribbean, and Afro-American History.* Amherst: University of Massachusetts Press, 1986.

O'Neale, Sondra A. "Ishmael Reed's Fitful Flight to Canada: Liberation for Some, Good Reading for All." *Callaloo* 1:4 (October 1978): 174–77.

Page, Thomas Nelson. *In Ole Virginia, or, Marse Chan and Other Stories.* New York: C. Scribner's Sons, 1895.

Painter, Nell Irvin. *Exodusters: Black Migration to Kansas After Reconstruction.* New York: Knopf, 1976.

Parkerson, Michelle. "Odds and Ends (A New Amazon Fable)." In *Afrekete: An Anthology of Black Lesbian Writing.* Ed. Catherine E. McKinley and L. Joyce DeLaney. New York: Doubleday, 1995.

Patton, Phil. "Mammy: Her Life and Times." *American Heritage* (September 1993): 78–87.

Penfold, Nita. "The Woman with the Wild-Grown Hair Relaxes after Another Long Day." In *Cries of the Spirit: A Celebration of Women's Spirituality.* Ed. Marilyn Sewell. Boston: Beacon, 1991, pp. 162–63.

Poitier, Sidney. *This Life.* New York: Alfred A. Knopf, 1980.

Polite, Carlene Hatcher. *The Flagellants.* New York: Farrar, Straus, & Giroux, 1967.

Porter, Nancy. "Women's Interracial Friendships and Visions of Community in *Meridian, The Salt Eaters, Civil Wars,* and *Dessa Rose.*" In *Tradition and the Talents of Women.* Ed. Florence Howe. Urbana: University of Illinois Press, 1991, pp. 251–67.

Potts, Stephen W. "'We Keep Playing the Same Record': A Conversation with Octavia E. Butler." *Science Fiction Studies.* 23:3 (November 1996): 331–38.

Rahman, Aishah. "To Be Black, Female and a Playwright." *Freedomways* 19:4 (1979): 256–260. Several articles in this issue are devoted to Hansberry.

Ramsay, Courtney. "Louisiana Foodways in Ernest Gaines's *A Lesson Before Dying.*" *Louisiana Folklore Miscellany* 10 (1995): 46–58.

Reed, Ishmael. *Flight to Canada.* New York: Random House, 1976.

Roberts, Diane. *The Myth of Aunt Jemima: Representations of Race and Region.* New York and London: Routledge, 1994.

Roberts, John W. *From Trickster to Badman: The Black Folk Hero in Slavery and Freedom.* Philadelphia: University of Pennsylvania Press, 1989.

Robertson, Nan. "Dramatist Against Odds." *New York Times,* 8 March 1959, p. X3.

Rosenberg, Ruth. "'You Took A Name That Made You Amiable to the Music': Toni Cade Bambara's *The Salt Eaters." Literary Onomastics Studies* 12 (1985): 165–94.

Rowell, Charles H. "An Interview with Octavia E. Butler." *Callaloo* 20:1 (Winter 1997): 47–66.

Rushdy, Ashraf H. A. "Ishmael Reed's Neo-HooDoo Slave Narrative." *Narrative* 2:2 (May 1994): 112–39.

Sanders, Ruby. "HUSH, HONEY." Unpublished manuscript, 2001.

Schopp, Joseph C. "'Riding Bareback, Backwards Through a Wood of Words': Ishmael Reed's Revision of the Slave Narrative." In *Historiographic Metafiction in Modern American and Canadian Literature.* Ed. Bernd Engler and Kurt Muller. Paderborn: Ferdinand Schoningh, 1994, pp. 267–78.

Seaton, Sandra. "*A Raisin in the Sun:* A Study in Afro-American Culture." *Midwestern Miscellany* 20 (1992): 40–49.

Shine, Ted. "Contribution." In *The Literature of the American South: A Norton Anthology.* Ed. William L. Andrews, et al. New York: Norton, 1998.

Smith, Jean Wheeler. "Frankie Mae." *In Black-Eyed Susans: Classic Stories by and about Black Women.* Ed. Mary Helen Washington. New York: Anchor, 1975, pp. 3–18.

Spillers, Hortense J. "Changing the Letter: The Yokes, the Jokes of Discourse, or, Mrs. Stowe, Mr. Reed." In *Slavery and the Literary Imagination.* Ed. Deborah E. McDowell and Arnold Rampersad. Baltimore, MD: The Johns Hopkins University Press, 1989, pp. 25–61.

———. "Mama's Baby, Papa's Maybe: An American Grammar Book." In *Within the Circle: An Anthology of African American Literary Criticism from the Harlem Renaissance to the Present.* Ed. Angelyn Mitchell. Durham and London: Duke University Press, 1994, pp. 454–81.

Stanford, Ann Folwell. "He Speaks for Whom: Inscription and Reinscription of Women in *Invisible Man* and *The Salt Eaters." MELUS* 18:2 (Summer 1992): 17–31.

———. "Mechanisms of Disease: African-American Women Writers, Social Pathologies, and the Limits of Medicine." *NWSA Journal* 6:1 (Spring 1994): 28–47.

Stowe, Harriet Beecher. *Uncle Tom's Cabin.* Boston: John P. Jewett, 1852.

Tate, Claudia, ed. *Black Women Writers at Work.* New York: Continuum, 1983.

Thompson, Robert Farris. *Flash of the Spirit: African & Afro-American Art & Philosophy.* New York: Vintage, 1984.

Traylor, Eleanor. "*The Salt Eaters:* My Soul Looks Back in Wonder." *First World* 2:4 (1980): 44–47, 64.

———. "Music as Theme: The Jazz Mode in the Works of Toni Cade Bambara." In *Black Women Writers (1950–1980): A Critical Evaluation.* Ed. Mari Evans. Garden City, N.Y.: Anchor Press/Doubleday, 1984, pp. 58–70.

Turner, Patricia A. *Ceramic Uncles & Celluloid Mammies: Black Images and Their Influence on Culture.* New York: Anchor Books, 1994.

Tynan, Kenneth. "Ireland and Points West." *New Yorker* 35 (21 March 1959): 100–102.

Walker, Alice. *The Third Life of Grange Copeland.* 1970; New York: Avon, 1971.

———. *In Love and Trouble: Stories of Black Women.* New York: Harcourt Brace Jovanovich, 1973.

———. *The Color Purple.* New York: Harcourt Brace Jovanovich, 1982.

———. *The Temple of My Familiar.* New York: Harcourt Brace Jovanovich, 1983.

———. *Her Blue Body Everything We Know: Earthling Poems 1965–1990 Complete.* New York: Harcourt Brace Jovanovich, 1991.

Walker, Margaret. *Jubilee.* Boston: Houghton Mifflin, 1966.

Wallace, Michele. *Black Macho and the Myth of the Superwoman.* New York: Warner, 1978.

Ward, Douglas Turner. *Happy Ending and Day of Absence.* 1964; New York: Okpaku, 1966.

Washington, J. Charles. "*A Raisin in the Sun* Revisited." *Black American Literature Forum* 22:1 (Spring 1988): 109–24.

Washington, Mary Helen, ed. *Black-Eyed Susans: Stories of Black Women.* New York: Anchor Books, 1975.

Weales, Gerald. "Thoughts on 'A Raisin in the Sun'." *Commentary,* June 1959, pp. 527–30.

Weixlmann, Joe. "Politics, Piracy, and Other Games: Slavery and Liberation in *Flight to Canada.*" *MELUS* 6:3 (1979): 41–50.

———. "Ishmael Reed's Raven." *The Review of Contemporary Fiction* 4:2 (Summer 1984): 205–208.

West, Dorothy. *The Living Is Easy.* 1948; Rpt. New York: The Feminist Press, 1982.

Wilkerson, Margaret B. "The Sighted Eyes and Feeling Heart of Lorraine Hansberry." *Black American Literature Forum* 17:1 (Spring 1983): 8–13.

Williams, Sherley Anne. *Dessa Rose.* New York: W. Morrow, 1986.

Williams, Shirley. "Tell Martha Not to Moan." In *The Black Woman.* Ed. Toni Cade. New York: Signet, 1970, pp. 42–55.

Woods, Paula. *Inner City Blues.* New York: Norton, 1999.

Wright, Richard. "Long Black Song," in *Uncle Tom's Children.* New York: Harper & Row, 1938.

———. *Uncle Tom's Children.* New York: Harper and Row, 1938.

———. *Native Son and How "Bigger" Was Born.* 1940; rpt; New York: HarperPerennial, 1993.

———. *Black Boy (American Hunger): A Record of Childhood and Youth.* 1945; New York: HarperPerennial, 1993.

Youngblood, Shay. *The Big Mama Stories.* Ithaca, N.Y.: Firebrand Books, 1989.

———. *Soul Kiss.* New York: Riverhead Books, 1997.

Index

Page numbers in **bold typeface** indicate chapters.
Please note: All names of characters are indexed by their first names. For example, Baby Suggs, not Suggs, Baby. All other proper names are indexed according to the surname.